Single Again

Single Again

Mildred Hope Witkin, Ph.D.

MASTERMEDIA LIMITED
New York

Library of Congress Cataloging-in-Publication Data

Witkin, Mildred Hope.
  Single again / Mildred Hope Witkin.

    Rev. ed. of: 45—and single again. ©1985
    Includes bibliographical references and index.
    ISBN 1-57101-001-7 : $12.95
    1. Single people—Life skills guides. 2. Divorced people—Life
skills guides. 3. Separation (Psychology) I. Witkin, Mildred Hope. 45—
and single again. II. Title.
HQ800.W56 1994
306.88—dc20   94-20693

Contents

Foreword to the First Edition

Mildred Witkin, first my student, then my colleague, is a re-markable person, a gifted therapist, and an inspirational teacher. Mildred brings her humanity, sensitivity, and empathy to her work and has healed countless troubled human beings. She is particularly drawn towards those who are hurting, who are vulnerable, who have suffered painful losses, and I have seen her instill hope and courage and mobilize the strengths of men and women crippled by their sexual and emotional diffi-culties. In this spirit, Mildred's book reaches out to people who have suffered the greatest stress we face in our lives—the loss of a valued mate. She has translated some highly technical psy-choanalytic and sex therapy concepts into simple and under-standable terms. The great ideas of Freud, Bowlby, Masters and Johnson, among other scientists, come alive and are expressed in useful, insightful, and practical suggestions to help persons who find themselves unhappily "single again" in mid-life and beyond build new and better lives. This book will help them make sense out of and cope constructively with their crisis, which contains great emotional hazards, but, as Mildred em-phasizes in this book, also great opportunities.

Helen S. Kaplan, M.D., Ph.D.
Clinical Professor of Psychiatry,
New York Hospital—Cornell Medical Center
Director of Human Sexuality Program at
the Payne Whitney Clinic of New York Hospital

Foreword

I believe there is no one in this world of the '90s who could guide us through the changes of becoming single again as well as my mother. Maybe everyone feels that way about their mother, but mine is not only loving and empathetic and wise, as I hope yours is, but she is also an assistant clinical professor of psychology, a sex therapist, and a marriage and family counselor. And she has been through my divorce and reentry into single life, her brother's reentry after my aunt's early death, and her own reentry and remarriage. My mother, after more than thirty years of marriage, has been single again like you and me.

The lesson she learned is the lesson she has taught me and will teach you: that becoming single again means change. Whether reluctant or chosen, tearful or joyful, change is somewhat frightening. We lose our sense of joy, we lose our sense of control, we cannot predict what's coming next. And the more we feel anticipatory about the future, the more we mourn our past and resent our loss. A future alone looms up as bleak. The weight of the past and the uncertainty of the future are more than illusions: They are financial, social, and emotional realities.

But to say there are real problems is not to imply there are no solutions. Over the years my mother and I have learned a great deal about the course of this emotional and psychological event. And some of what we have learned can be summarized in three sentences:

- There are some typical and predictable responses to becoming single again.
- It helps to go through it with information and preparation.
- It is possible to emerge from it better off—*on balance*—than before.

Of course, we can't guarantee you a happy ending, but knowing some answers will at least make the world livable again. To guarantee yourself a happy ending, you will need to be open to unexpected joy; laugh once again, particularly at yourself; accept what can't be changed; and change what you can't accept, when you can. My mother has taught me all this, and she can help you learn to be single again and enjoy it, too.

Georgia Hope Witkin, Ph.D.
New York, 1994

For My Darling Daughter, Georgia
          —you made it happen.

For My Darling Son, Roy
          —you have always been there.

For My Darling Daughter-in-Law, Laurie
          —you have always cared.

For My Darling Grandchildren, Kimberly, Nicole, Scott, Joshua and Jennifer
          —you have always brought me joy and pride.

For My Darling Husband, Jorge
          —you gave me faith and eased the way.

With Love

Part One
The End and
The Beginning

CHAPTER 1

The End: First Love, First Loss

First love—we all remember it. The loved one is the *only* one, the center of the world—no, the universe! We change the way we act, dress, or wear our hair to please the one we love. We who cannot comprehend poetry as we sit in a classroom suddenly are seized with the urge to write long odes dedicated to the beloved. Any words the beloved sends our way are loaded with special meaning. The yearning can be intense. And this tremendously significant relationship can occur without the beloved even knowing it exists.

When the relationship is recognized by the beloved—she gives you a toy, he gives you a bracelet, you both exchange words of loyalty that echo the marriage vows—the two of you move to a second phase. The beginning of this phase is sweet, and no young person should miss it! The kisses are passionate. These days, with about sixty percent of teenagers having sex by the time they're nineteen, lovemaking often deepens the relationship. The lovemaking (with appropriate precautions against the double risks of AIDS and pregnancy) can be sweet too.

Unfortunately, young love is fickle and often fades. Breakups are common and sometimes brutal. Rings are thrown down storm drains. Rumors of promiscuity are spread. Shouting and screaming are common.

When we're young, rejection by a loved one is a trauma of incomparable agony. It feels like the end of the world—no, the

3

universe. The trauma can be so intense that each year some young people commit suicide to escape the pain of a broken relationship. More often, however, our fears inflate to such grotesque proportions that we can't sleep, can't eat, can't show our faces in school or in social circles where the rejection occurred. The reason: because of youth or inexperience, we don't know we'll survive intact. Leaving or being left for the first time casts us into uncharted emotional territory, which we navigate in pain.

We also navigate in fear. The first time we love and lose—and almost no one escapes the experience by thirty—may be the first time since infancy that we feel helpless and desperate. And even though anyone faced with a loss will confront many painful thoughts, like "I didn't realize how much I still care for him," or "Maybe something is wrong with me," or "I feel so lonely," a younger, less experienced person may magnify these feelings. "I didn't realize how much I still care for him" becomes "I can't live without him!" "Maybe something is wrong with me" becomes "I am ugly and unlovable!" "I feel so lonely" may metamorphose into "I am lost forever" or "I want to die." In fact, the first time we are rejected, unfamiliar emotions can spin us out of control.

> Ray was a high-school junior, small for his age, with a high voice, who hadn't yet had the full benefit of male growth hormones. Rosemarie was a pretty girl: curly caramel-colored hair, flawless skin, voluptuous body. Rosemarie liked Ray and was happy to go with him to the pizza place after school now and then, but one day on the way home, he became amorous and she refused his advances.
>
> Ray couldn't accept her rejection and began to follow Rosemarie at odd times. She noticed him staring at her during basketball games, at her locker, in the parking lot.
>
> One day Ray came close, grabbed Rosemarie's

arm and told her, "You belong with me." She pushed him away, screaming, "Don't touch me!" Ray went home and drank vodka until he was numb.

The Grief in Brief

"I don't like you."
"I don't love you any more."
"We're no good together."
"I want out of this marriage."

Whether expected or unexpected, wanted or unwanted, words like these cause a shock that can reverberate for weeks, months, or even years after we hear them.

To be single again is to end a way of life. But sometimes it doesn't seem that way. Men and women seeking divorce, for example, may continue to do the same work, keep the same hours, engage in the same recreations, even see the same friends. Then one day they move from one bed to another bed, from a home shared for years to a home alone or one that's just created. That move, that shift, is a break in history. Nothing will ever be the same again.

For the abandoned person or the widowed woman or man, this dislocation is always more profound. Those seeking a divorce can prepare themselves, at least to some extent; it is their initiative, and they take steps beforehand to cope with the future. But those who have lost their mate through death or desertion are always shocked, even if the end was anticipated. No matter how long an illness may have lasted, we are rarely prepared for death; no matter how many "signals" a disgruntled spouse or love partner may have sent, the final act of separation is never really expected.

But shock alone is not enough to account for the onset of trauma. The fact is that life for the newly *singled* woman or man does not merely *appear* to be different; it *is* different in a thousand ways. The least of it is getting used to new routines, new customs, new ways of being perceived by friends and acquaintances. The most of it is the necessity to reexamine yourself, to discard much of what you have done for years and start all over again.

Three conditions characterize a traumatic event:

1. The change is drastic.
2. The change is both internal and external. It affects the way we see ourselves and the way we relate to the outside world.
3. The change is real. Our economic and social situation is different; people and institutions treat us differently. The change is not only in the mind, to be eradicated by mental exercise, but in the real world as well.

Just as all traumatic events have these three elements in common, all recovery journeys also will have common elements. If we look at enough recoveries, in fact, we can chart a pattern that most people follow. The pattern of recovery seems to consist of four stages:

1. **Denial**, or a refusal to accept the reality of the event.
2. **Anger** or rage at the partner.
3. **Withdrawal** or retrenchment—a regrouping of forces.
4. **Acceptance** and reintegration of the self.

These are more than periods to be lived through; all four stages can be fruitful and lead to a good recovery.

When we speak of stages, we don't mean sharply delineated periods, like a drama in which the curtain comes down on one setting and rises on a completely new one. Each stage merges into the other and erupts inside the other. For instance, the anger of the abandoned person exists from the beginning, during the stage of denial; periods of denial, anger, or shame can occur at any time, even long after you've recovered and are leading a new and satisfactory life. But even if the boundaries aren't precise, it's still true that in recovering from trauma we generally go through these phases.

The Four Phases of Loss

When we're young, in the throes of first loss, the future may seem to be a gaping emptiness, marked only by the absence of the loved one. It will help to know that the denial, the tremendous anger at our partner or ourself, and the withdrawal are all absolutely normal and necessary to getting on with life. Here is the map for those going through it for the first time:

Denial

He's gone. This thought occupies our mind, but in our heart he's still there and feels very close. We can still remember the smell of his hair, the slight scratch of his beard, his wonderful muscular body. We can imagine that he still loves us, even though he has plainly said he does not. (This just goes to show how much of a love affair happens in our minds!)

Denial has a purpose: to shelter us from the worst of the shock. While our mind is subconsciously processing the facts, we're medicating ourselves with a tranquilizer of denial. This allows some of the most difficult work of loss to be done while life goes on. Soon we can't bring up his image into our mind's eye. Soon we feel nothing at all. It is a combination of fatigue and the mind's way of protecting us from the roaring pain that threatens to invade. We may go to bed early and oversleep in the morning. Our appetite may disappear, or food may taste *too* good and we overeat. We may feel overwhelmingly sad and maybe even unable to go to school or work.

The first time we experience a loss, our denial may interfere with our life. But remember, most of us have our first losses when we are young, when all of our emotional and physical healing mechanisms are in better working order, and so we recover relatively quickly. Consider the experience of Jan, who's in her twenties:

> In the middle of our hot-and-heavy romance, Eric got transferred to another city. We missed each other so much that one morning, he woke me up with a 6 A.M. phone call to ask me to marry him. I said yes and rushed out to get plane tickets to visit him.
>
> The visit went well—his parents were there and we all adored each other—but by the next visit a month later, I could see he had lost his passion. Before I left he said he wasn't sure we should be married. I cried all the way to the plane and stared out the window for hours.
>
> Once home, I stayed by the phone, waiting for his call. When it didn't come, I went numb and stayed that way for a month, going through the motions of getting dressed, going to work, eating, cleaning. I still kept hoping he would call and tell me he had made a terrible mistake, but he never did. Then one spring day, I was looking out the window and . . . the haze lifted, just like that. I felt alive again and knew I was ready to move ahead.

Anger and Rage

How could she go? What does she think I am, just a meal ticket? How could she embarrass me this way? It's amazing how quickly true love can turn into true hate! This is more proof that love is based on what's in our minds rather than on the facts.

Many of us pass quickly through denial into anger or even uncontrollable rage. After all, even when someone dies, the person left behind may feel an irrational anger.

You may have heard about cases where rage is life-threatening. Many a rejected partner has acted on the thought

"Well, if I can't have her I'm going to make sure no one else can either," or "I'll make him sorry—I'll kill myself." But for most of us, the adrenaline of rage is more appropriately used:

> After Amy gave Mark his ring back and moved to another city, he threw himself into his work, arriving at the office before everyone else and staying until well after dark. On the way home, he stopped each day at the health club for a workout that would last until he was totally exhausted. Then he staggered home to bed.

Work and workouts are not a bad way to recover from a broken relationship. Besides being an outlet for all the adrenaline coursing through the body, they can help bolster any sagging self-esteem that has resulted from the breakup. Vigorous bread kneading, closet cleaning, nail hammering and the like also are fueled on adrenaline, bringing a reward for all that work! The first time you suffer a loss, you may be surprised at the intense feelings of rage that seize you. However, they usually pass quickly.

Guilt and humiliation are close cousins of anger and rage—in a sense, they're anger and rage turned upon ourself. Your partner has up and left; where do you direct the fury? You may begin to blame yourself, or even believe that the departure was your fault and feel humiliated. One vital lesson to learn from this book is that a voluntary departure gives far more information about the one who leaves than the one who is left.

Withdrawal

Once your rage is gone, you can expect to be completely exhausted. You may feel you are stuck in a twilight zone between the past and the future. Often we do not have the courage or the energy to start a new relationship yet. So we watch TV, take ourself out for coffee, see movies with friends.

The truth is that withdrawal from dating is not a twilight zone between the past and the future, but rather a very real present that can be filled with wonderful moments:

> In the months after Eric ended our engagement, I decided to try celibacy. That meant not dating, and certainly not sleeping with anyone.
>
> My little vacation from men turned out to be one of the best periods of my life. I shifted my focus to things that interested me—dance, music, calligraphy. Through the music I met the man who eventually became my husband. I will always wonder if the fact that I held him off for months before even kissing him had anything to do with it.

As long as the withdrawal does not turn into a severe depression, it can be a valuable and very personal time that actually can be enjoyed. Here's a period where self-parenting can flourish: do things that feel good, look for emotional and spiritual nourishment, maybe even repeat to oneself words that a parent might use to comfort a child. I've found that young people who have a strong sense of identity—and young people are indeed more independent today than they were just a few decades ago—will come out of withdrawal renewed and ready to move ahead. Their high energy makes it much harder for them to cloister themselves and mull over the past. Depression is less common in younger people as well.

Acceptance

Acceptance is the last phase of loss. If you're young, you'll probably find that this phase comes quickly. The years you've invested in the affair are relatively few; if you were married, children are less likely to be involved; physical aging isn't a major concern. Though young people may fear the future and have serious self-doubt after abandonment, hope seems to stir sooner in your heart.

This final adjustment we make to loss is more a phase of the mind than the heart. We stop reviewing the past, we stop redoing the present, we stop escaping from reality, and we look at the facts: The affair is over. We put our images of the former beloved into our memory book, close it, and turn the key in the lock. She's now part of the past; he's now a memory. We're ready to look around and see what the future consists of!

> Bob still thinks of Margie now and then. "She was my first love," he says nostalgically. But Bob has moved on. A year after Margie told him there was someone else (poor Bob also lost his job and apartment at the same time!), he met a woman who reminded him a bit of Margie. They dated, and Bob found out she was, in fact, nothing like Margie. He had a new love.

How quickly we arrive at acceptance varies enormously from person to person. It can take months or years.

A lot of that depends upon personality and childhood experiences. The person who will be slow to recover is likely to be someone who depends too much on other people, who feels that emotional wounds should be coddled, who takes any rejection as proof of unlovability, who believes humans were never meant to be single. All of these unproductive premises can be recognized, disputed, and brought under control.

A rejection need not ruin your life. It's an emotional experience to survive and learn from. If the process seems to take too long or causes you protracted agony, a trained therapist or support group may help.

Love on the Rebound

Sometimes we try to slip past the painful phases of loss by quickly replacing the one who left. This way we never have to miss the dear departed. Not so! The loss may slip in later and complicate the new relationship. Or the loss may make the new relationship a sham—a rebound sham:

> Just two months after Mike's divorce became final—the split had been his ex-wife's idea—Mike met Jane. A month later, Mike and Jane were sleeping together. A month after that, he introduced her to his closest friends at a small cocktail party. "What do you think?" he later asked them. "Isn't she fantastic?" His friends were shocked and concerned that Mike was moving so quickly.

But Mike's real question wasn't about Jane; it was about himself. "Aren't I fantastic to attract such a terrific woman?" was a thought he definitely needed to voice at this time of uncertainty and loneliness. And he needed someone to say yes. His friends, knowing that Mike had been devastated about the unexpected breakup of his marriage, told him he was lucky to have met someone so nice so soon. That seemed to be enough for Mike, and he soon found he was interested in seeing other women as well as Jane. However, he might just as well have believed she was finally "the one" and closed his options too. That's why I advise younger people to wait at least six months to let denial, rage, withdrawal, and acceptance play themselves out before beginning to explore the world again.

Abandoner's Emotions

Being the one who is left is certainly no pleasure, but the one who leaves also may carry some heavy emotional baggage. What seems to remain for the one who is left is a flotsam and jetsam of self-doubt and pain, accentuated by the fact that the one who is left feels no control over the process.

For the one who leaves, guilt makes up the bulk of the emotional baggage. Jillian was twenty-eight when this happened:

> Everyone said brides were supposed to be nervous, but the night before the wedding my head was whirring with so many fears and doubts I didn't sleep. By morning, I knew what I had to do: tell him that I couldn't get married now. I did, and he cried.
>
> This was the worst thing I ever did to anyone in my life. I regretted it for a whole year and anxiously pumped my friends for news about how he was doing. When he finally got married, I was enormously relieved.

In my practice, I see that the amount of guilt a young adult feels can vary tremendously. Some can end a relationship in the most callous way and feel no guilt at all—in some circles, the loved-'em-left-'em body count is worn as a badge of honor. This can be no surprise in our society, where child abuse, neglect, and selfishness are common, and simple human values go untaught. We see people treat others unkindly every day on television, and many young people assume this is the way to be.

A person with a conscience, however, can be consumed by feelings of self-reproach: *Why did I ever get involved with that person? I should have known I would hurt him. I wish it were me suffering instead of him.* People who feel this way must know that the romance took the course it did because there was no other course for it to take at the time. We can have a certain amount of control and self-discipline about the relationships we form, but sometimes not as much as we might like. The chemistry of attraction often works its magic without much input from the intellectual side of the brain. So don't expect to be completely logical about love. Still, guilt is a good teacher. Next time, perhaps, it will be easier to identify the threats to a good relationship before it proceeds too far and has to be dissolved by one of you.

The abandoner also is a likely target for stress. Even if *you* *chose* the separation and were thrilled with your decision, you can still be surprised by the amount of stress you feel. Think about it: Your social life is changing, your family life is changing, your financial life is changing . . . The sheer volume of trying to keep up with all the changes can be overwhelming. An awareness of what's happening—plus a little of that special medicine, tincture of time—can speed your recovery.

Last Word

No words can completely reassure you if you're young and newly single again. Recovery is a process we all must work our way through. But you can learn about where you're going by listening to other people who have gone before you. Here's what they want you to know:

- Now that you've experienced loss so profoundly, you know that you have the capacity to link, to care and bond. That means you can do it again.
- Young years are a time to meet many people, to find out who you are by seeing how you are with others.
- Trust the recovery process. Even the anger and sadness are necessary to healing—and will pass.
- As the old song says, "Got along without you before I met you, gonna get along without you now." (And you will!)
- And, as the old saying goes, "Love is always new." Anyone can love again. Anyone.

Recovery Readiness Checklist

To help you be more open to recovery, see how many of the following statements apply to you. Are you getting over the end of your relationship? Check each statement that describes your life now.

_____ 1. Most of the time, I don't hope or expect that my "ex" will return to me.

_____ 2. When the phone rings, I hardly ever find myself hoping that it's my former mate.

_____ 3. I rarely dream of being together with my former mate.

_____ 4. I don't spend much time imagining that my former mate is thinking regretfully of me.

_____ 5. Only infrequently do I feel angry toward my former mate. I rarely fantasize about hurting him/her, calling and saying how I feel, or sending awful things in the mail.

_____ 6. I am coming to understand that the breakup was caused in part by factors beyond my control. I hardly ever feel shamed or humiliated by the departure now.

_____ 7. My appetite and sleep patterns are closer to what they used to be before the relationship ended.

_____ 8. I'm dating exciting people, not just old, safe, "nonsexual" friends.

_____ 9. I go out in the evening, not just during the day.

_____ 10. I've had some new experiences lately.

KEY

If you checked:

- 2 or fewer statements, your emotional wounds are still raw and need nursing. Come back to this checklist in a month or so and see if you identify more closely with the statements here. Use the unchecked statements as a guide to what lies ahead.
- Three to six, you've made some progress since your loss. Keep up the good work. You're beginning to put some time and space between yourself and your emotional event.
- Seven to ten—full speed ahead! You're already trying new relationships, new experiences . . . The remainder of this book, with its specific guidelines on reentering the social scene, will be full of advice and ideas you can use now.

CHAPTER 2
Love and Loss Over Forty

Clara is in her mid-fifties, of average height, very slightly overweight, very well groomed. You would not call her beautiful except when she smiles, which is not very often. She works as a media analyst in an advertising agency.

> I've been divorced for four years now, but it started the year before that. That was when Dan said he had to have a serious talk with me. The talk was about how he was leaving. He wanted me to understand why.
>
> I understood why almost immediately. Dan's a handsome man, very distinguished, tall, broad, full head of hair, bright blue eyes. Women fall for him. He had had some affairs while we were married, but they hadn't lasted long.
>
> He wanted a divorce because I was holding him back. He works in a department store—assistant manager at major appliances. But it didn't give him enough . . . satisfaction, he called it. There were rich women out there, and there was no reason he couldn't get one. And though I was working and making a decent living, it wasn't enough for us both to live on. But if he had a rich wife, he could play the market, speculate, travel, open his own busi-

ness—do whatever he wanted. There was only one thing standing in his way: me. He had nothing against me personally; surely I could see how he felt.

I fought it. I told him I would make it hard for him and I did. I don't believe in divorce in the first place, not unless you're desperate. And he hadn't been so easy to live with; I had put up with a lot. Besides all that, I had gone out of my way to do things the way he wanted me to. The whole thing stank and I told him so.

So our lawyers went at it. Meantime he was trying to turn our daughters against me. We have two—Marsha was at college then, and Lily was a senior in high school. He wrote to Marsha that she knew how hard I was to live with, but now I was impossible. Marsha saved his letters and I saw them later—much later. What he meant was that when he was starting with another woman or doing other cute things, I argued with him. I'm not the crying type; I'd rather talk things out. With everybody else when I'm in an argument I can keep my voice at the talk level. But not with Dan: he has the knack of getting me right to the scream level. Which of course is all the girls heard, because while I'm screaming he's in total control.

He staged scenes for Lily. It took me a while to realize it. He'd make sure she was studying or reading—not listening to television—and then he'd start something. He wanted to make sure that the television didn't drown out my yelling. I always yelled on cue, and I was never drowned out.

I didn't tell you that he lived at home all that time, did I? Well, he did, until two weeks after the divorce was final.

I didn't tell you about sex either. It didn't stop. We slept together that whole time—more often than before. I'd spend the whole day thinking about how I hated him and the whole evening trying not to blow up at him, and we'd get into bed, and he'd touch me or say one word, and we'd be making love. Or whatever you call it. I'll tell you something else: if he didn't start, I would start. I'm not too happy about that when I think about it now.

So the lawyers did their thing and we went to trial. The girls testified how hard I was to get along with. Dan was the picture of a reasonable man who just couldn't tolerate any more. I felt like a piece of ice, and I guess that's how I came across.

He got the divorce and moved out. I was never so lonely in my life. Lily went off to college at about the same time, so I had nobody. I kept thinking he'd come back. I kept thinking about what I'd say when he did come back. Or when he'd phone. Or how I'd answer his letters—which was a joke, because he never wrote a letter unless he had to, as I well knew.

I don't know how I got through those first couple of months, coming back to that empty house, but I did. I was miserable. I said I wasn't the crying type, but I cried then. A lot. I stopped crying when the child support checks stopped coming. That's what the judge gave me: no alimony but a little money for Lily and Marsha, plus Dan had to pay their way through college. After the first few months he didn't pay a thing.

First I blew up. I don't think I was ever so angry in my life. Then I took him to court. He fought it. I'm still taking him to court every so often, over some other cute thing he does—like trying to sell my house from under me. He always fights it.

Basically, he's got what he wants. There are two women he goes out with, both wealthy. One's a little older than he is, one's a little younger. I understand that they're both beautiful. I'm betting he marries the older one; she's more likely to die first and leave him her money.

For a time the girls would hardly talk to me; they blamed me for everything. Things began to change when the support payments stopped coming. Now we're close again. Lily stays with me when she's not in college—the first year, they both stayed with friends on their vacations. We talk a lot. They don't have much to do with Dan, which is the way he wants it. That's one of the things we talk about. He used them and he hurt them, and they're still having trouble coping with it. But they'll be all right.

I haven't dated since the divorce, not anybody. I haven't had sex either. I thought I would miss it, but I didn't. Except lately I'm starting to think about it again and about men too. I suppose one of these days I'll go out again. I belong to a church with a good singles group, and they helped a lot while I was going through the divorce. But we do things mostly as a group. Anyway, there are no men there that I really want to date. As I said, right now I'm not that anxious to go out, though I wouldn't mind it. It's a question of when and where I'll start looking.

There's no doubt that Clara will come out all right: she's too intelligent, too determined, too well balanced not to. It's taken her a little longer than usual to get to the point of wanting to meet new people, but she's made it. We tell her story in such detail because most older people take a similar emotional journey to get to that point and to go beyond it.

As when we were younger, we must pass through the four phases of loss when we are older. But for an older person, the phases are more complex and take longer to pass through. We become "set in our ways"; our past as a couple has lasted longer and so will be harder to shake off; a future alone looms bleaker and more desolate than we could have imagined. Nor are the weight of the past and the uncertainty of the future mere illusions; they're realities that grow more pressing as the years pile up.

Younger men and women often can find another partner and resume a way of living very much like their earlier one; for an older person, especially an older woman, this possibility is more remote. The younger person can look upon being single again as an interruption in the flow of life; the older person must look upon it as the end of one life and the beginning of another, and most likely, very different life.

Denial

Denial in the Abandoned Woman or Man

The woman is about fifty-five years old, smartly dressed, attractive, verbal. It is three years since her husband left and she is still puzzled, still hurt and angry; and although she has a new life now, it is clear that the hurt and anger will remain a long time.

> I thought he was crazy. I mean literally crazy, insane, psychotic. How could he be sane and throw away thirty years of marriage and children?
>
> I told him he should see a psychiatrist, and he said he was already seeing one. That was the first time he mentioned it. From the way he spoke, I knew the psychiatrist was helping him leave me. That was why he was going—so he shouldn't feel guilty about leaving.
>
> We didn't tell anybody for a long time. I kept thinking he would change his mind. Actually, I

> thought he had lost his mind and it would come
> back again. Then when I did tell some friends they
> also said he was crazy and some day he would come
> to his senses and come back. They meant well, but it
> didn't help at all.

This is the stage of denial, of refusing to acknowledge that the event has actually occurred or is actually occurring. As when we were younger, we cannot believe that a mate is really going through with it, really means what he or she says, is really not crazy. And so we simply refuse to admit to ourselves that the event has actually taken place; in a part of ourselves we deny its reality. How is denial necessary to recovery? Shouldn't the attempt be to become reconciled to reality and begin from there? The answer is that certainly the ultimate goal is to accept reality, but first we must survive the shock, and it is here that denial plays its essential role.

In fact, denial plays two roles. One is to buy time to accept the idea of loss and its implications; the other is to allow the person to function in the world.

Of all newly single people, abandoned women and men usually have the most difficult time, and denial helps them get through it. Were the denial to persist or completely obliterate the reality of the situation, they would need professional help. But typically this is not what happens. Most often these people alternate between periods of despair when reality breaks in, and periods of relative calmness when the reality is denied. The denial helps them rise above the despair for at least long enough to see to their needs before despair comes again. Unconsciously the man or woman losing a spouse senses the finality of the separation and proceeds to make adjustments; consciously, however, until the initial turmoil has abated the finality is too much to endure. So they endure for as long as possible, and then their minds deny that the situation is final after all.

Thus one function of denial is to help us come to terms with the new reality. But exactly what is this new reality? In the initial shock the only reality for the abandoned person is loss. They face the prospect of beginning a new life with what appear to be no emotional resources. This reality also may include a deep sense of shame and humiliation, especially among older women. There is always anger at their partner, but there can also be a profound sense of their own inadequacy. For if they were not inadequate in some important way, why would the partner have left?

This is the reality that denial guards against, but in doing so it also allows us to function in another reality. This is the *reality of everyday competence,* of being able to do many things adequately and some things excellently, of having a role in the world apart from our role as a husband or wife. If we have been married for many years, this confirmation of competence is critical, because it provides a stable ground upon which to build a new life. Buffeted by shock, however, we tend not to see that stable ground except when the shock is denied.

It is denial that protects our reserves of strength; and as the awareness of those reserves begins to take hold, the denial decreases. Some measure of self-esteem returns, some sense of our own survival. It is usually at this point, when the abandoned man or woman can fully face the fact that the mate really wants to leave, that denial substantially ends and anger begins.

Denial may be indispensable for men and women being divorced, but it is the opposite of that for their friends: denial is not called for in friends. The woman we quoted earlier, who said that the friends who had predicted her husband's return "didn't help at all," was right; this kind of "help" never works. The reason is that the divorcing spouse rarely returns, and it is not productive for friends (or relatives, acquaintances, and the like) to reinforce unreality, to help create a fantasy of restoration and strengthen it. Women and men being sued for divorce are in a state of inner turmoil, and what they need most of all is an anchor to hold on to, an external source of stability. Good friends can provide that anchor by offering assurance through words, actions, and attitudes that the outside world is not also in turmoil, that it has not changed radically, and that warmth and understanding still prevail there. But to do this the friends must stand apart from the situation; they must represent the outside world at its best. (Suggestions for friends are discussed in Chapter 3, under Helping.)

Denial in Widows and Widowers

Although denial is most acute among abandoned men and women, it also appears in widows and widowers.

Faced with the death of a loved one, the first response is to deny it: it can't be possible; there must be some mistake. But death is obviously more final than divorce, more undeniable, if you will; and overt denial is replaced by covert denial in the form of blankness or forgetfulness. The bereaved person forgets that the spouse is dead, or encounters a blank numbness in which nothing has any meaning, including the death of the spouse. The belief that the dead spouse will be rejoined in an afterlife may also gain strength here. Whether true or not, the belief itself serves the same function as denial: to gain the widow or widower time to adjust to a new situation without simultaneously having to face an overwhelming loss.

Moreover, almost every human society has developed its own customs and rituals to ease the bereaved person through at least the initial stage of mourning. The rituals serve many purposes. They help discharge some of the emotions, help integrate the loss, and help keep the widow or widower occupied and connected with the outside world. Even after this initial period society still provides a breathing space in which incongruous or atypical behavior is forgiven. Friends may offer the solace of a future spiritual reunion, but this is clearly not the same as saying that the dead person will soon come to his senses and rejoin the living.

Denial of the death of the spouse may also take two other forms. One is to create a shrine to the loved one: leave all his or her things unchanged, speak as though that person were still alive, organize a whole way of life around the person who has died. Perpetual mourning is an aspect of this form of denial.

The other form is to take on some of the personality traits of the deceased: become neater than usual because she was neat, watch football on television because he used to do that—in brief, to recreate the lost spouse in oneself.

These two forms of denial may occur for brief periods of time. If they persist or if they interfere with the recovery process, then professional help probably is needed.

In most cases, however, it is not needed. Although the widow or widower experiences a greater loss than the person being sued for divorce, the blow to self-esteem is much lighter. And as friends and relatives volunteer their help and concern, the ego can be sheltered and even the sense of loss can be cushioned, at least for a while. So denial is not so acute, and the next stage may be entered more quickly.

Denial in Divorce-seekers

Ostensibly the person seeking a divorce has neither physical loss nor loss of self-esteem to cope with and thus should have no need to deny his or her new status. On the other hand what the divorcing person is sure to lose is history, and this poses its own problem.

Actually, denial on the part of the older person seeking a divorce usually takes two forms. One is urgency: everything must be done at once, signed and sealed, packaged and delivered; every delay is intolerable. Everything that was, the urgency is saying, must not be anymore, must never have been, must not be remembered; the landscape of the past holds too many memories and must be hurried through. For some people this form of denial is the hardest to overcome. Denial also takes the form of *spectatoritis,* of being outside ourselves, watching ourselves perform actions that seem to have no meaning. The world tends to lose substance and become thin and hollow; the divorcing man or woman often seems to float through a haze of activities and events and remain untouched by them—seems to be an observer rather than a participant. Even when involved with the actual divorce, with the ending of a relationship that is in fact the end of an era, the person may go through it as though surrounded by a bubble of air that keeps everything out.

The Value of Denial

The stage of denial is almost always necessary for the newly singled person. It provides protection against the flood of unbearable overwhelming emotions and allows these emotions to seep through gradually and manageably. At the same time denial allows the remainder of the self, the aspects of personality in which the partner is largely uninvolved, to be strengthened and confirmed, so that when emotions do break through, the man or woman is better prepared to meet them.

Finally, in a sense, denial is realistic, especially for the parties in a divorce, because some sort of relationship still exists. The former mate still exists; the children still exist; the old in-laws still exist. Even if there are no children or in-laws, the spouse's birthday still comes every year; his favorite movies still show up on television; sometimes a memory of her erupts on the most unexpected occasions. War, it has been said, is the continuation of diplomacy by other means; divorce is the continuation of marriage by other means. And so, to some extent, the denial of the finality of the divorce is a recognition of the continued existence of the other person in the real world. And since memory persists in everybody, denial on the part of the widow or widower is a reflection of the history of the relationship and the continuing presence of the past.

Anger, Guilt, Humiliation, Shame

Anger in the Abandoned Man or Woman

For both partners in a divorce, especially for the abandoned person, the first emotion to break through is usually anger, or anger mixed with shame. Anger is also the last emotion to leave and may linger in parts of the mind indefinitely. The woman— very wealthy, very successful, the mother of two very successful daughters—has been divorced for five years.

> I was sure I was all through with Carl. As soon as he said he was leaving I went to a psychiatrist, and she was very helpful. My colleagues were great. My friends encouraged me to get into my anger and that helped too. Carl and I had our battles during the divorce, but for two years now we've hardly seen each other. He avoids me and I don't chase after him. I don't think I've thought about him with anything but amusement for over a year.
>
> And then last night I had a dream. I'm in my classroom, talking to my students. And I'm saying, "He's damned; he's damned! He's going to hell! Some day he's going to pay for this!" *He* was Carl, and I really wanted him to go to hell—literally go to hell, burn and suffer. I thought I had gotten rid of that a long time ago.

Of all newly single men and women, the anger of the abandoned spouse is the easiest to understand. It is the anger at being betrayed and rejected, at having one's emotional investment in another human suddenly rendered worthless. Worse, the rejection is almost always felt to be retroactive, to go back to the earliest stages of the relationship, so that the divorcing partner is not only rejecting us now but has always rejected us, never loved us from the beginning. It is not only that the current situation is bad but that the entire relationship has been a waste: if the partner can leave now, then those twenty or thirty years together were a fraud.

Most abandoned people have no trouble admitting their anger. An older person with years of life experience may be more familiar with anger and can recognize it intellectually. Many, however, may have trouble expressing it and some deny most of their anger in a flood of self-recrimination: the breakup was their fault; the partner was perfect; they themselves were impossible to live with; who could blame anyone for leaving? Even if this were true (realistically, it is never true), it does not mean that the anger does not exist. It does exist; it is justified, and it must be acknowledged if this remorseful person is to move on to a new life. Professional help is sometimes very useful here.

Humiliation and Shame in the Abandoned Man or Woman

The humiliation and shame of the abandoned man and woman are also easy to understand. It is not only that they have been rejected, but also it is that the whole world knows of it. They are not good enough to remain married to. No matter how good a mate one actually is, when one partner announces an intention to leave, the other partner feels at fault and dreads the idea of exposing that fault to friends and family.

What exactly is shame, where does it come from, and what should one do about it? *Shame* replaces the sense of self-worth by a need to appear worthy to others. The actual feeling arises from a belief that others do not think us worthy, do not value us highly.

As such, shame is much more prevalent in older women, since these women, more than men, have been taught that their value lies not so much in their own accomplishments as in what others (mostly men) think of them. Trained to live reflected lives, such a woman's self-concept is more dependent than a man's on how she thinks she is perceived by others, and shame is the conviction that her reflection shows miserably.

The energy for shame, however, the drive behind the feeling, generally comes from anger at the partner converted into anger at oneself and placed in the eyes of others. It is commonplace that any emotion can be converted into any other emotion (the switching from love to hate and back again is the best-known example), but for most people—again, especially for women—anger per se is a difficult emotion to deal with. That is, we are taught that it is inevitably destructive and must be suppressed or risen above. So we change anger into something else, and if we have been indoctrinated to look to others for self-esteem, we color those others with our anger. We feel that they reject us also, and as a consequence, we are ashamed.

What can we do about shame, the feeling that we have been humiliated? Most psychotherapies treat it as something to be faced and mastered. We must assert our own worth and powers, they say; to invest them in others is to revert to being a child again, seeking the approval of the powerful adult world.

But this is precisely what happens in trauma: we are catapulted back into an earlier psychological state, the state of psychological dependency. The familiar world is collapsing and we feel unable to cope. Meanwhile standing like bulwarks are real people, family and friends, who are not collapsing, who still control their world. It is no wonder that in trauma we turn to the outside world for emotional (as well as physical) nurturing. However if we imagine that the outside world is disapproving then we feel ashamed of ourselves and withdraw.

Thus we should expect the person being divorced to have some feelings of shame. Friends and others can help by clarifying the destructive tendency and encouraging the man or woman to redirect the emotion outward, as anger at the partner, rather than keeping it turned inward toward the self—which inevitably leads to emotional and/or physical suffering. [In fact recent studies suggest a direct link between trauma involving a significant person in our lives (spouse, parent, child) and the onset of cancer.]

Anger and Shame in People Seeking Divorce

Anger and shame are also experienced by the divorcing person, although not as strongly as in the rejected partner.

The divorcing person becomes angry because, oddly enough, the spouse is letting go too easily. Much as we want to leave, much as we have pondered all the good reasons for leaving, much as we are entirely committed to obtaining a divorce, we still want the partner to woo us back again. More than that, we want our partner to transform himself or herself in the effort: to give up everything, adopt an entirely new personality, become the perfect fantasized other. If the partner cannot or will not do that, he or she does not love us and has never loved us. That is cause enough for rage and reinforces the reasons for leaving.

Later the divorcing person may recognize that these expectations are, to say the least, irrational. But this person, like the person being left, is in a state of turmoil. He or she has also been married for many years and is facing a new life alone (or with a new partner); he or she also is traumatized in many new ways; and he or she may also regress to psychological dependency. The impact is not as deep or extensive as that of the abandoned person, but it is still there.

Also like the abandoned person, the divorce-seeking man or woman feels shame at the breakup of the marriage; blame the other as we will, there is always the knowledge that at least part of the responsibility is ours. Even today, when almost half of new marriages end in divorce, divorce usually is still seen as a failure, proof of some sort of inadequacy. For the older person, raised in a time when divorce was a last, desperate resort, the deliberate breakup of a marriage is taken to signal a collapse in one's adequacy and a demonstration of that collapse to others.

With it all, the person seeking a divorce almost always feels a sense of guilt. We know that our partner is in emotional pain and that our actions have been the agents of that pain. So, typically, we go into psychotherapy or sequester ourselves from friends for a while or—taking the opposite tack—drink a little too much and socialize more than usual. Thus we cope with our knowledge of the spouse's distress, and thus we look for reassurance that we are not really to blame.

But reassurances—the break was inevitable; the mate was impossible; one person is not responsible for the emotions of another—all fail to some extent until the spouse starts to recover and emerge again into the world. At that point a paradoxical event may occur: The divorcing spouse grows angry with the recovering partner. Why? Because this is further proof that that person, the wife or husband whose pain evoked so much guilt, does not love us any longer, has gotten us out of his or her system. If the spouse had really loved us—ever—she or he would not recover but would be desolate forever. And so anger returns because the spouse's recovery seems to diminish the divorcing person's stature.

This also is a manifestation of regression to childhood dependency. For example, along with a knowledge that he or she is dependent on the parent, the child retains a portion of the infant's feelings of omnipotence, of being the most important person in the world to the mother and father, of living eternally in the center of their lives. And when the spouse (who to some extent has served as a parent figure, as spouses always do) has had the audacity not to be totally crushed by one's defection, the child in the divorcing person's psyche may become angry at this betrayal.

Grief in Widows and Widowers

Anger, shame, and guilt are usually the dominant emotions in the parties to a divorce, and in the widow or widower grief generally dominates.

In a sense grief is an easier emotion to cope with than anger and shame; just as in a sense widows and widowers have an easier time than the divorcing or the abandoned person. The major reason is that widows and widowers at least have not been overtly rejected: there is no shame attached to their new status, no aura of failure; they do not divide their friends and force their children to choose between them. Further, as we said earlier, society tends to protect the bereaved partner, not only by providing a buffer against the problems of survival but also by showing more empathy toward behavior that might otherwise be thought peculiar. Finally, grief is thought to be a "cleaner" emotion than anger, shame, or guilt; there may be some difficulty in allowing oneself to grieve, but, except among some dwindling areas of American society, there is no stigma in doing so.

The problem is that the widow or widower feels not only grief but also anger and guilt—again, arising from regression to psychological dependency. Anger comes because the partner has deserted the bereaved person and in that desertion has demonstrated a lack of caring. Clearly on a rational level this is absurd; and clearly no adult consciously equates the death of a loved one from illness or accident with desertion. But we are dealing not with the adult but with the child in the adult who believes that real adults can do anything and that if the deceased partner had wanted to he or she would not have died.

Because this anger is irrational and is felt to be so, it is typically denied; and this denial is reinforced by a reluctance to speak ill of the dead. So the bereaved woman or man has trouble expressing anger at the dead spouse—and not only expressing it but actually experiencing it, actually being aware of it. It seems wrong, sinful, somehow shameful to feel anger at this dead person. But until that anger is accepted, the working through of the bereavement can scarcely be completed.

And the bereaved woman or man almost inevitably experiences a sense of guilt at not having been a better mate. Sometimes this can be overwhelming. Frequently it is mingled and cleansed with grief, but often it lingers for decades. The speaker is a small, quiet woman in her seventies, whose husband has been dead for twenty years.

> I was always smarter than Joe and he never really made a good living, and when he died I was sorry but I thought, well, he was never the best husband. He had never made me really happy, and I can learn to live without him very well. And I did. But lately he's coming back to my mind, and now I'm thinking that I wasn't the best wife to him and never made him very happy. What can I do with that? He's been dead twenty years.

And a fifty-year-old man recalls the death of his wife five years earlier in an automobile accident. Married twenty-two years, they had been growing apart for the last ten, and it would have been only a matter of time before he asked for a divorce. . . .

> What saved me was that I bought tickets to a play she wanted to see. She had been talking about it for a long time, and I finally bought us some tickets. They were for a Friday evening, and that Wednesday afternoon she had the accident. She was conscious for an hour or so, and I like to think that she

remembered we were supposed to go out together. I like to believe that was the last thing she thought of—that I still cared for her. If I hadn't believed it, I think I would have gone crazy. I still believe it. I have to.

It is also true that, like shame, guilt is fueled by anger; it too consists in large measure of anger turned inward. This is not to say that guilt is always irrational; it is that very often guilty feelings are inappropriate, exaggerated, unrelated to the real situation. A man who beats his wife may legitimately feel guilty; the wife who flees the brutal husband and feels guilty when he turns to drink is in another category.

The guilt we call irrational involves unrealistic expectations of the self—impossible ideals; and it is this guilt that is very often anger turned inward. It is the anger of the oppressed child, unable to defend himself or herself against his adult oppressors or take revenge on them. So he has one recourse: He identifies with them. He does this out of necessity. They are strong and he is weak; and he identifies with their strength because otherwise his own weakness would, he feels, be fatal. But having made the identification, he must now be angry at what makes them angry: that is, at himself. The anger thus reflected inward is what people often experience as guilt.

Handling the Emotions

No matter under what circumstances we become single again, there is no escape from anger, guilt, and shame. Whether they have a real basis or not, these emotions are consequences of the trauma, of seeing the world through the eyes of a helpless child. Because they are painful emotions to express as adults and because American society is still generally intolerant of the expression of strong emotions, they are typically repressed. But this repression carries penalties: at best a lengthening of the recovery process, at worst the onset of severe psychological or psychosomatic illness.

What is to be done with those emotions? In one sense, nothing; we do not have to do anything with them. We do not have to punish the rejecting spouse, expiate the guilt, redeem ourselves for the shame. But we do have to acknowledge them and express them.

The pressure of these emotions constitutes a form of stress, and many people have developed their own stress-handling methods: meditation, exercise, a deep plunge into work. But most people do nothing except repress the emotion and deny the stress—and the outcome can be devastating. During the course of a thirty-year marriage a woman's husband threatened to leave her on three separate occasions unless she changed her ways. Each time the woman swallowed her pain and anger and gave in to the husband's demands; and each time within a year she developed cancer. Fortunately in each case it was discovered early enough to allow a complete recovery.

If friends have any role during the phase of anger, it is to offer a chance to let go, to offer the chance to express the feelings that may otherwise cause real physical harm. But this is not always an easy job for friends, or even for professional counselors and therapists. Conditioned to distrust the expression of strong feelings, many Americans fear that strong anger will always lead to blind fury, that strong pain will always lead to uncontrolled hysteria. This rarely happens, but the fear alone is enough to make people pull away from strong feelings and attempt to damp them down. Thus friends will tell the deserted woman that her husband isn't worth getting angry over. They mean to be helpful; but the important factor is not what the man deserves but what the woman needs. She is full of anger, and she needs to work it out of her system. And therefore she needs her friends to tell her, by their words and attitudes, that the expression of her anger—and guilt, pain, humiliation, shame—is acceptable to them.

Withdrawal

After denial and anger have been worked through, the single-again man or woman may want to spend more time alone than usual. This is the beginning of the return from the helplessness of the child to the autonomy of the adult. Being alone, or simply doing things alone, brings a deep feeling of contentment. The woman speaking is in her fifties and has been divorced for three years.

> We had money, and we could have afforded good restaurants and good vacations and orchestra seats to plays and a little bit of fun. But he was always too stingy—everything for the office, nothing for the two of us. So after he left I did it myself—paid my own way, sat by myself, ate by myself, treated myself like a queen. I never felt lonely, and I loved every minute of it.

It turned out that what this woman loved most was not the experience of eating well or sitting in the orchestra nor even—though this was part of it—of being her own person, not having to defer to another's preferences. What she loved most was the sense of being a whole person, a sufficient person, fundamentally an integrated person.

But this feeling comes toward the end of the reintegration process, not the beginning. For later the woman remembered that this period had been preceded by a period in which she seemed almost to be marking time. The worst of the shock was over; she was well into her work again, and yet nothing gave her a sense of satisfaction. The men she met were not ready for her or she was not ready for them; her colleagues suddenly seemed not hostile or antagonistic but somehow more fallible than before, more error prone, more apt to show a lack of sensitivity or sympathy. She had begun to see a psychotherapist, and she complained with some irritation that the therapist didn't understand her.

What this woman was, in fact, doing was reintegrating her life, regrouping her forces. Because this now was her most important task, everything else became a distraction or an irritant. For most people there is a natural healing process for the mind as well as the body, and she was guarding this process, unaware (as are most people) that it was taking place.

But the process is crucial. This odd space, this misunderstood, awkward, uncomfortable, grumpy feeling, is actually the feeling of being in transition, of being detached from the past and the present, of being, in a sense, in a state of timelessness. The initial denial, followed by the expression of anger and the other emotions, has served to wrench us free of our former life, and we do not yet have a clear sense of what our new life will be. So we are traversing a gap, an emptiness, and this part of the recovery process is the experiencing of that gap.

Reconsideration

It is now that another phenomenon sometimes occurs, the phenomenon of reconsideration. The person suing for divorce begins to think that he or she may be making a mistake; the abandoned person, accepting the finality of the situation, finds herself or himself thinking of reasons for making one last try together. The widow or widower may develop an unrealistic belief in an afterlife, consult mediums—or simply begin seeing the deceased mate everywhere, at supermarkets, office buildings, all public places.

For most people the phase of reconsideration is an attempt to dispel the discomfort of the transition by returning to a familiar situation, the old relationship. But usually the attempt is futile: they have come too far, committed themselves too much to a new life. And even though some couples do get together again for a time (sometimes only for an evening of sex), it is usually just that—only for a time. The situation has changed and they have changed, they are not really the same people they were before the breakup, and they cannot behave as though they were.

Last Word

With all its confusion and humiliation the transitional period sometimes makes possible the creation of a new personality, in which repressed potentials can emerge, in which previously un-expressed talents and abilities can flower. Hurry the process and the chance to build a new world and a new self may be lost; let it happen and the chances are good that it may happen for the best. When the woman dined alone in a good restaurant on food she enjoyed in surroundings she admired with a waiter whose attentions she relished, that these externals were doing something good to her is not what mattered. What mattered was that somewhere inside her there was finally an inde-pendent person who could enjoy these things whether alone or with others.

The final stage is the acceptance of the new status and the birth of the self—and that is the subject of most of the remain-der of this book. But first we want to go more deeply into this phenomenon we call regression, since it is a central experience of the newly single woman or man.

Transforming "The End" into a Beginning

If "All the world's a stage, and all the men and women merely players" (as Shakespeare said in *As You Like It*), right now it may seem to you that your stage is dark and the actors have all gone home. Here's a synopsis of tips from this chapter that will help raise the curtain and bring up the lights:

- DO be ready for some unexpected emotions during this time: rage, shame, mood swings, surges of emotion you thought you had dealt with.
- DO express your feelings (without hurting anyone else, of course). Holding in strong emotions may make you sick. Acknowledging them speeds emotional healing.
- DON'T rush into new relationships. Don't make any permanent decisions (such as marriage or moving in with someone new) for about two years.
- DO remember the four stages of loss—denial, anger, withdrawal, acceptance. They're the steps to a more emotionally stable and satisfying recovery.

CHAPTER 3
Regression: The Helpless Child

The woman was in her late thirties, small, dark, and pretty. At first she spoke rapidly. One night a few months earlier her husband of fourteen years announced that he wanted a divorce. He had fallen in love with another woman; he couldn't live a lie any longer. . . . It was all over. But this wasn't her problem.

She hesitated a long moment. "This is going to sound crazy," she said, "but I have to ask you something." We waited, and she waited. Then: "When I came in here," she said, "did you smell anything? A bad odor?" We shook our heads. "You don't smell anything now?"

"No."

Now her words came rapidly again. "A few weeks ago I began to smell this odor coming from me. It was very bad. I could smell it and I was sure everybody near me could smell it too . . . only they were too polite to say so.

"I wash myself," the woman continued. "I take showers, and I soap myself all over, and I scrub myself. It doesn't seem to help. I still smell that bad odor coming from me." She paused. "You don't smell anything?" And then: "Am I going crazy?"

Of course this woman was neither emitting an offensive odor nor going crazy. What she was doing was experiencing the feeling of shame that many people feel when their spouses leave them. And she was connecting this shame with an earlier episode in her life: when, as a very young girl, she had had to sit for over an hour at a church service and had soiled herself. In an apparently bizarre way she was regressing to a time thirty-five years earlier to find an "explanation" for her pain. If she felt so crushed, so ashamed of herself, it must be because she had done something bad.

To our way of thinking, regression is a central concept in understanding the consequences of the separating event. It is a return to an earlier psychological state, and we have divided it into two types. One is regression in the classical sense, which occurs inevitably as a result of trauma, of having been shaken to the very center of the self. This we call *traumatic regression*. Desperately needing something or someone to hold on to, in traumatic regression we psychologically return all the way back to early childhood. The other type of regression we call *situational regression,* and it can occur when we are confronted not with a whole new life but with a new situation, a new set of circumstances that challenge our confidence. To help meet the challenge, we go back to similar circumstances we encountered years before, often during adolescence. Traumatic regression and situational regression are related to each other, but occur at different times and are experienced in different ways.

We also want to add that as therapists we are aware that the word *regression* itself may have negative connotations. In our view, however, it is a defensive maneuver that is essential to the psychological survival of most people in trauma.

Traumatic Regression

The most important fact about traumatic regression is that it is completely normal: it happens, literally, to everybody who suffers a trauma. But what exactly does happen?

What happens is a pervasive feeling of helplessness. The world and the self have become completely undone, and we

simply do not know how to cope. We are too weak; our powers
have dwindled; our capacities have shrunk; we are just not up
to the task. This feeling, this conviction of being helpless, is the
core condition of traumatic regression, the center from which
all the other symptoms radiate.

Helplessness—and Hiding It

The experience of being helpless is expressed differently by different people. Sometimes it is translated directly into behavior:
The person states that he or she cannot perform as expected, as
had been done in the past, and makes an explicit request for
help. But this is not very common. More often, we put on an
elaborate and transparent show of independence: For example,
we refuse to accompany friends on an outing, telling them to
go ahead anyway; we will be fine. But at the same time our
manner is saying how sad we are, how depressed; and how can
they leave us alone? Or we put on a show of doing things for
ourselves or returning to old routines again, and somehow
never get very far. Or our work is punctuated by sighs, mutter-
ings, or expletives. In brief the overt behavior says "I'm all
right"; but the message, which is usually clear to everybody, is
"I can't do this alone; help me."

For most people in this country the need to dissimulate,
to hide the helplessness under a tattered cloak of confidence, is
very strong. So they create three typical self-images to conceal
the truth from others and from themselves.

"I'm still in charge." The first self-image is related to denial. The person wants to think of himself or herself as still being competent, wants to preserve a self-image that has been
severely undercut in other quarters. So some men and women,
once they have recovered from the initial shock, work harder
and more desperately than ever before: partly to drown their
pain in details, partly to prove to themselves that they can still
function successfully. They have not been affected; they have

not been shaken; they are just as good as they always were. But the desperate quality of this behavior, the unyielding insistence on total competence, is a giveaway: secretly, in a manner that they will not admit even to themselves, they want to be taken care of.

"*I'm not a child.*" Related to the need to feel in command is its obverse, the shock at feeling childish. For some women and men there is something shameful in the very thought of not being able to take care of themselves, of revealing to the world their inability to cope. And not only to the world but also to themselves: they are acutely sensitive to the fact that in feeling helpless they are like children, and they find this disgraceful and, yes, shameful. Adults are not supposed to act like children—at least, not like incompetent children. So these men and women grit their teeth and slog ahead, deriving their deepest satisfaction from the fact that they have not given in to the shame of feeling helpless.

"*I will not be a burden.*" The final self-image is one of grim independence, and it is a reaction to the fear of imposing on other people. Regardless of our needs and desires, we have no right, the feeling is, to burden others with our problems. Other people are busy with their own lives and it is not fair to involve them in our weakness. The good friends and even the close relatives, the sisters, brothers, mothers, fathers, do not want to be around a crybaby and should not be forced to bother with somebody who—at bottom—has problems that are not their own. It is better to be strong, wear a stiff upper lip, straighten one's shoulders, stand erect, and make believe that either nothing has happened or, if something has, that it can be handled without a fuss.

The Voices From the Past

All three self-images have common aspects. First, they are based to a great extent not on our own feelings but on our expectations (fantasies, usually) of how others will react. This is clearest with the person who will not impose on others: his or her behavior is absolutely determined by the anticipated responses of friends and family. Similarly, the person ashamed of behaving and feeling like a child is reacting to the supposed opinion of others; their anticipated accusations are feared; their imagined scorn is fled. These accusations seem to belong to the self; but the outside voices came first, telling the young girls and boys not to act like babies, to be grown-up, saying that big girls and boys take care of themselves. It was those voices that evoked shame in the child, and it is the fear of those voices, now internalized, that evokes in the adult the fear of being childish.

The person driven by the fear of failure, by the need to be in command, is usually male. He hears the same voices but they carry a different message: that to be a real man is to be un-bowed in the face of catastrophe, to act always with grace under pressure—never mind how intense the pressure is or how much self-destruction the demonstration of grace demands. But the message says more: that to fail as a man is an occasion not for shame but for extinction. The equation reads: performance equals manhood equals all value; and when performance is gone the man might as well be gone also. Thus it is not uncommon for men to commit suicide when they feel they have lost the ability to perform as before.

A man's identification of performance with self-value also comes from outside the self. It begins in childhood with the standards imposed by adults. This is more common in men than in women because until recently competence was valued more highly in men than in women; little boys were expected to grow into big men who could do important things while little girls were expected to become sweet and charming mothers, wives, and secretaries. The pressure on boys was greater than that on girls and started earlier; it was and is thus more established in men than in women, more integrated into the personality, harder to separate out. But the man in trauma, driven to prove his competence, is responding just as much to those early voices as is the woman, driven to avoid shame.

Hypersensitivity

Although feelings of helplessness can sometimes be hidden, it is harder to conceal the other consequences of traumatic regression. One of the most striking consequences is a heightened sensitivity to others. It is the sensitivity of a frightened child, both parents suddenly gone, thrust into a new world dominated by adults he or she does not know. Dependent upon these adults, the child becomes extremely sensitive to their moods, because the only way to feel safe is to know if either they like him or her or if he or she is doing something wrong. So the child sifts through the grown-ups' words and gestures, actions and intonations, tuning herself or himself especially to signs of danger: that is, displeasure, impatience, anger, indifference, annoyance.

The person in trauma is in an analogous position. The world has been completely altered, and although the people in it are familiar, the relationships feel different and strange. And so women and men become sensitive (actually, hypersensitive) to others, to the nuances of initiative and response, and especially to the negative nuances—or what, in one's pain, are taken to be negative nuances. In a divorce particularly, the question of whose side the friends and family are on becomes overwhelmingly important, and the slightest hint of partiality toward the other is taken as a deliberate insult to the self.

Passivity

The third symptom of traumatic regression is passivity: The person in trauma often doesn't want to do anything beyond taking care of her or his immediate needs—if even that much. But at the root of the passivity is fear.

The man or woman in trauma has been wounded by another person, and there is a great reluctance to go out among people again and face the possibility of being wounded once more. This is especially true of people wounded in self-image, such as being asked for a divorce; for them the world has become so cruel that the prospect of actually doing something in that world, taking any initiative, carries too great a foreboding of disaster and more pain. Even the widowed person experiences the fear that he or she is not the same as before, doesn't have the same social skills, is not as attractive, doesn't play the game as well—in fact, doesn't even know what the new games are. That person also hesitates to move. And so we tend not to take initiatives in dealing with others, no matter how familiar and beloved those others might be.

Unconscious Manipulation

If helplessness, hypersensitivity, and passivity are some of the symptoms of regression, how are they handled? One possibility is to ask for help directly, but as we said, the internal prohibitions are usually too strong. In addition asking for help also means taking an initiative, and this also is avoided.

The typical method is unconscious manipulation—the attempt to induce others, *by indirection,* to respond to our unspoken needs. The main recourse of the hurt man or woman in a world that seems dangerous is that of the child in the same circumstances: to manipulate the adults into doing what she or he wants. In trauma we want to be taken care of, and we ask in the only way we think is allowed: by denying the wish and hoping it is granted anyway.

The wish to be taken care of is there even with people who succeed in masking it completely; the women and men who vow *not* to complain but simply go about their business and bother nobody. The manipulation is there also. The woman avoiding feelings of shame assumes unconsciously that if only she acts maturely her friends will reward her by taking care of her of their own free will—by reading her mind, so to speak. And the man driven by fear of failure is engaged in manipulation—not so much of others but of himself, of the inward voices that define manhood for him. He feels that if only he behaves like a man in these most difficult circumstances, then those voices will let up, cease their demands, and tell him what a good boy he is. But they rarely do.

Nor do the external manipulations invariably work. Friends and counselors do not read our minds; brothers and sisters eventually do go out without us; the effort fails. If it does not always fail, it sometimes fails, and every time it does, it erases all the times it has succeeded. The results of failure are anger and depression, while the results of success are typically elation and optimism.

This is to say that the unconscious manipulations attempted by the person in trauma contribute to the mood swings that are characteristic of this period. And this brings us to the final symptom of traumatic regression.

Mood Swings

In the recovery period states of elation and depression alternate regularly and without apparent reason; and even as recovery proceeds, periods of depression seem to strike unaccountably. By no means does depression result only from failed manipulations; the loss itself is a major factor and so is all that the loss represents. What hurts is not only the specific event (I am no longer living with this man or woman), but also the associations carried with it (I am no longer a married person among married people; I am no longer a "normal" adult; my attractiveness is now in doubt; my life-style feels all wrong; my old relationships are suddenly strained). More troublesome, the trauma dredges up feelings buried deep in childhood: I am inherently unlovable; I cannot trust anybody; everybody will leave me; I cannot survive alone.

So there are good reasons for the attacks of depression that accompany every trauma. The point is that failed manipulation can trigger these depressions and intensify or prolong them.

Depression during trauma is fed from many sources: a realistic source—things are not the way they were; a regressed source—all of my bad childhood fantasies are true; and a reactive source (unsuccessful manipulation)—I have failed again; nobody really loves me; nobody does what I want. Elation during trauma is fed by three very comparable sources: a realistic source—I am taking care of myself rather well; a regressed source based on the child's feelings of omnipotence—I can master anything in the world; and a reactive source (successful manipulation)—they love me; they've done what I want. And so, just as failed manipulation drives the depressed mood deeper, successful unconscious manipulation pumps the elated mood higher.

In summary regression in trauma shows itself primarily in five symptoms: helplessness, hypersensitivity, passivity, manipulation, and moodiness. All of these patterns are seen in children: their real need for adults coupled with a flat denial of that need, real helplessness and sensitivity, real swings in mood. Passivity alone is usually absent in the child except for the child who has been deeply wounded. For this child, as for the man and woman in trauma, nothing is worth doing because doing something brings hope, and hope only brings pain.

Recovering From Traumatic Regression

Moving Backward

A trauma is an event that has two dramatic effects: it changes life drastically, and it may rob us of some of our capabilities. This is where trauma differs from crisis, which also imposes drastic change but usually leaves our capabilities intact. In a crisis the ground starts to collapse underfoot; in trauma the ground starts to collapse and, at the same time, our legs grow weak. For the person in crisis the best move may be to leap ahead, to an unfamiliar but potentially promising future. For the person in trauma this course is much too terrifying: safety, not opportunity, is the first concern. And for the person in trauma safety lies behind, in a place we have already lived in, whose terrain we know. But safety here means psychological safety, emotional safety, and so the person in trauma retreats to the last psychological, emotional state in which he or she felt safe.

This is always the state of childhood. It is safe for two reasons. First, it is familiar: no matter how bad your childhood has been, at least you know what to expect. It will probably hold few surprises; and if it also holds terrors, at least they are familiar terrors. And second, even if your childhood was bad indeed, for you to have survived into adulthood intact in any degree, there must have been a bedrock sense of being taken care of, a sense that, in the final extremity, some adult would offer at least a crumb of help.

How do we know how far to regress? We recognize the match between our current emotional circumstances and our earlier circumstances. We do not retreat just a little way, to the stage of the young adult, for example, because that stage is one of self-responsibility and expansion into the world. We need support, and we go back and back until we reach the psychological state in which we needed support in the same way—and got it. In brief we retreat to a place where, psychologically at least, our feeling of helplessness is justified.

Moving Forward

But if one moves into regression, one also moves out of it. The regressive flight is natural under the circumstances, as is the return to adulthood. The reason for this is that children want to grow up; because helplessness is an uncomfortable feeling and dependency is an uncomfortable status. For most people the dream of an eternal, carefree youth is not a reversion to childhood, with its lack of autonomy, its lack of independence, its fundamental lack of meaning; instead they dream of a reversion

to adolescence, to a great gulp of autonomy and a small swal-
low of responsibility, to the tasting of one's powers and capabilities before their limits have been tested. Many people would
remain in their adolescence if the world would let them, but—
Peter Pan notwithstanding—practically nobody wants to remain a child.

In our return from regression, we are helped by an important fact. If in trauma we regress to a familiar stage in the past,
then, as we recover from trauma, we will tend to vault to a familiar stage in the present. For many of us that stage is the
stage of maturity. There also we are comfortable; there also (the
initial helplessness gone) we feel secure, and there also we feel
relatively safe because in that world we know how to take care
of ourselves. The child does not want to remain a child; but he
or she faces many years of learning how to become an adult.
The regressed adult does not want to remain regressed but
wants to become an adult again. She or he has already been
there, knows the way, has a familiar life waiting. For the great
majority of people regression is a temporary phenomenon, a
period that will sooner or later come to an end in the fully
functioning adult.

This must be emphasized because many people in trauma
fear that its results will last forever, that the feelings of helplessness and dependence will remain central to their existence.
This is also feared by some friends and family, and it is this fear
that drives the man or woman away from help and into solitude or grim resolution, and drives the friends into behavior
that can only seem uncaring or hostile. The victim fears that to
ask for help is to remain helpless; the friends fear that to offer
help is to be obliged to help eternally. But everything we know
about trauma shows that this is false. The person wants to recover and will recover, even in poor circumstances; in good circumstances the recovery will be faster and more complete. In
short, adult functioning will almost surely return to the man or
woman who had been functioning as an adult before the
trauma.

But what happens when the man or woman who had been the dependent partner is suddenly confronted by being newly single? Sometimes that person finds reasons to remain dependent or, even, to become more dependent than ever. But this is not inevitable. It is equally possible that the formerly dependent person, bereaved of support, finds that she or he actually enjoys standing alone—and is, in fact, rather good at it. Some newly single people, especially more mature women, may have spent most of their lives never having known real independence, may have gone from child to work to wife without ever having to test themselves. But it is never too late for autonomy; and sometimes these women—when the recovery period is over—find their freedom to be a revelation. One woman, widowed at the age of fifty, who had proceeded from school to marriage and motherhood without a break, spent two years in mourning; then, using most of the small estate her husband had left her, opened her own business—a fashion boutique. The business was a success; two years later she opened a branch; the year after that she married again—and now she is healthier, happier, and more vibrant than ever.

Still, the fact is that most people enter the trauma at some reasonable level of adult functioning and will leave it at about the same level. What, then, is the best way for that person, while still in trauma, to act—and what should friends, family, and counselors do? The answers can be given in nine words: *ideally,* help should be freely asked and freely given.

We have talked about manipulation as a way of coping with trauma. Manipulation is, of course, the opposite of freely asking: it tends to be counterproductive, and yet for many Americans *it is the only way of coping they know,* and for most Americans in trauma it is the only way they can think of. Children often *do* get what they want by manipulating their parents; and when we regress to the psychological state of childhood, that is how we try to fulfill our needs. There is nothing abnormal about it; for many if not most people it is a necessary part of the recovery from trauma.

But, as we said, manipulation tends to be counterproductive: it often doesn't fulfill our needs; we manipulate ourselves as well as others to the detriment of our relationships; and after a time it can retard the recovery process. So the best recourse is to state our wishes or needs clearly and openly.

Why don't we do this? Primarily because we are ashamed of being or seeming to be weak. We are stuck in our old syndrome; adults stand on their own two feet *under all circumstances.*

But there is no shame in weakness when we are weak, as there is no shame in asking for help when we cannot help ourselves. The man on crutches with a broken leg may need help in negotiating stairs; the woman after childbirth may need help until she recovers some strength. In neither case is it childish to ask for help directly; rather it is a sign of maturity. Women and men in trauma are "weak" in the same way: they are temporarily unable to cope, temporarily in need of assistance, temporarily needing others to provide a structure for their lives. But after a time the condition is cured, and that is the end.

Helping

For the people close to the man or woman, there are two broad ways in which help may be offered.

One is simply to listen while the other talks, but that may not be so simple after all. Most people are not accustomed to simply listening; they are accustomed to giving advice and comment, and especially to making judgments. But the person in trauma wants to talk and be understood, not advised and especially not judged. He or she uses words not only to communicate ideas but also to do two more important things. One is to express emotions. The blow to the self is tremendous, and for many people the hurt and anger evoked by that blow can only be discharged in words. Sometimes the words are spoken more intensely than usual, so much so that the listener may become uncomfortable. Still, the best thing to do now is to do very little except listen and encourage that person to keep talking.

But there are different ways of listening, and it is important to try to listen as empathetically as possible. What does this mean? It means tuning in to the speaker's *feelings* rather than the *ideas*. If a man, for example, is proclaiming the viciousness of his wife in leaving him for another man, the poorer response is to concur in the wife's wickedness. The better response is to understand the pain the man is feeling: *That really must hurt; it sounds like you really hurt; I can imagine how bad you feel; that does sound terrible*—these are the kinds of words that tell the wounded person that he or she is being understood at a deeper and more important level than the level of judgments and right or wrong.

Besides talking to relieve emotions, the person in trauma also talks as a way of putting himself or herself back together again. These words are exploratory, the concepts half-formed, the ideas sometimes half-baked. The person in trauma is like a woman or man caught in a flood, clutching at straws—at every idea or notion, no matter how unrealistic—that the mind throws off. But people caught in a flood soon recognize by themselves that straws cannot sustain them, and people in trauma soon recognize by themselves the ideas and decisions that are not sustaining. For many men and women, however, this recognition is the result of talking, not of being talked to; it is the process that helps, not necessarily the content. Giving unsolicited advice, pronouncing judgments, may interfere with the process and add to the confusion. Thus, except for factual assistance in specific areas (legal rights, for example, or accounting procedures), the best help for the person deep in trauma is to listen and understand and not try to change very much.

In addition to being listened to, men and women in trauma usually need help in breaking out of their passivity, their unwillingness to take initiatives. This being so, friends and relatives (and therapists and counselors) may properly take the initiative themselves. The single-again person will probably not ask friends if he or she can join them on some outing; the friends must do the asking. It is they who must invite the man or woman to go shopping with them, or to a ball game, or the opera or library. The friends must actively offer to include the single-again person in the activities from which he or she may feel totally detached.

These offers are helpful even if they are not accepted. What is important is that the offers be made, that one is told that he or she is still good company, useful, productive, valuable. Similarly the professional counselor may have to be more outgoing than usual, more willing to proffer direct suggestions. The person in trauma finds it hard to make even simple decisions and may need explicit directions—if only to buy new clothes, have a haircut, eat more regularly—as well as meet new people, start a new life.

It is worth emphasizing once more that the single-again man or woman will eventually assume control again. Helpers should realize that their job is part-time; they need not be on call twenty-four hours a day, seven days a week. But during this period they should also realize that they must take the lead in helping the person reconnect with reality.

Situational Regression

When traumatic regression has begun to fill its role, when some sense of security is restored, the single-again woman or man begins to move out into the world. But now they encounter another class of uncertainties: the uncertainty of social contact. Almost surely they will be undertaking new activities and meeting new people, and almost surely the most important new people will be those who are possible mates. Here is where uncertainty becomes most acute; for the fact is that men and women who become newly single have never before been single at this age or under these circumstances.

The resolution of this uncertainty is the same as the resolution of traumatic uncertainty: regression. Not to childhood, because there is no need to go back that far, but to a previous stage in which we were single, apprehensive, and feeling our first sexual stirrings. This is the stage of adolescence and young adulthood. When the single-again person returns to society, she or he very often brings along the attitudes, emotions, values, and expectations of ten, twenty, thirty, forty years before—attitudes and values that may not be appropriate to the new circumstances.

The Inadequacy of Adolescence

For most adults the outlook and behavior of adolescence are no longer appropriate; they were not really fruitful then, and they are less so now. Nor are the goals of adolescence ordinarily right for the adult. Normally, what satisfies a sixteen-year-old boy or girl is not the same as what satisfies a fifty-year-old man or woman. Sex, sharing, work, understanding are important at all ages, but their relative importance changes with time. Many men and women, however, thrust into a strange situation, act as though their needs are the same as they were years ago, as though nothing has changed at all.

Not only needs are different: the means for realistically meeting those needs are not the same. Most obviously, one's body is not the same. But also the ratio of the sexes has changed: from rough numerical equality in the early ages to a great preponderance of the female sex at older ages. Inequalities of wealth weigh more heavily: in early adulthood all the people we knew seemed to have the same amount of money; and if there were exceptions it made little difference, because everybody would soon be rich and successful together. As we get older, we know people who are much richer or more successful than we are, or much poorer and less successful; we are acutely aware of disparities of wealth and can no longer believe that time and luck can close those gaps.

Nevertheless, for many newly singled adults the internal agenda returns to what it was years before. Wanting, on the one hand, to satisfy their need for security, they still seek in others the qualities they sought when younger: In fact, men often seek youth itself—the company, sometimes in marriage, of women much younger than themselves. So they think that living out their fantasies will create the reality, and they will actually *be* young again. But they cannot be, and almost always they are bitterly disappointed.

Leaving aside the search for a young partner, men and women often revert to the fantasies of youth and the main criterion by which the young, inexperienced person evaluates another: nothing less then perfection. What they sought for then, they seek for now: eternal love, the unique one-and-only created just for themselves alone, the happy-forever-after relationship with never a need for anyone or anything else, that marvelous person with whom—and here is the heart of the fantasy—they can be perfect themselves.

Nobody consciously believes that perfection is obtainable in this world. But sometimes odd strands, residues of some of the incongruous values of youth, remain. How do we respond to a potential partner; what criteria are valid? Clearly, affection and response should be spontaneous and unforced, but still . . . a widower tells his daughter why he is indifferent to an attractive widow who is clearly interested in him. "She's older than me," he says. He is eighty; she is eighty-two.

It is not just superficialities of age, accent, dress, appearance that can carry at any age the undue weight they carried at twenty-one; it is also more profound expectations: of what relationships should be like, of what sex means and should be. For many men, for example, sex becomes again a matter of "scoring," of successful seduction (although seduction, in this climate, is hardly the right word); for many women sex becomes again a test of their attractiveness, their ability to arouse desire in a man. Both attitudes lead not only to unsatisfactory relationships but also to unsatisfactory sex.

These are the attitudes men and women have brought to their first marriage, but then there was time to either work out the difficulties or mask them. Now there is less time to work things out and less reason to mask anything. And so for many older people sex becomes more of a problem than it should be. And in the same way one's attitudes and beliefs and expectations, insofar as they represent earlier, unproductive habits of thought and behavior, bring more problems than solutions, more frustration than fulfillment. We go back to the way we were when younger; but those ways are often wrong.

This condition, situational regression, may cause more complications than traumatic regression. Traumatic regression is a clear upheaval: we feel ourselves acting uncharacteristically and attempt to recover; and on the way to recovery many people help. The majority of newly singled men and women are over the worst of the trauma in about six months, although it is usually two or three years before most of the effects have become insignificant.

But situational regression is not a clear upheaval: in fact, it feels comfortable. Those patterns of behavior, those goals, are what we have always had; they are familiar; they are our natural ways of interacting with the world of people. And the people themselves, the friends and family, are accustomed to us and see nothing wrong in how we behave. So the old attitudes are not recognized as being useless or counterproductive: like an old favorite pair of slippers, lopsided at the heels, we think we feel good in them when actually they are spoiling our postures and hurting our backs. They are best discarded: the single-again woman and man need to stand as tall as possible.

Last Word

The fear of failure or shame, the hypersensitivity, the passivity —these signs of regression almost always fade with time, sometimes quite suddenly as you prove your new strength and independence. As time passes and you move away from your trauma, the child in you will emerge less and less. Meanwhile, *all* the different parts of you that were hurt are finding a more mature harmony as you become more and more the adult you want to be.

Help for the Helpless Inner Child

To hasten your passage through regression—to help you grow up again!—remember:

- Understand, as you recover from the shock, that almost everybody who suffers a trauma feels like a helpless child for a while. It's normal. Don't fight it; note what's happening with interest.
- Know that you'll pass through this phase and reclaim your adult strength once you're over the shock of your loss. You'll feel much more in control once you've made some plans and done a few things for yourself.
- Don't use sex as a measure of your power or attractiveness. This is a shaky foundation for a real relationship.
- Ask for help if you need it. You'd be willing to help someone in need. Someone else may be very glad to give you support now. Recognize that it's for a short time, and you'll assume control again.

CHAPTER 4

The New World, The New Self

After two or three years of being single again—sometimes more and sometimes (for the person seeking a divorce) much less—a double synthesis has occurred: the world has come together again and makes some sort of sense; the self has come together again and confronts the world. The process is not abrupt but gradual, the accumulated result of time, friends, and one's own efforts. The trauma and its effects are mostly dissipated, and the single-again person resumes control of his or her own life.

What we do with that life depends on both the new self and the new world, for the world can be very different for different people (generally it's better to be male and it's better to be wealthy). But economics are not the only constraints: the world tries to impose on the single person certain psychological and emotional constraints that are more subtle but equally pervasive.

The World and Sexuality

Your dating and mating experience will depend greatly on how old you are when you become single. The world for those under forty-five and single may seem more difficult than for older people: the pressure to find a mate, or at least a partner, is high.

Up to about forty-five the norm for adult Americans is the couple, not the single, even if the coupling is only temporary, for a few months or a few hours. For the younger person to be without a partner is somehow to be a failure; the assumption is that one is without a mate not out of deliberate choice, but due to a lack of attractiveness or adequacy. Singlehood is also sometimes attributed to deep neurosis or other psychological causes.

Further, the younger person who is again single is expected, sooner or later, to begin looking for a partner—and not only to look, but actually to develop, at least occasionally, some sort of relationship. That is normal behavior. But many attempts to connect—either briefly or possibly permanently—can hit blockades. Lee is in her late thirties and divorced:

> When I was single the first time, it was basically, if you wanted him, you just had him, no problem. So after I got over the shock of my husband's defection and found myself single for the second time, I assumed the rules were the same. One evening I'd been out for drinks with a friend and was returning to my apartment in a cab. The driver was nice-looking and I thought it might be fun to have him up to the apartment for a brief encounter. I did that another time, before I was married, and it was a lot of fun.
>
> So I asked the cute cabbie if he wanted to come up for a drink. And you know what he said? First he looked at me, then he said, "No thanks, lady."
>
> I paid quickly, went right upstairs and made myself a drink. Then I got up and looked in the mirror. Was I so bad? No. Then after a long time I figured it out: AIDS. He was afraid of me. Smart guy. He taught me something I won't forget: Times are different now.

The world is not the somewhat safe, somewhat innocent place it was in decades past. Until researchers come up with a vaccine, the specter of AIDS will be a wedge between any two people trying to connect. (See Chapter 9 for more on AIDS.)

For the older person society offers a reprieve: deliberate single-hood, especially for the once married, becomes acceptable; the stigma is almost gone. But there is a catch: sexuality is presumed to be gone also. In spite of all evidence to the contrary, many people assume that at some point in middle age men and women lose the sexual urge; and the failure to seek a partner is attributed not to personal deficiency but to exhaustion or a "natural" waning of desire.

If this were all, there would be no problem; one could connect again or not, as one chose. But if one does choose intimacy with another person the paradox becomes clear: to look for a partner is acceptable, to look for sex is not. The older we are, the more society tends to dismiss the desire for passionate intimacy, and it is hard to persist in the face of that dismissal. A sixty-year-old woman tried to explain to her son why she wants to marry a man her own age, but she says her son "doesn't seem to understand. He says I can get all the companionship I need from him and his children. Of course I love my grandchildren . . . but I don't know how to tell him that's not the kind of companionship I'm looking for."

Blindness to the sensuality of the older person is bad enough, but more often the attitude is one of uneasiness and hostility. The older one is, the more society frowns upon coupling, and if not coupling per se then the activities that lead to coupling, especially activities that smack of sex. It is nice for older people (over fifty-five) to get together as a couple, but nice in a quaint, "cute" way. It is not nice for older men to groom themselves carefully and worry about the scent of their after-shave lotion or the cut of their trousers, as though they really wanted to attract a woman, as though they really were making a statement about their sexual prowess. It is not nice and it is not acceptable, or if it is acceptable, that is because the energy behind these activities is denied; he's not sexual; he's fastidious. But one could never really believe that that old man could still . . . get it up?

This attitude persists even among people who should know better—counselors, psychiatrists, physicians. Not all, of course, but many of these professionals, having read the scholarly articles, attended the seminars, spoken with their colleagues, still cannot admit that older people have specifically sexual desires and needs. One hospital was conducting an open-house blood pressure screening program for people in the neighborhood, and there was a physician in the room just to keep an eye on things. A man in his mid-fifties stopped to speak to the doctor on his way out.

> My blood pressure checked out pretty good, and I
> wanted to find out about sex—how often, that kind
> of thing. I was a little embarrassed, but I asked him.
> He asked me how old I was, and I told him fifty-six.
> So he said it was okay to have sex twice a year. I
> thought I hadn't heard right, and I said, "You mean
> twice a week?" "No, no," he said, "twice a year is
> plenty."

The doctor, the man reported, seemed to be in his early thirties. Perhaps in twenty years he will remember the incident and feel ashamed of himself. So one strong message from the world to the older single person is to deny sexuality—or if not to deny it, at least to conceal it. If this were the only message it would be bad enough, but at least it would have the virtue of clarity. But today there is another message transmitted by all the media—television and films, books and advertising—to all ages and both sexes, in all circumstances and conditions: that sex is a positive good, an end in itself, practically the birthright of every American. And this complicates matters enormously.

For one thing it makes it harder to opt out of the search for a partner. Twenty years ago the older single person could decide rather gracefully to give up being half of a couple and assume a different role: to be a parent, grandparent, aunt, uncle without also being a mate. In those days sex may have been less rewarding for many people, and it made little sense to again pant after an experience that never meant too much in the first place. The family was not so dispersed then, and the need for warmth and support could be met by sisters and brothers and cousins and did not have to be met, as seems true today, by one special person. And finally in those days people expected less for themselves and from the world; they settled for less, settled, usually with gratitude, for being comfortable.

Today most people want more for themselves and demand more from the world. Whether or not we have ever been satisfied sexually, we still want that satisfaction, will not settle for permanent frustration even if we have always been frustrated. We want to be fulfilled, not just a little but totally, to overflowing. Other people, we have been informed countless times by television and the other media, have achieved the good sexual life, and it is somehow our obligation to do the same—and the older person does not have much time left.

So the single older person is given a double message: on the one hand, she or he is too old for sex, shouldn't want it, is a little dirty or laughable for seeking it; on the other hand, sex is marvelous, wonderful, rejuvenating, the most worthwhile thing in the world, to be enjoyed by everybody—and not just your old everyday sex but supersex, multiple orgasms for women, the thrill of a lifetime for the man, practically the be-all and end-all of existence. With the belief structures of the past, it is no wonder that sexuality becomes such a problem for the older single person—for many, the most troubling problem by far.

The World and Security

But sex is not the only problem, and its resolution is complicated by many other problems. These usually center around security, and the situation can be stated very simply. For most

people over forty-five the loss of one's mate, through divorce
or death, means less security than before, sometimes much
less.

The suddenly single mother or father of small children
may have to carry an unbearable burden: the cost of child care
may, for example, cancel out job earnings. We may have to give
up the house for an apartment, may have to do without a car
for a while, may have to skip nursery school for the little ones.
But the younger single does have hope: in our twenties and
thirties we are advised to go into debt, reach for the good life
on borrowed money, because dollars will inevitably grow
cheaper and we will be earning more and more of them. And,
in fact, for more people than not this tends to be true. It stops
being true at about the age of forty-five. Although success and
money can come at any age, the decent prospect of a continually increasing income begins to fade at about forty-five, to be
replaced by an uncertainty and fear that increase as the years go
on. Similarly the single-again housewife turned worker at forty-
five or older cannot count on an income that will let her live
comfortably or as comfortably as when she was married.
Women today may rise much further in business than previously, but the double barriers of age discrimination and sex
discrimination are still hard to overcome. The economic future
for the older woman alone without an independent income is
at best problematic and can be bleak indeed.

Even if there are no current economic problems, the possibility of a sudden illness, accompanied by a drastic loss of income, can be frightening. A woman in her late fifties, divorced
two years, needed a hysterectomy—a "minor" operation. But
suddenly she became apprehensive, more than seemed appropriate. "I suddenly thought, what happens if I get really sick,
chronically sick? Who takes care of me? Where do I get the
money to lead a decent life?" For the past half year she had
been dating a divorced man about her age, and they had always
shared expenses. For the first time she spoke to him about
money problems. "He became very upset," the woman says.

"He said he couldn't handle it. His wife got most of his earnings when he divorced, and he had nothing to fall back on. He doesn't make that much money anyway. He was all shaken up." The man put it simply. "I can't carry more than my share. It's not possible. I love her, but if I ever had to pay any of her bills—*any* of them—I'd have to break [it] off." The woman recovered from the operation; she and the man are together again, and everything is the way it was. "Except now I'm scared," the woman says, "and I don't know what to do about it."

On the other hand if the world for newly single men and women of any age is in some respects more difficult than the old world, in some respects they are better able to meet it. The separating event has brought problems, but it has also brought opportunity, opportunity in the form of freedom. In brief the women and men need no longer consider other people's needs as being on a par with their own.

Children of any age always need parents for a special kind of emotional support, but above the age of sixteen or so they do not need parents to supply their physical needs (except, perhaps, for money). Nor do they need the parents' physical presence. Much more than in the past, the single-again person can give priority to her or his own desires.

But freedom can be a source of anxiety as well as opportunity. The anxiety comes from the realization that we are truly alone and not needed; there is no comforting, familiar function that must be performed, which can act as an organizing center for life. Suddenly we are faced with a chaos of choices or an abyss of emptiness. How are we to spend our days, evenings, and weekends? How are we to cope with them? The anxiety can sometimes overwhelm the sense of opportunity, but for most newly single people that feeling does come: the realization that for the first time in a while they can put themselves first without guilt or apprehension. Still attached in many ways to the old life, still bearing old scars as well as new uncertainties, the older person also feels a new sense of possibilities, a chance to make something new and different out of the rest of his or her life.

Diving In or Opting Out

What is made from this sense of possibilities depends on the individual. For many people life has been the experience of turmoil or conflict, of deep disappointment; and for them the goal becomes the experience of calm, a retreat from passion or possibly demanding interactions. They have had their fill of life with a partner and want nothing more than the feeling of relief that it is all over—that and the friendship of a few people (usually of the same sex) whom they can leave at night and go home to their own apartment and sleep undisturbed in their own beds. Intimacy has been too wearing, too unrewarding, ultimately barren or painful or exhausting. So just being released and just tending to their own small needs and pleasures can become a source of deep satisfaction. "I've done enough," one fifty-year-old woman says. "I took care of my husband; I took care of my children; I took care of my sister when she was sick. I was always the good one. Now I only have to worry about myself." Was she ever lonely? "Sure. But I go shopping or play cards with some friends and I'm all right."

Similarly many men and women are relieved at the end of sex or at least at the end of the necessity of having sex with a partner. Perhaps never fully experiencing their own sexuality, women for whom sex has been a demand for compliance and men for whom sex has been a demand for performance welcome the chance to be rid of those demands. Or rather, since in most cases their sexual activity had dwindled long ago, they see no reason to seek out unrewarding obligations all over again.

Other men and women retreat from intimacy not through exhaustion but through fear. These are people who always doubted their own adequacy—as lovers, mates, parents—and tended to marry people very much like themselves. For many people marriage can be a chance to grow and explore, to overcome insecurities and fears and find new strengths and satisfactions. But for people trapped in the conviction of inadequacy, marriage is not an opportunity to grow but a place to hide, an excuse *not* to explore. Further, expecting to be rescued or redeemed by the partner, they are always disappointed and this disappointment turns into an endemic desperation or hostility or both. Nothing gets resolved, not their personal problems nor their problems with others. Still, they often remain married to each other for a long time, married and miserable. When they do become single again, some of these women and men set out to make the very same mistake, but many simply withdraw. They cannot risk revealing themselves again; they cannot cope; in some way they know they fall short and are bound to disappoint anyone who comes close. They cannot stand the sense of failure that comes from disappointing others and themselves, and so they back away from intimacy, from the effort to connect again.

Last Word

No matter what the reason, the decision to opt out of the search for another partner is clearly valid. Certainly people differ greatly from one another; and certainly men and women of any age can find other things to do with their energy and time than spend them in the pursuit of a painful intimacy. The world itself at any age can be fulfilling and rewarding in at least a dozen different ways, and an intimate relationship is only one of them.

But many men and women who opt out would rather not. Many would welcome intimacy again if only they knew how to handle it, if only intimacy would not—as it did in the past—

invariably result in disappointment, anger, shame, and guilt. But these are not invariable. In the long run and the short run for the woman and man whose sensual being remains strong, nothing is as life-giving as an intimate, sexual relationship.

Reentry Dos and Don'ts

The world "out there" is not as big and scary as it may seem. You have little to lose and much to gain by taking steps that lead you outside your circle of familiar experience. Just remember:

- DO follow your own path back into the world. Death and divorce involve not only changes around us; they involve changes within us. You may need more time or less time to adjust than someone else.
- DO remember that friendships, romance, and sexual relations can bring joy and keep us feeling young and vital.
- DO consider that there has never been a better time to explore than now. You're free! Seize the moment. Meet people, taste foods, travel, try a new hobby, take a class, sign up for a sport, go on a retreat. You will return refreshed and revitalized.
- DON'T let anyone stop you!

CHAPTER 5
The Social Scene

For the single-again person hoping for intimacy, it usually takes not less than six months nor much more than two years to begin the serious business of looking for a partner. The exceptions occur principally in the very early stages. Often the blow is so great that the man or woman rushes into an affair. This is an attempt to prove that he or she is still attractive, or to make up for all the time "wasted" in being married to the wrong person, or to fill some suddenly empty hours. But the affairs are typically short-lived and tend to defer the recovery or mourning period.

When the recovery period is waning, when one's new status has become at least partially integrated, a more deliberate, active seeking (or active receptivity) begins to take place. Out there is the society of other single people, and into it ventures the newly single man or woman. But they enter it shaped by years of marriage and recalling the patterns of their original singlehood; they find a society that in many respects defies their expectations. Often disoriented, sometimes acutely distressed, many of them experience what has been termed in other contexts *the shock of reentry.*

The shock is not fatal; people recover and go about their business. But the fact that it is a shock, that the new world can be so different from what we expect, poses two dangers. One danger is that our old attitudes and beliefs will harden, leaving us without the freedom to experiment, to try new ways of thinking, feeling, and relating. The other danger is that our old attitudes and beliefs will rupture, leaving us without the ability to discriminate (especially in the area of sexual conduct), to sense what in the new world is beneficial and what is not. As in most cases the early problems generally arise with regard to sex.

The First Singlehood Revisited

In a sense the rediscovery and reintegration of sexuality becomes the central task of the period of reemergence. What complicates the situation is that this was also the task of our first singlehood.

When we were young and dating we had little doubt that sexuality was the organizing force of male-female relationships, the magnetic field around which the other aspects of the relationship were arrayed. Today the "rules" and conditions have both changed, but sex remains the core of most new male-female relationships. This is not to say that all such relationships should be sexual, nor that a sexual relationship should be the central part of life. But where men and women are involved with each other, sexuality tends to enter, sometimes seriously, sometimes in the nature of a sauce to a meal.

Further, although all female-male relationships need not end in either sex or separation, the question of sex almost always arises. And it arises not in general, hypothetical terms but quite specifically. For the single-again person sexuality usually involves some very basic choices: who to sleep with, when, under what conditions, and after how long a time—or whether to sleep with anyone at all. How we react to this issue depends not only on the self but also on the circumstances, on the sexual charge of the occasion. The different ways of meeting people carry different sexual charges, and it is important not to generalize from one or two experiences and not to assume an old attitude without at least reexamining it. A sixty-year-old widower flatly refused to go out with divorced women because he knew "what they were like." What were they like, we asked him. Never mind, he said, never mind; he knew what they were like. (They were promiscuous, of course; and for this man promiscuity in a woman was not only immoral, but it also triggered anxiety over his own sexual performance.) The idea that divorced women might be as varied in their attitudes toward sexuality as married women never occurred to him. And in fact many men do prefer widows because somehow they are supposed to be "safer." Other men will have nothing to do with women who have children at home, because through some roundabout path they might end up being responsible for those children, and responsibility is the last thing they want.

The other major element of reentry shock is *insecurity*—again, of a very specific kind. We do not know whether others are lying or telling the truth. This man claiming to be single may really be married; this woman hinting at a large income may be desperately poor; the man who seems so fascinated by our conversation, charm, and personality may use us as a receptacle for three minutes' worth of sex; the woman who seems so attracted to us, so willing—even eager—to yield, may actually be in desperate need of a whiskey sour and nothing more, or a ride home and nothing more. As with sexuality, the different modes of meeting can carry different cargoes of insecurity.

How do most people meet? In bars, at dances, in singles clubs, fitness groups, temples, churches, and through third-party introductions—friends, dating services, singles parties. But these imply an active seeking; clearly they are not the only ways of meeting people. Thus some men and women who are single make a point of doing nothing unusual: they go about their ordinary business and make no special effort to find someone new. If something happens, fine; if nothing happens, that's the way it is. Some take what might be called passive action: show up more often at church or temple services, become more active in local affairs; attend the theater or the ballet or the ball game more often; take up tennis or bowling. In brief they place themselves in situations where they are likely to meet more people than usual and hope that some of those people will be potential partners and that some of those people will wander their way and be attracted to them.

Still others go to singles bars or singles dances or otherwise enter the new world of meeting people.

The Singles Bar

In the singles bar both sexuality and insecurity are highest: the sexual charge is at peak intensity, and ignorance of the other is most complete.

Sex and the Space-Time Continuum

At the singles bar sex is paramount, the major element in the atmosphere. Further to sexuality is added urgency, the urgency of time that must not be wasted, not even half an hour, and for some people not even ten minutes. Conversations in singles bars tend to move swiftly and often bluntly: an offer to buy a drink, ten or twenty minutes' worth of talk, and then an offer for dinner, often with the barter made explicit—if we have dinner first, will we go to bed later? In your place or mine? Sometimes the offer of dinner isn't even made. Many of the married men who populate singles bars have to be home by a certain hour and have no time to waste on preliminaries. Otherwise they might miss their train, and then there would be hell to pay with their wives.

Another example of the pressure of time is that of women in cities who must get back to their dwellings while it is still safe to travel. If they cannot find a partner at least to see them home, they leave early, so as not to have to walk unattended in the dark, lonely hours. And that leaves fewer women for the remaining men. The urgency arises also from the need of men and women, no longer youths, to wake early and go to work the next morning. And it arises from the desire to realize a return on one's investment. We can enjoy ourselves at dances simply by dancing, but at singles bars we do not enjoy ourselves simply by drinking: we usually go specifically to find a partner. We have invested time and money in this search, and as the time runs out and the money runs down, we become increasingly desperate to get *something* in return. The sense of urgency becomes almost tangible.

There is another fact that adds to the sexual charge at the singles bar: space is limited and the people are usually crowded close together. Given that most of them are looking for partners and that this is known, given that their bodies are inches away from other bodies, and given that their senses are flooded with scents and sounds, laughter and perfume, after-shave and cigarettes, it would be strange if sexuality were anything but at a peak.

It is the combination of sexual pressure and the urgency of time that accounts for many of the characteristics of the singles bar: the inspection of one sex by the other; the immediate closeness, or semblance of closeness; the brevity of the introductory phases; the rapidity with which decisions are made. All responses are magnified and quickened: we can stay by ourselves and be almost completely alone; we can join a group and be instantly scrutinized by everyone nearby, instantly evaluated. We are, of course, doing our own evaluating; and the result of this scrutiny and evaluation is an illusion: the illusion that we know a lot about these people, about this particular person that we are talking to. But nothing could be farther from reality. "I feel sorry," says a woman, "for widows who loved their husbands. They come here and believe every story any man tells them, and they always get hurt."

Turn-offs and Temptations

Singles bars have been called jungles but they are not: there is no anarchy here; the rules are observed. But the bluntness, the directness, the inspection and appraisal, the almost exclusive concentration on sex can be repellent. Women do feel that in singles bars they are reduced to little more than sexual organs; men do tend to feel more predatory than usual and also more driven to score, to display their prowess.

Still, for the reemerging man or woman, sex is easiest to come by at the singles bar. A relationship that lasts more than a night (or even that long) is generally unlikely, although there are a few people who do find a permanent partner. On the other hand women with some degree of comeliness and men with some degree of initiative have a good chance of finding a sexual partner for at least a couple of hours.

Also, with all its hyperpressures of sex and time, there is one way in which the singles bar is comparatively benign: it is noncompetitive. In part this is due to the very pressure it exerts: the emphasis is on connecting as quickly as possible, not on fighting over a prospective partner. The time spent in fighting may be precisely the time in which one could have found someone else. In addition men and women are there in roughly equal numbers; there is no gross proportional imbalance between the sexes. So there is not the sense of many people of one sex competing for a few members of the opposite sex; the sense is that, at least in terms of quantity, there is enough to go around.

Apart from the sexual connection there is one other quality of singles bars that attracts people, that may turn a somewhat repelled first-time visitor into a regular (or semi-regular). *It is the quality of excitement.* It is a hectic, tense, feverish excitement, but it is there nevertheless. It crystallizes from the tension of being too close to people, from sexuality like a tide lapping at everyone in the room, from the movement and maneuver, the watchful eyes, the ceaseless shifting of patterns of emotion as couples form and break apart. Men and women talk to each other but continually look elsewhere, checking other parts of the room, making sure they're not missing anything. It is the feeling that here there are a hundred opportunities to do what has been forbidden before.

Sports and Health Clubs

After aerobics came on the scene in the '70s, physical fitness became part of everyone's good grooming, and it also happens to be fun. Even someone who prefers the solitary sports—running, swimming, working out on a weight machine—can parlay that interest into a way to meet people. And that way is called a health club.

At the club, you're shoulder-to-shoulder with other people interested in the same type of workout you are. It's possible, for example, for a woman running on a quarter-mile rooftop track to make eye contact or even bump into a man doing the same thing. Then comes the "excuse me," the "that's okay," and maybe even "shall we have some juice at the health bar in half an hour?" Not all such meetings lead to the couple running off into the sunset, but at least you know from the beginning that you have one shared interest.

Many clubs, villages, and other groups run sports for singles, and such activities can be very low-key and unpressured ways to meet people and make friends. One young, single doctor we know plays volleyball once a week in a group at the Young Men's Hebrew Association. "It's a Jewish Y, but lots of other people come too," he says. "And not everyone plays volleyball. Some people who come are *bad* at volleyball. They sit on the sidelines to watch and cheer. Afterwards, we all go out for coffee at a diner." In the three years he's been attending, he reports that three couples have become engaged and one couple has married.

Quality Control

One great thing about sports activities: they're not exclusive. All you need is a few dollars for a sports night or a few hundred dollars for a year's health club membership. But that's also the problem with sports activities—they're not exclusive. Anyone who can pay the money is *in*. Our young doctor reports that his volleyball group attracts some people who might be emotionally dangerous, like those who come in just to watch other people work out in tight and sexy aerobicwear. A few clubs advertise classes for women where men are not allowed to watch!

When you meet people in a sports setting, just remember to use the same radar to spot mismatches that you would in a singles bar or at a party.

The Singles Dance

At singles dances, which are popular with older singles, the women begin to outnumber the men: the proportions are about sixty percent women, forty percent men. And at singles dances the competition is more intense than at singles bars, but the sexual charge and sense of urgency are lower. Further, if the first exposure to the singles bar can be jolting, the first exposure to the singles dance can be unsettling in a more subtle way. For the singles dance, to the man or woman who has not been at dances for years, is a mixture of the familiar and the odd that can give rise to a strong feeling of disorientation.

The Past Revisited

What is familiar is the milieu: the dance floor seems the same as it did years before; there are the same mixed groupings, the same knots of people who seem to know each other (and the same people who seem incapable of knowing anybody), the same variety of clothing, even the same music: fox-trots, Latin rhythms, a rare waltz. What is different is that all these people are older. And the disorientation arises because we do not expect people in this setting, behaving in these ways, to be so old. The couples are doing the dances of our youth but they are not young; the perky blonde in the short, swirling skirt has the face of a fifty-year-old. It often takes time to get used to it.

More troublesome, for many people, is their unexpected confrontation with overt sexuality. Couples do more than dance: they hold hands; they reach for knees; they rest on thighs. It seems inappropriate, somehow wrong, for these people to engage in such "youthful" activities.

So many men and women react *to themselves* as older adults the way they reacted when they were younger—and the way many younger people today react. They think it is improper to behave this way; they are too old for that kind of thing. And so their youthful prejudices, never outgrown, can come back to disrupt their new life.

Finally, as in singles bars, we cannot be sure that the person to whom we are attracted is as single as we are. "I'll tell you what bothered me the most," says a woman in her late forties. "You can't tell what's going on. You can't tell who's married and who's not; who's going together and who's not, or what's happening. For thirty years when I went out I *knew* who was married, and if I didn't it made no difference. Now I didn't know and it made a big difference. And I didn't like it one bit."

In brief married couples (and "steadies") also go to singles dances, but their reasons are not sexual but financial. For (usually) not more than five or ten dollars each, they can have a supper snack, as much dancing as they want, and a chance to meet their friends. These couples seem to know each other and congregate together. And for many people, as they grow older still guarding their independence, the chance to have an evening of conviviality and a full stomach for only a few dollars is not passed up so lightly.

Competitiveness

For single people, however, competition starts to emerge. Not all men are friendly to the unfamiliar single man who enters the scene; not all women will show even the slightest courtesy to single women they do not recognize. At singles dances there is simply more time; people tend to come by private car, not public transportation, and the women usually arrive in groups. (And usually they have a pact: if the driver of the car finds a partner, the others must manage to get home by themselves.) Most dances start about eight P.M. and end near midnight; there are four hours in which to meet, talk, and try to impress someone, but there are also four hours in which other people are doing the same things, perhaps with potential partners to whom one is attracted. In brief if there is time to maneuver there is also time to be outmaneuvered; if we have a chance to be charming, we can also be outcharmed.

Nor does the competitiveness lead to stable, long-term relationships. Regulars will tend to dance with each other, but this is usually as far as it goes; the percentage of people who meet at dances and later marry appears to be (in the absence of any real data) about as low as for singles bars, although it does occasionally occur. And the dance is less promising in terms of surefire sex: sexuality is in the air, but not with the same intensity as at the singles bar, and the unattached man or woman looking for a quick connection is more likely to be disappointed.

One reason is that many of the people at dances do not come primarily to find a sexual partner; they come primarily to dance. In fact, simpleminded though it may sound, the enjoyment of dancing is the best reason to go to dances. For a few dollars the older single woman or man can have four or five hours of dancing with a light supper thrown in. But if one cannot dance or is not interested in dancing, then one will miss a good deal of the enjoyment—and may not find a partner either.

Shall You Dance?

Like the singles bar, the singles dance offers attractions beyond its basic function of allowing people to meet and dance to- gether. One attraction is the chance to be with people in a so- cial setting. Many newly single people lead lives that are unremittingly solitary or allow only very limited human con- tact: office or business acquaintances during the day, the televi- sion set at night. But these satisfactions are partial at best, and so are the satisfactions offered by higher leisure activities: read- ing, drama, the opera, museums. Most people need a measure of personal, free flowing communication with others; and if we cannot have a large measure, a small measure helps, even sim- ply being in the presence of social activities. For the nonpartici- pant there is the pain experienced by the outsider, but the sheer, almost physical, reward of simply being with other peo- ple often outweighs the pain.

There is a final reward for going to dances that is so obvi- ous it is usually overlooked. Dancing is a way to hold and be held by someone, to feel our body in contact with another body. For many single people this is the only real chance to physically touch another human being: once a week in the company of fifty or one hundred other couples on a dance floor moving to the sound of music. In Florida (and perhaps else- where) some Senior Citizen's centers hold dances for a dollar per person—one dollar for touching, feeling, holding another person for an hour or two. It is not everything but it is infi- nitely better than nothing, for it is mainly touching, especially touching with a hint of the erotic, that keeps us alive—and lively—a little longer.

The Singles Club

The singles dance and the singles bar exist primarily for strang- ers to meet each other, perhaps only once; in contrast the singles club exists for friends to meet each other at least occasionally during the course of the year. From this difference in purpose spring many differences in character. Sexuality is less intense; the urgency of time is much less pressing, and the competitiveness is more severe.

Getting In . . .

Admission to the singles club is by invitation and approval by a screening committee. For the man there is no problem: being in short supply, he does not have to meet very stringent criteria. "If a man can breathe without help," one long-time club member says, "and not act like a lunatic, he's in." It's also necessary to pay dues, typically forty or fifty dollars annually.

Paying dues is the easiest part of it for a woman. Although most singles clubs start with a roughly equal number of men and women, women tend to be faithful club members, while very many men—about sixty percent as a broad estimate—drop out or become inactive. This means that the woman applying for membership is almost always placed on a waiting list. And the wait can last two years or longer.

Willingness to wait is not the only trait a woman needs. She also must be attractive, well-groomed, and socially adept, and she must have a house or large apartment. The reason is that the club, although usually sponsored by an umbrella organization, is not so much a location as a group that holds affairs and functions. Many of the functions are held in member's homes, and the woman needs a home in which she can entertain about twenty-five people. Men also act as hosts, but women much more so; the main reason is that this is a way for a woman to take the initiative with a man. If a woman wants to get to know a man, all she has to do is sponsor a function in an area she thinks to be of interest to him and invite him to come. If he accepts, she invites other members; if not, all she has wasted is a telephone call—and a certain amount of hope.

. . . And Staying In

Why do women join singles clubs, wait up to two years to get in, and then, once in, seeing themselves outnumber the men by more than two to one, remain faithful? Are their chances for marriage increased? In one singles club with over four hundred members the first seven years of its existence resulted in only three marriages; another singles club saw only two marriages in ten years. Do they remain members to connect with a man, never mind marriage? With almost two women for every man the prospects are unlikely. Or do they stay to become part of a new "family," one that can provide the nurturance she can no longer count on from her real family? The singles club, she soon learns, is not like a family and does not provide a familial kind of nurturing. Then why? Why do women—most of them attractive, intelligent, more youthful then most of the men, more careful of themselves, more *desirable,* to put it plainly, than most of the male members—strive to get in and stick it out once accepted?

There are two reasons for wanting to join. First, the singles club provides reassurance in some important areas. The atmosphere is relatively dignified; there is not the "meat-market" feeling that characterizes singles bars and (to a lesser extent) dances. More important she knows that the men are in fact single; she may waste her time but at least it will not be with a married man. She knows also that the men are at least minimally acceptable. Usually men who apply for membership are friends of members; further the man with serious problems will soon be found out. So the woman can be sure that in a profound, personal sense she is at least safe with the men in the club. And second, despite all the odds, she might be the exception and find a man of her own.

For men the reasons for joining are simpler. The singles club is a way of meeting unattached women in substantially large numbers without a lot of male competition. It is a way for a man to establish a connection, sexual and otherwise, with a

woman more or less of his choice who is at least minimally sol-
vent, attractive, and solicitous of his well-being. It may be, in
short, a pretty good deal.

The Old-Girl Network

But the preponderance of women in the singles club and the
fact that they tend to be more active than most men and to remain longer may have some unexpected consequences. Primarily these have to do with power.

Typically the president of the club is a prestigious male,
but there are usually four to six vice-presidents, almost always
women. Women are also in charge of most of the committees:
entertainment, food, fundraising, culture, weekends away—
everything. With all the committees and functions, there are
usually things to do five nights a week; and for the active man
this can mean five nights a week in an attractive home, being
fussed over by at least one—and sometimes as many as
twenty—women at a cost of about five dollars per night (to
cover refreshments).

But vice-presidencies and committee chairpersonships
are positions of power, and power is sometimes abused. In the
singles club the abuse of power takes the form of limiting the
access of other women to new male members. This is done in
two ways. The easiest is simply to deny membership to women
who might provide too severe competition, who seem to be too
attractive to men. The denial is not overt: the new name is
merely placed on a waiting list and never moved off. Women
sponsored by other women members, or women who seem unthreatening, will usually be admitted within two years. Women
sponsored by male members may never get in; one such
woman has been "waiting" six years so far without hearing
from the club.

Another way women keep other women away from new
men is by getting there first. The first time a new man attends a
function, the officers and other old members gather around

him immediately to make him welcome, see that he's comfortable, answer questions, tell him about the club—make him feel at home. What could be more natural? But it is hard for other women to break into this circle or for the man to break out without seeming rude. So at least at that first function the man rarely has a chance to meet other women, and women outside the inner circle rarely have a good chance to meet the man. And if the man is desirable, then their attention, their assault of care and concern, will continue at function after function until the new man becomes an old member.

The Quick Connection

An old member is one who is essentially settled in the role he has elected to play and the people with whom he plays it. When this happens, the game, such as it is, is basically over; and it usually happens within twelve months—the period covered by dues. For practical purposes if connections are not made within that time they will probably not be made at all. Consequently when a new man comes into the club, the women have a relatively short time to meet and establish a relationship with him, and he with them; and the same holds true when a new woman joins the club. Connections are made with new members almost exclusively; and if they are not made at the beginning, when the member is indeed new, they will probably not be made at all. In the initial stages the new man may connect with several women, but after a time this almost always ceases.

Sexual connections, intimate, passionate connections, are rarely made between two old members of the club. Those connections that are made are rarely acknowledged publicly. A man and woman sleeping together will not advertise that fact nor allude to their relationship and will tend, in fact, to behave as though it does not exist.

But while in their public demeanor partners treat each other as they would any other member of the club, in private members discuss their affairs in great detail with their friends; and what the detail largely consists of is the sexual behavior of the partners. Men usually discuss among themselves the details of the sexual act: how well they "satisfied" the woman and how much they "got" the woman to "do." The fact that most men exaggerate in these areas is well-known; on the other hand there is always the possibility that the story might be true. If the woman has been a total disaster—a "stick," a "stone," a "dishrag"—that also is talked about.

On the other hand what women discuss mostly is not the sexual prowess of the man but his lack of sexual prowess. (To talk about sexual prowess is to invite competition.) Let a man fail to perform "adequately" in bed and all the woman's friends soon know it—and the man knows they know. This is the man's area of greatest vulnerability, and the mockery of women can feel as if it is too much to bear. No matter that the problem may be temporary or the result of nervousness or overeagerness or a dozen other causes; very few men can take such a "failure" in stride or tolerate the thought of it being common knowledge.

Patterns of Male Retreat

It is much easier to drop out; and the dropout of the denigrated male is one reason for the imbalance of the sexes. Another reason is the initial surrounding of the man by the inner circle of women. At first the attentions are gratifying, but after a time they often begin to feel smothering; many men feel hemmed in, restricted as to their choice of women, coerced, in a sense, into contact with only a small group. Unless they have connected with someone in that group, the smothering may be too great and they may leave.

Finally some men—the sexual "failures"—retreat, in a sense, without leaving the club. They become squires; the perfect nonsexual escort. The man who is a "closet" sexual failure with women may still enjoy their company, may still experience sexual excitement in their presence, may still feel more alive when he is with them. And so he may establish a courting, nonsexual relationship with one or a few women: buy them lunches and dinners, take them to the theater or ballet or ballgames or department stores, do anything except take them to bed. It is, for both the woman and the man, a relationship that is better than nothing: nondemanding, companionable, convenient. And a bit more: for the woman it is at least partial confirmation that she is still desirable to men and an announcement to the world that she is still attractive enough to have a man. For the man it is a chance to be with women and to let the world know that he is still a "man." There is also the hope that the sexually "successful" men in the club will think him one of them.

Competitiveness Again

In bars and at dances the competition among women for available men is muted, in part because of the pressure of time, in part because as long as the initiative is left to the man there is not much a woman can actually do—except be as inviting as possible. In the singles club time is ample and men are approachable as fellow club members, and so the competition is more intense and overt. Any unmarried man is a potential partner; any unmarried woman is a potential competitor. One unattached woman was escorted to a luncheon as the guest of a male club member, and not one of the women at her table spoke to her. Later, in the ladies' room, she encountered a woman to whom she had just been introduced. The guest spoke a few pleasant words; the woman looked at her, looked away as if she weren't there, and walked out without speaking. "It happens every time I go there," the woman says. "It's weird, but by now I'm used to it."

One would suppose that the situation would be different for men, that with a surplus of women the men would be more relaxed with one another. But this is not the case, for the men compete for new, attractive women. And as with women, no connection short of marriage is considered permanent; there are no hands-off situations; everyone is fair game. If an attractive "date" is left alone for a few minutes, other men gather around her with talk and questions. The questions, presented as if in jest, often center around why she is seeing that particular man, and they are asked with an intonation that suggests she is wasting her time, that she might do much better with a man like himself.

Incentives

As far as sex is concerned, the singles club has few advantages for women. For the quick connection bars and dances are better; for the long-term relationship it seems to make little difference. The same, oddly enough, is true for men. One would expect that men who remain in the club, having a relatively large number of women to choose from, could find someone with whom to establish a more permanent relationship. But this rarely happens: the great majority of men who do enter long-term relationships find their partners outside of the club. Typically they bring these new partners to a few functions, but the hostility of the women members is so great that the partner usually becomes uncomfortable—and the man becomes irritated. So he often either drops out of the club or cuts back sharply on his attendance. In brief, except for a flurry of activity when a new member arrives, the singles club is not the best way for men and women to find a sexual relationship.

Sex aside, however, the singles club offers real rewards. These are, first of all, the rewards of structure, acceptance, and activity, and these are especially important during the recovery period. The club is a place to go to with things to do and people to be friendly with; and these are powerful benefits indeed for the person still immersed in a sea of self-doubt and self-reproach. For that woman or man the singles club provides a foundation, a way out onto dry land again.

Even when the transition is passed, the club offers rewards. These are people, after all, with whom one can feel comfortable, people who may be competitive but will otherwise be unthreatening, whose values and outlook on life will be familiar. The club provides the opportunity to go to places and meetings that may in fact be interesting; to say that the principal purpose of a discussion on equal rights is to bring men and women together is not to deny intrinsic interest to the subject itself. The club keeps people active with other people, and this is important. Knowing what to expect, the single man or woman over forty-five can often find great satisfaction in belonging to a singles club.

Party Poop

It's a private house or apartment with the rooms lit up, waiting for guests. If you're like the typical guest, you arrive with one or two friends, although many people do come by themselves. As at any party the hostess (or host) greets you at the door, takes your coat if you're wearing one, ushers you in, introduces you to a group of people—and the party has begun.

One of the fastest-growing ways for single people to meet, the private party is becoming popular all over the country. The affair is held in a private residence with a hostess or host and a number of guests. Actually, both *private* and *party* should be in quotes, since the hostess personally has not met nor invited most of the guests—and a fee is involved, usually about twenty dollars. Nor is the affair given to celebrate any occasion: it's run solely to bring single people in contact with each other.

But the growing popularity of the private party for singles is no accident, because it does provide some significant benefits. First the number of men and women is just about equal. To go to a singles party you usually have to phone in for a reservation; and the person in charge keeps track and makes sure that

that the sexes are in balance. While you can't be sure of finding the partner of a lifetime, you can be quite sure that there won't be a glut of one sex or the other.

Second, it's very unlikely that you'll meet any real "crazies" there. An experienced call-taker develops a good instinct for the unfit or unsuitable potential guest and finds ways of keeping him or her out. The fee also discourages party spoilers, and the fact that parties are usually held on weekend evenings discourages a married person from attending. You can go to one of these parties knowing that the people you meet will be relatively normal and almost certainly single.

Third, if an age group is announced, most people probably will fit in—or at least, look as though they do. It's true that older people sometimes go to a party advertised for younger people (the reverse rarely happens), but they stand out as older and they're not very happy. So they tend not to repeat. There may be one or two people who are obviously the "wrong" age, but not many more than that.

Fourth, generally you get good food and a reasonable amount of liquor. The food is almost always served buffet style but usually includes hot as well as cold dishes; and although in some states the party giver can't advertise that alcoholic beverages are served, once you get there they're usually available. If you drink too much, you'll be asked to leave, but this too is a rare occurrence: people don't go to these parties to get their drinking done.

This brings up the fifth, and what is to some people the most important, benefit, the hostess or host. To some extent the "party" is fiction, but the hostess or host is real and does perform the required functions. He or she mixes and mingles and gets guests to mix and mingle; the host or hostess introduces people to each other, leads the loner to a group, starts conversations—in general, helps the evening go smoothly. You're not totally on your own unless you want to be. (At parties, as everywhere else, there are always a few people who seem to be born sideliners—who stand on the outskirts of every gathering, every occasion, always looking in and never joining. The hostess will try to get them into the mainstream but can't make this an evening's project.) What happens finally is that the fictional party becomes almost real. The food, the drinks, the hostess or host, the other guests, the talk, the general atmosphere, all contribute to the partylike feeling. So the ambiance does take hold, and so the evening—the time and the money-can be well spent.

Satisfaction depends on your objectives. If your goal is to find a long-term partner, the chances may not be much better than at any other type of meeting. For shorter-term relationships the chances would seem to be somewhat better.

In general, as with all ways of meetings, singles parties have disadvantages as well as advantages. For example, the parties are usually very crowded, since the party giver wants to have as many guests as possible. Second, although there's a general equality between the sexes, in numerical terms there may not be many people to choose from—a party for forty people, for example (which is fairly large), means that there are a total of only twenty people of the opposite sex who might be suitable partners. Third, there are age limits. Many party givers will not accept women over a particular age; some have an upper limit for men as well. If you're in the "wrong" age category, you can forget the whole thing. And finally, for many single people, twenty dollars is not a little money to spend for what may turn out to be nothing more than a decent supper.

Are singles parties for you? The answer depends on whether you're a party person or not. If you are, then of course they're for you. If you're not, they might be for you anyway—if not to meet the love of your life, then perhaps to give you an opportunity to sharpen your social skills. If you're the kind of person who's turned off by parties, the singles party is not for you.

As with all the other ways of meeting, you get the most out of parties if your main goal, at least for the evening, is to go to a *party*, to enjoy the atmosphere, the warmth, the food, the talk, the pleasures of civilized social interaction—and if you do meet someone special, all the better.

Advertisements, Etc.

There are thousands of ways of meeting people, as many ways as there are for people to come together. One man in a singles bar proclaimed that he was a superior type who came there only for fun; when he wanted to meet superior women he went to a museum—one specific museum on one specific day. People meet in supermarkets and bowling alleys, shopping centers and parking lots. Resorts have singles weekends; churches and synagogues have special services for singles. And sometimes fashion dictates meeting places: yesterday it was bars; today it is athletic clubs; tomorrow, who knows where?

People also meet less randomly and more purposefully. There are many publications devoted exclusively (or principally) to classified ads for single people: "Slender woman, age 33, home-loving but likes theater, walking, dancing, looking for compatible man 35–42, 6 feet tall and over. Send photo if possible. All letters answered." Sometimes the respondents send photos and sometimes they're even recent photos, but the connection rate doesn't seem much better than average.

Dating services can be traced back to the matchmaker of early times, but the newest type offers technological advantages: videotapes of potential partners. Although this may be effective in preventing complete mismatches, the "success" rate (long-term relationships) doesn't seem much better than the old-fashioned type.

One advantage of dating services for the woman is that she's not likely to encounter married men, since there are easier ways for married men to connect for one-night stands. On the other hand it appears that sexual and other connections are not very frequent. To a great extent the dating service connection is like a blind date again, with both parties somewhat on their best behavior, dressed a little more formally than usual, taking a few more pains to impress the other. And because the expectations are not primarily of sex and connecting but of dating and evaluating (as on blind dates years before), very often the dates end in a pleasant, ultimately disappointing evening.

In addition some dating services have been accused of deceptive practices, specifically, of supplying in-house dates for their clients. These are men and women who are attractive, charming, sensitive, all that a partner could want. But the woman client never gets a follow-up call from the man, and the male client always finds the woman too busy to see him again. Still, the date has been so desirable that the client is inspired to resubscribe (at a typical fee of five hundred dollars per year) and to recommend the service to friends.

Last Word

What is clear about social activities, especially for women, is that they should not be aimed exclusively at meeting and connecting with new people and so finding happiness. We can meet new people in many circumstances; we can connect with only a few of them, and we can get real satisfaction out of only a few of those connections. The person who goes to singles bars or dances, or athletic clubs or parties, or joins a singles group, for the sole purpose of establishing a good connection will often be bitterly disappointed.

The secret is to engage in the activities mostly for their own sake, because they are enjoyable per se: go to bars because they are exciting; go to dances because they're fun; join a singles club because the activities are interesting and the people congenial. Even with dating services and classified ads, avoid the attitude that the rest of your life is at stake, approach new people with an attitude of exploration: what will he or she be like, what will the evening be like? Most often the person and the evening will not be exactly what we had in mind, but the encounter itself can be interesting, if only because no two encounters are the same. And if the evening has been a total disaster? A disaster from which we can awake the next morning with all faculties intact is perhaps more to be laughed at than agonized over.

With this it remains true that in general men are better off than women. Any man of reasonable attractiveness and in reasonable health can probably find a bedmate for an evening or establish a longer relationship if he cares to. He can often find a younger woman to be his partner, sometimes a much younger woman. Women are at a distinct disadvantage in both areas: in no way can they be certain of finding someone for a night, still less of establishing a more permanent relationship.

Yet it makes a great difference whether the woman comes to the encounter wearing an armor of restricted attitudes and values or with a sense of openness and inquiry. Reentry into the world is always disturbing and unsettling, but it is also a chance to learn about ourselves and others in a new context. What do we really want? What is important? What aspects of life have been and are still the most disappointing—and why?

To enjoy ourselves, or at least to begin to enjoy ourselves, *in the moment,* in activities practiced for their own sake in the present and not for what they might bring in the future, is the crucial first step. It is not an easy step for many people to take.

Once this is accomplished, however, once the woman—or man— realizes that she has nobody to please but herself and that she might just as well follow her own inclinations, the feeling of desperation and anxiety dissipates. Now, of course, is precisely when the new partner arrives, the man or woman who may just be right, because nothing is as attractive as the sense that we are at peace with ourselves and at home in the world—and enjoying every minute of it.

Up-to-Date on Socializing

Knowing a few basics can boost the enjoyment factor of
your social encounters:

- INSPECT the venue you've chosen—singles bar, singles dance, sports club, dating service, health club,
  party. Are the people there about your age? Are they
  doing things (whether it be dancing, drinking, or
  working out) that you enjoy too? Is the ratio of the sex
  you wish to meet favorable to you? If so, stick around.
  If not:
- REFLECT on what kind of activity might be right for
  you. Sports bars, for example, attract men; dances
  often attract women. If large parties make you shy,
  maybe you'd prefer a one-on-one date set up by an
  agency. But no matter what you choose,
- EXPECT to feel out of place the first time you try any
  singles activity. You haven't been in this type of environment for a while, and things have changed. But you
  can also . . .
- EXPECT to eventually feel comfortable and enjoy the
  activities you're taking part in. And no matter where
  you are,
- DETECT insincerity in people who approach you if
  you can, especially where unknowns meet unknowns.
  She may just want sex; he may just want a woman to
  talk to over his beer. Or they both may just want someone, anyone, to be with them to prove they're not total
  misfits. As for yourself,
- PROTECT your own sincerity. After a few bad experiences, you may develop a calloused heart that's imper-
  vious to genuine loving and caring. Avoiding predators
  can help keep you open to the real thing.

- CONNECT in a friendly way. Don't expect love at first sight—statistically, the chances are slim! But do look for good conversation, a pleasant encounter, an evening that was worth your time.

Meeting in Comfort

To be most comfortable—and therefore most cordial and relaxed—as you meet new people, find the situations that best suit your personality. Which do you prefer?

_____ **Intimate situations.** Consider dinner parties, blind dates, dating service dates, personal ads, dates your mother arranged.

_____ **The excitement of large groups.** Consider dances, singles parties, political events, rallies.

_____ **Special interest groups.** Consider book clubs, professional organizations, "meets" where people gather to exchange information, health clubs.

_____ **Spontaneous meetings.** Look around wherever you are! Matches are made not only in heaven but at the supermarket, the beach, the bus, the bank, the dog grooming shop.

_____ **Getting to know people without pressure.** Keep your eyes open at the office, in your religious group, at the block party. Love could be blooming right under your nose.

No matter which way you like to meet other people, one thing is certain: You won't meet anyone if you sit on the couch watching TV all day. Get up! Get out! Get going!

CHAPTER 6
Dating Again

Dating: It can be delightful and delicious. It also can be difficult, disturbing, or disastrous. But most dating disasters can be avoided, and those that can't can be neutralized with the proper perspective. This chapter will tell you how.

If your dating skills are rusty, they can be polished. Dating is a skill, and though you can survive the experience without understanding it, you will get much more pleasure from the process if you bring a few insights along each time.

What Is a Date?

Ask five people for a description of dating and you'll probably get five different answers:

"A date is a time set aside for two people to get to know each other."

"It's a chance for you to get out and do something that's fun or interesting."

"You go to a movie and dinner and make a lot of small talk."

"You're stuck with someone you hardly know for a few hours. It's a pressure cooker."

"He pays a few dollars for dinner, then he thinks he bought you."

If only dating in our species were as simple as it is for some of the animals! The male comes around, performs his mating dance, the female indicates a "yes" and suddenly they're married, or the animal equivalent. Human males perform a mating dance of sorts as well, but it's much more complicated. Just sit at a singles party for a while and you can witness the look, the walk-by, the approach, the well-chosen opening words. This is just the beginning of a longer dance that can take days or even years.

Date Psychology

As you can see from the comments collected, many humans find courtship excruciating. That may be because they're not looking at it with curiosity. If you do, you'll see that when you go on a date with another person, there are actually six people on the date:

- Two people who see the other person the way they want him or her to be. Your date is the one you always knew would come, perfection personified, the answer to your prayers. Your date sees you the same way.
- Two people who are what they want the other one to think they are. You're sweet, charming, eager to please, not quite your honest self. Your date is the same.
- Two people who are their real selves, complete with foibles and fallibilities. You each bring with you all your previous experience—the hurts, pain, anxiety, suspicion, and defenses, as well as old tapes you've heard about yourself that may not necessarily be positive. Your date, of course, has a real self too.

To sum up, the reason this number of people exists is that we fantasize our perfect partner, we want to please that perfect partner, and we want to be seen as perfect too. Finally, we are

our real selves. Earlier, in the competitive arena, all our energies went into just getting noticed. Now someone has singled
us out, and our stomach is quivering like Jell-O. We're about to
be checked out at very close range, and that thought may be
very scary. And the thought of *failing* to hold up to the glare of
scrutiny—agony! It's not just our work or our singing or our
smile that are being examined, it's our very selves.

If he doesn't call, or she always says she's "too busy," that's
all the information we may get. We may never know why we
were rejected. No one will tell us if it's the way we look, or
something we said, or the fact that we forgot our mouthwash.
So we often prefer to stay home or go no farther than the big
parties, where no choices have to be made.

With so many negative overtones, it's amazing anyone
goes on a date. But we do. In fact, many good friendships, serious romances, and marriages result from courtship. If you're on
the threshold of a dating period, remember that much of the
joy in life comes from getting out and doing things with others.
All those "extra" people who come along on the date with you
are there to help protect you until you develop some trust in
yourself and your dating partner.

Removing the Mask

If the two of you continue to see each other, the four "idealized
others" eventually will depart, leaving only the two real people.
This is a turning point in any relationship, and one that should
always be passed before you decide to marry or perhaps even
go to bed.

The first to go are usually the two fictitious people we're
trying to be, but are not. Keeping up these appearances is very
strenuous work and most of us find it much easier not to do it,
even though it is accompanied by a few twinges of anxiety:
what will he/she think of me? we wonder.

This is still far better than the way things used to be. Not so long ago, a woman was *never* supposed to reveal the "real me" in a relationship. Instead she wore a Mona Lisa smile, always asking "How was your day, dear?" and saying "Let me get you the newspaper." A dissatisfied or angry wife often was replaced with a fresher, more youthful substitute who had less hurt, pain, anxiety, suspicion, and defenses than more experienced may women carry with them. Even today, women may find that some men expect a one-way deal in which she is supposed to study *their* sport, cook food the way *they* like it, wait home while *they* work late or go out to play.

Fortunately, in the '80s a "new man" came of age (and a man can come of age at any time in his life). This "new man" did not expect a woman to be a doll. He'd become accustomed to the idea of equality. He was a better listener and did not expect waitress service. Occasionally, he regressed to the old ways—particularly if this is what he was accustomed to in the home where he grew up—but a reminder of new approaches is usually enough.

Men may encounter the same major differences in the women they date. The woman who was married in the '50s or '60s and is newly single may have very traditional ideas about her role and her relationship. She may keep her mask on for a long time. For a man who's accustomed to this, there's no conflict. But for a man who's used to giving a woman a bit more space, her one-dimensionality may be terrifying. The good news here is that after a period of adjustment, most newly single women embrace their whole selves, including their strength, intelligence, and independence, with enthusiasm. And once they've embraced it, they're often unwilling to let go of even one little piece of it.

So the first two to go are the "perfect" you and the "perfect" dating partner. Two "idealized people" and the real two still remain.

Where Did the Love Go?

The next to depart are the two "idealized" people who exist in the minds of their dates. Men and women find it very hard to let go of the person of their dreams. She wants to keep forever that man who is unfailingly kind, sexually tender, possessed of great business acumen. He wants her to be ever sexy, intelligent, flawless, and perhaps a little submissive.

Our culture fuels this idealism. Our girls dress Barbie dolls in fluffy dresses and play board games about meeting Prince Charming. In their teens, many of them romanticize relationships with sex-hungry boyfriends. Our boys see sexual images of women from the moment they are able to turn on the TV. They see ads for dial-a-porn that make them think that women secretly want aggressive men, that a "no" really means a "yes." As the boys grow into men, they may continue to respond to media titillation and expect real women to behave like the caricatures they've grown up with.

A couple can become very involved—even marry—before they notice who their mate really is. She may suddenly realize that Prince Charming is selfish, sexist, or has a few truly annoying habits. He may be rudely awakened when the Girl of His Dreams gets tired of sex his way, acts moody, or competes with him careerwise.

Prince Charming and Cinderella have vanished. In their places are a real woman and a real man. At first we may feel that love has gone for good—but the truth is that real love was never there. So what was that incredible thrill, that amazing rush, the fantastic sex? It was infatuation. Georgia Witkin, Ph.D., a well-known psychologist who happens to be my daughter, explains in her book *Passions* that infatuation is an altered state of consciousness—a temporary trance. We can't stop thinking about our love, and we can't slow down our racing heart. The object of our infatuation seems bigger than life, so attractive to us that we can't understand why everyone else doesn't see it too. We fantasize constantly, can't concentrate anymore, need him or her to give meaning to our own life.

Sometimes infatuation wears us out physically and emotionally, and then we feel like we're falling out of love. But infatuation can sometimes lead to a lasting love that's quieter and more solid.

That's when the two real people meet at last.

Dating Theory

Developing a relationship takes time, and it's very unlikely that a date or two can do that. That's why it's not wise to think of a date as a means to getting somewhere—married, attached, in love, or sexually released.

Dates are supposed to be fun. If you've spent time stuck at home with small children or trapped behind a desk at work, you know just how pleasurable the thought of a movie or restaurant meal can be. Or maybe you prefer a beer, a burger, and a rock concert. Whatever it is, think of finding someone who will go along with you as a great opportunity for enjoyment.

This means you should accept that blind date! He or she may not turn out to be someone you want to spend the rest of your life with, but he or she has already agreed to be your companion for the evening. Make the most of it. As the saying goes, "You may have to kiss a lot of frogs before you find the handsome prince." Another way to approach it is to use a trick borrowed from successful salespeople: You need to collect a lot of "nos" before you get a "yes." Each boring date paves the way to a better one.

So don't look for anything more in your date than a companion for the moment. As you do so, you'll effortlessly get to know each other better and maybe even enjoy yourselves. Your first dates with a new someone are not a time to do a lot of analysis. Does he have money? Would he be a good father to the kids? Will she get fat as she grows older? Will she try to stop me from going running? Don't worry about that now. Just see if you can enjoy yourselves together. Pat, age thirty-nine, is glad she didn't let some early stumbling blocks get in the way of a good relationship:

> When I met Dan, I was attracted right away. He was tall, exotic-looking, good-natured, and very bright. But around our second or third date I found out we had some differences. He liked chrome and glass; I like English chintz. He liked to travel; I'm a homebody. We had a major religious difference, too, and his mother made it clear that if we married I would be expected to convert.
>
> Dan and I are now married. Our house is decorated in a simple style that is neither his ultra modern nor my flowers and ruffles. When he wants to travel, sometimes I go and sometimes I stay home. The religious question was the tough one. I didn't convert but we'll raise our children in his religion.
>
> Our eight-year marriage is better than a lot of the ones I see around me, and I would say that our differences add a lot of spark.

The only analysis you want to do early in a dating relationship is about the basics: Is she or he abusive? Does she or he have a severe alcohol or drug problem? In cases where the incompatibility is obvious or the problems of majestic proportions, it's time to end the relationship before someone gets hurt.

Otherwise, suspend your judgment for the moment and relax. Your date may sense what you're doing and do the same. Throw your energies into attentiveness to your date and into making yourself presentable, then let the date go where it may. Every new relationship deserves a chance! It may blossom in spite of itself.

From Discomfort to Discovery

To add to the fun, see if you and your companion can find something to do that will get you talking or laughing. The traditional movie and dinner are enough for movie mavens and food lovers. But many other people find the movie-dinner formula to be stiff, and so is the conversation. Use your creativity to dream up a date that will be pleasing and memorable. The elements of a Great Date can include:

- **The interest of both parties.** Gone are the days when a woman would tag along with a man just because he wanted to see a wrestling match or drag race. Likewise, no man has to sit through a romantic movie he finds a bore and a snore.
- **The comfort of both parties.** If bugs and sitting on the ground make her uncomfortable, don't plan a spring picnic. If the date involves transportation, the one who's not driving must trust the one who is.
- **Simplicity.** Many a date has failed because the plan was too complicated or involved an overnight stay.
- **A chance to talk.** Though you don't want to judge, you do want to at least make a connection.

Here are some Great Dates to get you started:

— a flying lesson, bike ride, rollerblading session
— a hike in the woods with a group of friends
— watching or playing a sport, with great snacks afterward
— a religious or political event
— a concert, perhaps outdoors
— a class or workshop, such as cooking together gourmet style
— a horseback ride or picnic

To Bed or Not to Bed?

We are all adults here, and most of us have some sexual experience. Why, then, is sex such a point of discussion? Because no two people are the same, because times change, because HIV/AIDS kills, because sex can be emotional or mechanical, ecstatic or insulting, hot-hot-hot or a chill wind of guilt or discomfort. You may not know which it will be until you're there. On a date where the chemistry is right, going to bed is tempting. Says a forty-one-year-old divorced woman:

> After ten years of marriage to the same man—who was never inconsiderate in bed but also never too thrilling—I am rediscovering sex. There's more power in my sexual response now.
>
> Either my husband and I got into a rut, or the man I date now is more creative. Things like this: He comes up behind me, puts his hands on my shoulders and kisses my hair. I can feel his warmth but there's space between us. Then he very slowly closes the space. I can feel his erection and begin to melt. I turn around, we kiss for a long time, he carries me into the living room and we make love on the floor. My husband never kissed my hair, never left any space between us, and never carried me anywhere!

Love the second time around can be like this—a new beginning just when you thought there could be no more beginnings. Here's a time when maturity has value: your sexual experience allows you to choose a more exciting partner and more freely enjoy what he or she has to offer. The novelty itself can be exciting.

Your maturity also can help you handle whatever follows—your date will either be back or not. Can you deal with not seeing the person again after you have had sex? This is something to consider *before* you have sex. Some men and women can give themselves completely on a date and then say goodbye with no regrets or thoughts about the future. Other people take sex more seriously, as a true connection between body and soul.

Still other sexual encounters are less than honest: some men and women use it as a way to insure another date, or make themselves feel less lonely or more attractive. Too often, when two people are intimate too soon, one may be just using the other, and it's not always easy to tell. Men and women have been deceiving each other and themselves for years.

The best advice? Make sure you know yourself intimately before you agree to know your partner intimately. Ask yourself what sex will mean for you, and ask yourself if it will have the same meaning, whatever that is, for your partner.

What Will the Kids Think?

The single man or woman with children has an extra consideration: what will the kids think about Mommy's new love interest or Daddy's new sweetheart? Here's what: they *don't* want to see their parent as a sexual being, and they *don't* want to feel their real parent is being replaced.

This is why bringing a new friend home to bed when the children are around is a bad idea. If not openly hostile, they may manufacture reasons to knock on the bedroom door or create a disturbance (almost always at a peak sexual moment). Only a partner with kids too would understand.

It's better to find trysting places outside the house. Your date's place—providing no kids are there—is a good choice. Or you can borrow a friend's apartment or beach house. A hotel room can be fun as long as it's a nice room. Some trailers and "recreational vehicles" have large beds. If you're athletic, there's always the car.

Date Rape

You thought you knew him, you thought he cared about you, you thought he was a nice guy, but then the inexplicable happens: a light kiss becomes a heavy hug becomes forced sexual intercourse that he wants and you don't. This is date rape. Just because it happens on a date makes it no less a rape. In fact, in date rape, the psychological attack is even more brutal than in a stranger rape because:

- Your trust in him makes it more difficult to see the point where an amorous advance becomes a threatened rape.
- He forces you with words; it isn't a purely physical assault (although one in three women raped by an acquaintance has the cuts and bruises to show for it).
- Afterward, he seems truly sorry and continues to call. One woman said the man who had raped her then offered to walk her back to her place so she'd be safe!

In one study, one in four male university students admitted being sexually aggressive despite a date's protests. In her interviews of 1,300 women for her book *The Female Stress Syndrome*, Georgia Witkin found that date rape was surprisingly common—*at least* to the one woman in four who has reported it in national studies. And we know that at least half of all date rapes go unreported, so the toll is even higher.

Too often, victims don't call rape when they should, says Dr. Witkin. That's because the victim often suffers serious doubts about her own perceptions and judgments. She may feel disillusioned, distrustful, powerless, less confident, and less safe. She may also develop a psychiatric problem, such as obsessive-compulsive disorder, phobias, or panic disorder. The victim may even blame herself for what happened, but it's important to know that the course of the evening was probably decided by factors other than anything she did.

Step one in dealing with a rape is reporting it to the police—the sooner the better. Step two is getting counseling, even if you don't think you need it. Almost everyone can benefit from it. You'll know that you're not finished dealing with the issue if you're reluctant to talk about it even with close friends, blame yourself, ignore symptoms that came on afterward, or are oversensitive to events that symbolize rape, such as a gynecological exam.

You're over the incident when you're free of bad dreams and intrusive memories about it, when you can talk about it with appropriate anger and not unreal detachment.

Blowing It

A date should be a situation in which you can be yourself. And you can take comfort in the fact that it's almost impossible to blow a date by being yourself. If, for example, you really like your date but your date doesn't like you, or if you disagree about the president's policy or whether chiropractors are worth the money or whether life is meaningful, and you end up tense and irritated with each other, that's not an indication that you blew it. It's an indication that you're not compatible, and going your separate ways is probably best.

That said, it is possible to make errors on a date. We often put our best foot forward, then trip over it. Getting drunk, throwing up, excessive sarcasm, rudeness, flirting with people other than your date, leaving your date stranded somewhere— these are serious breaches of dating etiquette that you should meditate on. Why did you act that way? Could it be that you're angry with the opposite sex? Have you not yet recovered from your previous loss? Is someone else setting up dates for you and you resent it? For your own sake and the sake of an innocent date, settle these issues before you start.

Last Word

So here you are, on the threshold of a dating relationship. Suppose you go out, have a wonderful evening, fall in love just a bit, and never see your date again? The reigning queen of etiquette, Judith Martin (better known as Miss Manners) has this advice. "The greatest comfort, when one is rejected, is to believe that the other person is making a mistake, which will be bitterly regretted sooner or later," she says. "Such thinking is most easily achieved when one is rejected on vague and flimsy grounds." Of course, if the rejection has been more specific—if, perhaps, attributes such as your personality, appearance, intelligence have been described critically—then you must stand up straight, set your chin, and move resolutely forward.

And what if it's you who must end the relationship? In most cases, give reasons that will leave your partner's self-esteem intact. Never treat someone you have loved with less kindness and consideration than someone you're first meeting.

Dating Dos and Don'ts

To make your dates the pleasurable experiences they could be:

- REMEMBER to keep your sense of curiosity. You're getting a firsthand look at some very interesting human mating behavior (including your own).
- FORGET ABOUT judging your date. You hardly know him or her, so judging isn't fair. Plus, you may cheat yourself out of a special friendship or romance.
- REMEMBER to be yourself. There's no point in getting to know someone else if you won't let someone else get to know you.

- FORGET ABOUT those extra "idealized" people you brought on the date. The sooner you and your date stop deceiving each other, the better your relationship will be.
- REMEMBER that a date is supposed to be enjoyable. Think "fun" first and foremost. Plan activities that meet this criterion.
- FORGET ABOUT sexual intimacy until you've made sure that you and your date are on the same wavelength. This way no one will get hurt.
- REMEMBER your manners! Etiquette is designed to help social encounters roll along more smoothly.
- FORGET ABOUT having sex when kids are around.
- REMEMBER that rejection will not ruin your life—and a new friendship will enhance it greatly. You and your date have nothing to lose and much to gain.

PART TWO
The Sexual Self

CHAPTER 7
Sexual False Starts

For many women and men the hardest part of being single again is getting over the initial shock. Next hardest is finding another partner: someone in whom they can be interested and who is also interested in them. Whether the interest is for a long-term relationship or a short-term interlude, once that person is met, things are supposed to go smoothly—depending, as usual, on luck as well as on personality.

But many men and women never seem to reach the smooth stage. They meet somebody and things always seem to go badly; something always turns out wrong. And the trouble often occurs in the area of sex. What makes it worse is that these men and women know others just like them who seem to have no trouble at all, who seem to find satisfying partners with satisfying regularity. And so to sexual frustration is added a more general frustration: things are working out very badly and there seems to be no way of improving matters. That's not the way it was supposed to be, but that's the way it is.

What went wrong?

The Frustrated Woman: Evelyn

Evelyn is in her late forties, thin, attractive, intense, trying to start a new career as a stockbroker after having been a homemaker since her late twenties. She has two daughters, twenty and seventeen.

After we finish talking I'll go to this nightclub. It's not really a nightclub—they have a piano, and somebody sometimes sings. But they know me there, and it's no hassle.

I know most of the regulars there too—the men. I had kind of an affair with one of them, but I broke it off. He was really disgusting—I mean, you wouldn't believe it.

I got divorced from my husband because he was a baby. He had other women—tons of them—and I wasn't supposed to care about it. Whatever he wanted to do, I had to want to do. I had to give up everything for him, because otherwise his feelings were hurt. I hurt his precious feelings. And then he went out and screwed another woman.

Money was never a problem—he had a lot and he spent a lot. More than I wanted to. Now, of course, he's absolutely tight. Sex was okay.

I'm not sorry I left. The girls are still a little crazy from the divorce, but I can handle it. And I'm hoping to get a decent job and make some money of my own.

Men are a problem. There are no good ones around. If they're not married by this time, they're sick. Or they're going out with young chicks. There's something wrong with them. I went out with a guy in his sixties and he was so weak he could hardly unzip his pants by himself, but he's coming on to me like he's a stud.

I haven't had that many men since the divorce. I don't like one-night stands, but sometimes I get desperate. And then nine times out of ten it's lousy. I mean *lousy*. As far as marrying again—sure. Just show me the right man. But there's no such thing.

I shouldn't say that. There's this woman I know—we met at a dance a few months ago and got to talking. She was my age, same kind of husband, everything. Then we said goodbye, and I didn't see her again until last week. I ran into her in some department store, and she had found this marvelous guy and was having a marvelous time. This was the second one. The first one she met wanted to get married and she didn't, so she dumped him. And she's no more attractive than I am.

Maybe she was lucky. Or maybe she knows something I don't know.

There are many women like Evelyn—vigorous, unsatisfied, bitter—at all ages and under all circumstances. They want sexual connections; they usually have much less than they want, and they find most of those connections unsatisfying. And they all know one or two women, "no more attractive" than they, who seem to be fabulously successful with men.

To some extent these other women *are* lucky, because there is always an element of luck in finding the right person. But Evelyn's surmise was also right: those successful women do know something she doesn't know. What they know is that sex is more than a matter of limbs and organs coming together in the right way. They know that sex is primarily the enjoyment of a physical *relationship*, even if the relationship lasts only a short time. And they know that they have a part in making the relationship work—and that, as women, they usually play a more important part than the man; that, at least in the first few encounters, the man may initiate but the woman tends to sustain. These women are able to sustain relationships with confidence and pleasure. In return they receive a great deal of pleasure for themselves, as well as the envy of other women whose men always seem to be "sick" or "disgusting." What these successful women are aware of is the anxiety many men feel concerning their sexual prowess. And what they are able to do is accept that anxiety as a "given," a part of the situation, and *not something that they are responsible for.* They are aware, that is, of the problems of the woman-wary man.

The Woman-Wary Man: Barry

Barry is a high-school teacher in his mid-fifties: medium height, balding, nearsighted. He speaks softly but with great precision. Married twenty-five years, his wife left him and their three sons five years ago for another man.

> I had a hard time at first. Marie was the only girl I had ever known—I mean, I never had sex with any-one else. I knew we had problems, but I was sure we could work them out. We always had before. So when she left, it was a real shock.
>
> I didn't get over it for years. I mean, I didn't look for another woman. But after a while I began want-ing sex again. I would have these fantasies, and I caught myself staring at women as they came by—in elevators, on the street, everywhere. Even teenagers. You name it.
>
> So I wanted a woman. But I have this problem: I come too fast. It never made Marie too happy, but we managed. I've always thought that was one of the reasons she left me, but I never asked. But every time it happened I felt lousy, and it happened all the time.
>
> I really wanted a woman, though. So I went to this singles bar. There were some really attractive women there, but they were surrounded by men,

and I'm not the pushy type. Finally I saw this other woman standing by herself. She was a little heavy, but she seemed all right. Her name was Joan.

I'll make a long story short. I bought her a drink, and we went out to eat, and then I brought her to her place. I was getting more nervous by the minute. I was sure I was going to foul the whole thing up.

Anyway I finally blurted out about going to bed, and she said okay. So she goes to the bathroom and then I go to the bathroom. And while I'm in the bathroom she's taking off her clothes in the bedroom. And I'm taking off my clothes in the bathroom. I don't even know if I like her. And I'm sure I'm going to come too fast.

But I'm not feeling like coming too fast. I'm feeling numb. I walked into the bedroom and I'm naked. And I'm limp. She's sitting up in bed, with the blanket up to her waist. So the first thing I look at is her breasts, and the first thing she looks at is my penis. And I'm limp—there's practically nothing there.

So we start making love. We're kissing each other, and I'm feeling her breasts. But that's not what I'm thinking of; I'm thinking of my penis. I'm waiting for it to do something. And it's not doing anything. And every so often she moves around so she can feel what's happening, and nothing's happening. And I'm getting panicky. So finally I start praying inside my head; I mean really praying. "God, let it get hard; God, let it get hard." God had better things to do.

So after five or ten minutes she pushes me away. She says, "Get off me," and pushes me away. As though I were some kind of insect. So I get off, not knowing what to say. The fact is, I *felt* like an insect. I didn't know whether to apologize or not, or even *how* to apologize. She told me to get dressed, and I

did, and when I came out of the bathroom, she had
a robe on. And she said, "Why don't you practice at
home before you try it with a real live person?"
Which didn't make me feel any better. And then she
said, "I can't tell you how marvelous it's been," and I
left.

I didn't try again for a few weeks, and the same
thing happened. And it happened a few more times.
I won't say I've given up, but I haven't looked for a
woman for a long time now. I masturbate—as Joan
said, I'm practicing at home. I'm starting to have
trouble there too. And in the last couple of months
I'm cutting down on that also. I just don't seem to
care anymore. Maybe I'm getting too old.

It's very unlikely that Barry is getting too old; since as
long as a man is fairly healthy, age is hardly ever a bar to having
some sort of erection. Nor is there a physiological reason for
his impotence. He—and Joan, and Evelyn, and many other
frustrated women—are trapped in a common and unfortunate
syndrome: the getting-together fiasco.

The Getting-Together Fiasco

What really is happening to Barry, Evelyn, and Joan? We'll begin with Barry, because his problem is central.

Barry and the Enemies of Male Potency

For almost every male his first erection is a mystery, and even
though later he may learn all the physiological details, something mysterious always remains. He looks at a woman,
touches, smells—or he only imagines, closes his eyes and fan-
tasizes—and the most exquisitely sensitive part of his body
swells, grows larger and rigid, and changes its outlook, gazing
up instead of down between his legs. How does it happen?

It's easy enough to find the answer, but even when he does, the man also learns that he cannot fully control his erections. Sometimes, especially when he's young, they come involuntarily and undesired, such as while he's riding on a bus. Sometimes when he wants it, the erection just won't come, even though he uses all the tricks he knows.

Because erections may be to some extent uncontrollable, when they come on schedule, they are like a precarious achievement, which the man cannot take full credit for. As Norman Mailer put it: " . . . a man is not often ready to explain that a phallus is not a simple instrument but a contradictory, treacherous, all-too-spontaneous sport who is sometimes the expression of a part of oneself not quite under Central Control, indeed often at odds with the will."* And when it doesn't behave as it's supposed to, when the penis lets him down, it's like a mysterious punishment.

There is nothing new in saying that for the vast majority of men, self-esteem is closely tied to sexual potency, the ability to have an erection at appropriate times. Most women know this, but many women are unaware of the depth of the connection, the intensity of the emotions tied up in sexual potency. Some men can accept occasional impotence with calmness, but most men grow panicky at the prospect. Impotence strikes at the very root of their self-image and ramifies into every part of their lives. What are the enemies of potency? Physiological problems aside, the two most prevalent are anger and anxiety; and of these, for the older man and woman, anxiety is by far the more important.

Anxiety. It's been said that no matter how experienced a man may be, the first time he goes to bed with a new woman he's a virgin again. That is, he's full of anxiety. But his anxiety is different from that of the youthful virgin. The young man is apt to

*Norman Mailer, *The Prisoner of Sex* (Boston and Toronto: Little Brown and Company, 1971), p. 7.

worry about his lack of skill or finesse, perhaps about some details of his physical appearance, most likely about his staying power. What he usually knows about himself is that his orgasms come quickly, and this is typically a major fear—he won't last long enough to satisfy his partner. Another fear is that he just won't know what to do.

The older man may have all of these fears and more. By this time he knows generally what to do, but he doesn't know what his new partner likes. And it seldom occurs to him to ask. (For one thing he thinks he's supposed to be an expert.) He also is more worried about his physical appearance. His skin is rarely as tight as it was or his muscles as firm; he's probably inclined a little to flab and sag and wrinkles and baldness; veins are beginning to stand out and blotches appear—and not just on his hands and feet: on his penis as well. So he is afraid that just looking at him will turn his partner off.

Also like the young man, the older man may be anxious about premature ejaculation. It has been estimated that at least fifty percent of American men are premature ejaculators—that is, lack ejaculatory control—with some authorities placing the number as high as ninety percent. And although there's some evidence that premature ejaculation diminishes as men grow older, for many men it doesn't diminish enough to allow complete control. So perhaps half of the older men in America taking a partner to bed for the first time begin with the same anxieties as the youth: will I be attractive to her (or at least, not repulsive); will I be able to satisfy her? But the older man has one other great anxiety: *the fear of impotence.* Impotence is not usually a problem with young men, and they don't usually worry about it. (If a young man does experience primary impotence—that is, if he's never had an erection and seems unable to—then he needs medical or psychological help, or both.) But as men grow older their potency tends to diminish, and for many men this causes tremendous anxiety.

We'll talk more about diminished potency in Chapter 11; for now the main aspect is that erections don't come as readily.

Young men can have erections simply by *thinking* about sex or through indirect stimulation. A young man and woman can dance together with only their arms touching, and if it's the right woman at the right time, the penis will become erect. If the young man does have an ejaculation at the wrong time, in only fifteen minutes or so he can often have another erection and another orgasm.

As time passes, both the ease and frequency of erections tend to diminish. Fantasies and mental images may no longer work, nor may indirect nonsexual contact. For many older men the only way to have an erection is by direct manual or oral stimulation of the penis. Even when fantasies and indirect stimulation do work, the sense of the years passing creates the fear in the older man that maybe next time they won't work, maybe next time he'll be a "failure." He also knows that next time is farther away than it used to be; the older the man is, the longer is the refractory period—the time it takes to get over an ejaculation and have another erection.

The fear of failure, the fear of impotence, afflicts men who are married as well as those who are single again and is one reason for the lower frequency of sexual intercourse among many older couples. But it's worse for the single-again man because now he has to prove himself all over again. It is with this attitude—fear of failure—that he meets a new woman and escorts her to bed. And then there comes the moment, as it did with Barry, when there she is, waiting for him. And what is he thinking of?

What he is *not* thinking of is his coming pleasure or the woman's desirability or warmth, stimulation, excitement, joy, passion. What he *is* thinking of is whether he'll have an erection—in fact, whether he is having, *right now,* the erection he is "supposed" to have. And what he is doing is checking himself to see what's going on.

Spectatoring. The technical term for this process is self-observation; the more colloquial term is spectatoring. Under any name it is probably the single most prevalent cause of sexual impotence among otherwise normal men. In brief the man worries about his coming sexual performance, especially about getting an erection, and keeps himself under observation to monitor the status of the erection—and by this process alone practically eliminates any possibility of having one. His anxiety has led to the impotence he has been anxious about.

That's what happened to Barry. The second time was even more of a guaranteed failure; whereas at first, with Joan, all he had was the anxiety itself, now he had anxiety buttressed by "evidence"—he had "failed" the first time. So his spectatoring became even more obsessive, and the likelihood of having an erection was even lower.

This is the classic case of *secondary impotence,* the impotence of a man who has been potent before. Barring physiological problems, it is completely curable: the spectatoring is curable and so is the impotence itself. *The cure is to flood the mind with erotic fantasies and images, sensual thoughts and memories, at the time of lovemaking.*

Sometimes it's hard for the man to do this because his anxiety is too great; in that case some relaxation techniques are called for. They're discussed in Chapter 8. And sometimes the man has problems because he's with a woman like Evelyn or Joan, and while he is trying to think sexy thoughts, he's aware that *she* is waiting, checking up, appraising his performance, which immediately sinks to zero.

It's easy to see why men like Barry can become angry with themselves and with women like Evelyn. But Evelyn has problems also, and it would be helpful if Barry knew about them.

Evelyn and the Curse of Creepy Men

Sexually speaking, women have several advantages over men. First their sexual powers do not diminish with age, or diminish much more slowly: if they were orgasmic before they are equally so now, and the amount of stimulation they need to have an orgasm doesn't change very much. So they do not have the specter—and the fact—of waning sexual competence to cope with.

Another advantage, well-known indeed, is that, unlike the man's, their performance, their orgasm, is hidden and can be simulated. Nobody has to know. So even if a woman *were* worried about her sexuality, she wouldn't have the added worry that this would abort the sexual act or that her partner might find out and label her a failure. But the most important difference is that she doesn't need an erection to prove her sexual prowess. So diminished sexuality is rarely a problem for older women. But older women do bring their own problems to that first sexual meeting, problems that can lead to exactly the wrong kind of behavior. Like the man's problems, the woman's problems arise from low self-esteem. Just as self-esteem for many men is based on their ability to have erections, self-esteem for many women is based on their ability to attract a man. Physical attractiveness becomes for many women what a big penis is for many men: something desirable to others and therefore valuable to themselves. It becomes a symbol of their femininity. But not the proof of femininity, just as the mere existence of a penis is not the proof of masculinity. If the proof of masculinity for a man is the ability to have an erection, *the proof of femininity for many women is the ability to stimulate erections in men.*

Until recently, in America and in many other parts of the world, the first job of a woman had been to attract a man, and when she did this society seemed satisfied and she was considered partially successful. She felt "normal" in the eyes of others. But in her own eyes she did not feel normal unless she completed the second part of her job: arousing the man sexually. That still seems to be the ultimate test. And how does she know when she has passed the test? She knows because the man has an erection. The man's potency becomes the proof of the woman's attractiveness; it not only confirms his basic value, but it also confirms hers. And if he doesn't have an erection, then not only he has failed; she has also failed.

But women, like men, cannot easily stand sexual "failure," especially when it is visible to others. Women can simulate desire but they cannot simulate the man's erection. And for those women whose sexual value depends on the man's response, the sense of sexual devaluation caused by the man's impotence is very profound.

The woman, however, has an advantage: she can shift the blame outward to the man. Men cannot really do the equivalent. Theoretically, an impotent man can lay his problems on the woman's shoulders: she has turned him off; she has not turned him on. But most men hate to consider themselves as being only conditionally potent, potent only under the proper circumstances. If they did, they would have a lot less trouble with their occasional impotence. No: most men secretly nourish the image of super-potency, the mile-long penis, the magic wand that cures a woman of frigidity, transforms lesbians into lovers, mesmerizes multitudes, the mighty tool of his masculinity. And when the tool breaks down, generally he breaks down also.

But after all it's his penis and not the woman's, and when it doesn't work, she is able to shift her response outward. If the man is impotent, is she sexually undesirable? In her heart she often feels that she is, and this is hard for anyone to face. But the woman is able to redirect the emotion away from herself and to the outside—specifically, to the man who has been impotent.

And so, to protect her self-concept, she makes him the object of her contempt and ridicule—a container, in a manner of speaking, for the emotions she carries but cannot acknowledge. She dumps on him because the load of shame and self-reproach is too great for her to bear. And so women who in other circumstances might be understanding, helpful, and relaxed become contemptuous, sarcastic, destructive—the "castrating bitches" of male legend.

Impotence on the part of the man arouses the greatest apprehension in the insecure woman, and premature ejaculation can do nearly the same. It's not as bad, because the woman can always assume that she is so desirable that the man cannot control himself. On the other hand women are trained to be responsible for the men in their lives, and so his early orgasm is again her fault in some way; and as before, she turns her self-reproach outward and attacks the man. (Not all self-reproachful women do this, of course; many apologize to the men!)

Just as a string of sexual "failures" can condition the man to expect more failures, they can also condition the woman in the same way: she expects each date to fail. And so all men become creeps or psychos or anything else—and so she is protected against experiencing her own negative feelings toward herself. But the price she pays—Evelyn and her sisters—is bitterness and frustration. Barry, of course, is frustrated, too, and wounded and full of self-doubt. And so they both go on their ways, with their sexual encounters becoming less frequent and more unsatisfying.

It doesn't have to be this way. What Barry and Evelyn have to do is accept themselves and each other as basically normal, basically agreeable people—and then recognize that *basically normal people experience basically normal anxiety at their first sexual meeting.* They both should recognize that *the normal physiological response of the human male to anxiety is to restrict the flow of blood to the penis, and the penis remains limp.* The man fears that he will not be able to please the woman and literally scares himself impotent.

Knowing the facts, however, doesn't help many men. They still demand performance from their penis, still become anxious, still "fail," and still feel crushed. But the woman is in a different situation. Aware that his problems are not her fault, she has a chance to take the initiative in a sense: to help the man and especially to help herself.

The Wise Woman: Estelle

Estelle is in her mid-fifties, a cheerful, no-nonsense, somewhat overweight woman born in Colombia, living for the past thirty years in the United States.

I came to this country as a bride with my husband, but as soon as I'm pregnant he ran away. I was good-looking then—skinny, you understand—and I supposed I'd get a job as a receptionist. But my English wasn't good enough then. So I become a file clerk, and I have my son, and in a year I look for work again. My mother takes care of the boy. I want to be a typist—I tell you, I'm a super typist—and I get a job with an electronics firm. Later they bring in a word processor and they want me to learn it—me and the two other typists, young girls. This is a new thing, and the other girls do badly. They're afraid of the machine, you see? But I learn it very quickly. Because I treat this machine like a man—I conquer it.

What do I mean, conquer? I mean I'm not afraid of it. It's a good machine; I'm a good typist. You handle it right; it does what you want. Nothing to be afraid of.

It's the same with men. They're like little boys. Maybe not like little boys, but not so complicated. They want to feel good. I make them feel good; they make me feel good.

They know that. That's how I get my second husband—I make him feel good. He was crazy about me. He wanted me to stop work and just take care of him, but I'm too independent. I do what I want. He died six, seven years ago, and it wasn't so easy. But I'm fine now.

I miss him a little, but I don't miss men. I get all the men I want. Look at me. I once was pretty, now I'm too fat. Especially fat legs—thighs. I'm really ugly there. Bosom is okay, and so is backside. So I say, if men don't like fat thighs, that's their problem. What I have is plenty. I don't have so many men—I don't need it. One at a time. Soon they want to marry me, then they get jealous, then I send them away.

The first time you go out with a man, he's a boy. Very nervous. Afraid he won't be able to get it up. That's good for me. He's so worried he doesn't even notice my fat thighs.

So what do I do? First I get comfortable. There's no sense doing anything when you're not comfortable. Then I talk a lot. I'm a big talker—I can talk a lot in two languages. Sometimes I don't shut up—that's my problem. I talk all the time.

I talk about how sweet the man is. If he has a lot of hair, I talk about how I like hair; and if he has no hair, I talk about how I like smooth. And meantime I'm reaching down and touching it—his penis. And I'm massaging it. And I'm telling him how sweet he is. And soon it starts getting harder—not all the time, but most of the time. A lot of the time.

So then I ask what they like to do in bed. Sometimes they say they want head [oral sex]. I give them head. I like this. They get hard so fast; they do anything I want. I have the power. They think they have the power, but what do they know? I don't do anything I don't want to do.

Sometimes when a man starts to get hard, he wants to come inside right away. He's afraid he's going to lose it. But I don't allow this. I'm not ready. I have my needs. I do for him; he has to do for me.

Most men don't get mad; in fact, they like it. It makes them feel necessary. Plus, they get excited when they see me getting excited. It's the same with me. Sometimes I have to show them what to do— where to put their hands, how to move. Men hate to admit they don't know something—they think they're supposed to know everything. Especially about sex and women. But they don't know anything. And they hardly ever ask. That's because men are shy—they're more shy than women. I always ask. I don't believe in guesswork.

What if a man won't do it? Then we're finished. I don't get mad—I'm nice and polite—but we're finished. He's got to go. I have my needs, and I have my respect. I don't mind a man being too anxious. I don't mind if he can't get it up. I don't mind if he comes too fast. I can handle it. But I won't start cold and he has to respect that. I need a warm-up. I need to feel I'm a lady and not a whore.

With some men you have to do everything yourself—I mean take their hand and put it where it belongs. That's just the first time; then they get the idea fast. That's because I'm a good teacher. With other men they don't need help; they're all over you. That doesn't bother me. I'm an easygoing type. And if they do something I don't like, I tell them.

What if a man can't get it up? It happens a lot. It's no big deal. They still have fingers and a mouth. They still like being touched down there even if nothing happens. And as long as they're willing to use what they've got, that's fine with me. I tell them how sweet they are, and they love it. Well, they *are* sweet. They're so relieved I'm not going to laugh at them or put them down. I could make them my slaves if I wanted to. It's a fact. Like I said: I make them feel good and they make me feel good.

What makes Estelle successful? Obviously, there's a basic self-respect there, a sense of self-worth that comes from within, not from the outside. So she can take care of herself; she assumes the responsibility for her own sexual satisfaction, and she does this primarily by communicating with her partner. Sometimes she communicates by actions, as when she guides the man's hand, and sometimes by explicit verbal instructions. But the man knows soon enough what she feels she has a right to expect—which is *not the perfect orgasm but a willingness to please,* a sense of relationship. And, of course, she takes care to learn what will please the man as well.

She also has a feeling for the dynamics of the sexual response. She knows that in the initial stages of anxiety the man will tend to be so worried about his own problems that he won't see her flaws—her fat thighs, as she says. She also knows that once desire begins to quicken it sweeps everything before it, so that the flaws (if that's what they are) cease to exist at all. In brief she accepts herself as she is, trusting her own essential worthiness and the arousal of sexual passion to overcome any problems along the way.

Beyond this, she is able to help the man relax. How? Fundamentally *by not asking him to do anything he cannot do.* For a nervous, fearful man, an erect penis is not always available, and if that is the only acceptable instrument, then the old cycle sets in, the cycle of anxiety and impotence. Once the demand for performance ceases, the entire atmosphere changes. And that is when performance—and an erect penis—usually come about.

Last Word

The secrets of Estelle's success lie in her skill in communicating and her ability to help her partners relax. These are also the secrets of men who make good lovers; and by no accident they are very important ingredients of any sexual relationship at any age, under any circumstances.

Secrets of Great Lovers

Think about the best lover you ever had (either in reality or fantasy!). What made the experience so wonderful? Chances are your lover gave you the feeling that *you were loved*. He didn't demand sexual tricks; he didn't jump on you. He held you close, made you feel special, had *your* feelings in mind. She didn't act self-conscious or make you feel self-conscious. She calmed you, caressed you, kissed you, made you feel *good*.

How to become a great lover:

- GET LOST. Fill your mind with erotic thoughts. Any time a nonerotic thought creeps in, erase it with an erotic one. Lose yourself in love.
- GIVE PLEASURE. Be generous. Ask your partner what he or she likes. If you can, fill the order! Wanting to please is a turn-on.
- RELAX. Let the joy and passion bloom as you make love. Take it slow and easy. Let your senses pull you in and sweep you away.

CHAPTER 8

Contact and Pleasure

This chapter is about relationships; why they work and why they don't. We'll talk specifically about the sexual relationship, but what we say applies to all relationships. Why they work is easy: because communication, relaxation, and self-responsibility are working in the relationship. And why some relationships don't work is also easy: because something has gone wrong with at least one of these three factors, and the whole relationship is thrown out of balance.

The fact is all of these factors are closely tied together; affect one and you affect them all. You can't communicate productively unless there's a basic trust involved—that is unless you can relax with your partner. You may not have much worth communicating unless you take responsibility for yourself and your own actions. You can't relax if you're withholding something important to you or if you feel that your partner is withholding something important to her or him.

Without responsibility communications become accusing and guilt-evoking, and the relationship becomes nasty. *Without communication* relaxation vanishes as the partners try to read each other's minds, expect their own minds to be read, and fail at both. So the relationship grows tense. *Without relaxation* communication becomes strained and guarded, misunderstandings pile up, and the relationship becomes explosive. It's a three-part package, and you can't do really well if one of the parts is missing.

Self-Responsibility

Self-responsibility doesn't mean selfishness or solitude; it doesn't mean living *for* yourself or *by* yourself. It means recognizing the fact that human beings are neither transparent to each other nor identical to each other, and that, therefore, *we cannot know automatically what any other person wants, feels, hopes, and dreams.* Somebody has to take the responsibility of making one person's needs known to another, of making one person's actions compatible with those needs. *Self-responsibility simply means that we take those responsibilities for ourselves.*

In sex taking responsibility for ourselves involves a mutual satisfaction of needs and desires, of what we feel we must have and what we feel we would like to have. Most human beings are comfortable with mutuality; most partners, especially intimate partners, do not want all for themselves and as little as possible for the other, but do want a reciprocal, caring relationship. The human want to be needed, the human need to be desired, is strong, and at the start of most relationships, even brief ones, some kind of care and concern for the other person is usually apparent.

On the other hand we may not know exactly what our partners expect of us. Nor, to be sure, are we always clear in our own minds exactly what we expect of them. Since neither we nor they are mind readers, *we must tell each other what we want.*

Self-responsibility in sex means knowing what we want and communicating this to our partners—and then reconsidering the situation if our desires are not met. That's what Estelle does, and that's why her sexual relationships are usually good. She asks; she tells; she shows; and if her partner really refuses to help, she ends the relationship—without rancor, without feeling used. And of course self-responsibility in sex also means knowing what we *don't* want and communicating this, too, to our partners.

Well, what do most people want in sex? They want what Estelle wants: a warm relationship and concern for her sexual needs. Most of her partners are more than pleased to be able to provide them; and in return Estelle offers a warm relationship and concern for their sexual needs. This is what they sense, those men who meet her, and this is why Estelle—and women like her—has less trouble sustaining relationships than many other women. They radiate an air not of imposing a test that must be met but rather of an experience that might be fun to share, and most men are grateful for the chance to share it.

Communication

Communicating With Yourself

Sexual self-responsibility consists mostly of telling your partner what you do and do not want. But this assumes that you yourself know what you want and don't want; and the fact is many people don't have a good idea at all.

We're talking in specific, not general terms. Most adults know their sexual preference in the common sense—whether they prefer males or females—but when it comes to actually experiencing the sexual act, these same men and women have only a diffuse idea of what really turns them on.

This sounds farfetched, yet we have found it to be true. Men and women enter a sexual relationship with a general idea of what they like but with much confusion as to the details. And there, of course, is precisely where sexual pleasure lies: in the details.

So the idea of self-responsibility suggests that we learn our own sexual sensitivities, and there's a way that most sex and marital counselors recommend. It serves some good purposes besides sexual self-awareness: it usually leads also to greater relaxation and better communication. On the other hand it does require an interest on the part of both the woman and the man that goes beyond a couple of hours. This technique, developed by Masters and Johnson,* is called sensate focus. The basic idea is that you take turns physically stroking and caressing each other and offering feedback on what's happening. Two sessions are recommended: in the first the genital and other erotic areas are skipped; in the second they're included. (Actually there's no reason why you can't bypass session one and go right to session two, but it seems to work better if you give it more time.) In each session both of you are nude throughout, and you don't have intercourse.

Before you start, there's one question you should answer: How do you feel about being nude in front of a partner when all the lights are on? If you're bothered by it, and many men and women are, then hold off. Wait until you've known each other longer and try it then. If you're somewhat embarrassed but not to the point of panic, and if you're both willing, try it. It usually helps.

In practice one partner starts as the caresser or the toucher, and the other partner is the touchee—the one who is caressed. You're both nude. The touchee is lying on her or his stomach; the toucher is *comfortably* alongside. If the toucher is in a physically uncomfortable position, the discomfort becomes transmitted to the partner and the results suffer.

The toucher begins to caress the touchee sensitively and lovingly, starting with the back of the head and continuing over the back of the entire body, down to the toes. Then the touchee turns over and the process is repeated. Again in this first session it's best to skip the genitals and other erotic areas.

*William H. Masters and Virginia T. Johnson, *Human Sexual Inadequacy* (Boston: Little, Brown and Company, 1970)

While this is going on, the toucher basically doesn't say anything; this is the touchee's inning. *The touchee concentrates on her or his own sensations*, doesn't worry about the toucher, what's going on with that person, whether he or she is growing tired, bored, or whatever. The touchee is exploring her or his own responses to physical caresses and is concentrating on those responses.

When something feels good, the touchee says so, using as few words as possible. "That feels good"; "I love that" are fine. When something feels bad, it's the same idea: "That feels bad"; "Uh-uh, not so hard." The touchee can also give directions to help the toucher; usually all you need are "faster," "slower," "not so much pressure," "a little harder"—some such phrases. When both sides of the body have been caressed, the two partners change places. To repeat, hold off from intercourse on the evenings (or whenever) you're experimenting with sensate focus, because you want to eliminate any feeling of obligation or tension relating to sexual performance. When you're both finished, it's time to talk about what you've experienced.

Are there any problems with sensate focus? Sometimes. Often they arise because most American men and women—especially if they're older—are not accustomed to playing the role of touchee. (Neither usually minds being the toucher.) Men view being the touchee as a passive, feminine role rather than an active masculine role; women feel uneasy because it somehow seems selfish to think of their own responses and not those of the man. But the whole point is that each partner receives and gives the same kind of sensual pleasure, so there's no question of selfishness, passivity, or initiative. And there's no question of sexual roles because there's no sex: the object is sensual awareness, sensual pleasure, and relaxation, not passionate arousal.

Another possible problem is that the toucher may try to take charge of the exercise: she or he will decide what's best. But the one in charge must be the touchee. *The toucher is learn-*

ing what pleases the partner and does this best by listening carefully and responding sensitively.

Communicating With Your Partner

People communicate with others constantly: through body language, tone of voice, gesture, a hundred different ways that do not involve words. And many messages are conveyed thereby, but often they're of attitude or emotional tone, not of explicit meaning. It's hard to say "I love when you caress my back around and around but not from side to side" in body language alone.

The two principal ways of making reasonably sure you're understood are "show and tell": demonstrate what you're after or use words to describe it. In sex the best way to demonstrate something is to take your partner's hand, place it where you'd like it to be, and move it the way you'd like it to be moved. It doesn't take most partners long to see exactly what you want. If this is physically impossible (as when the back of the body is involved), then tell is appropriate.

But you don't have to wait for the middle of intercourse to tell. A good time is after sensate focus exercises or after pleasurable intercourse or after any intimate encounter when you both tend to be more open and relaxed than usual.

If you're still embarrassed, the classic way for people who want to convey information but can't bring themselves to say it out loud is to ask the other person to read something: to give the teenager a book on sex, the new bride (or groom) a cookbook, the overweight husband (or wife) a book on dieting. Thus you can give your partner this book and ask him or her to read the portions you'd like him or her to. If you're interested in sensate focus but don't know how to introduce the idea, let him or her read that section; you'll have much to talk about, and the ice will be broken.

So communicate your needs and preferences, but don't stop there. Listen properly to your partner's communications.

Listen carefully, listen openly, especially listen nondefensively. Sometimes we become so tense in our relationships that any suggestion that we do something differently is taken as an attack on our intelligence and skill. But that's not usually what the communication is about.

So listen, talk, show, read, demonstrate, pay attention, until you both know exactly what you want and what the other person wants. Then, with the right chemistry between you to begin with, there's an excellent chance that the time you spend together will be happy.

Relaxation

When a couple first comes for sex therapy, most often the first goal of the therapist is to help them relax. There's a good reason: in terms of relationships, sex included, relaxation is practically synonymous with a word we haven't used before, perhaps the most important word in any relationship. The word is *trust*.

The connection is direct: if we trust somebody, we can be open with her or him; if we don't trust, we can't. If we can trust our partner not to laugh at us, or think we're peculiar or odd or crazy or perverted, or put us down, or tear us apart, we can say anything we want. If we cannot trust our partner in this way, then we can say practically nothing of importance except goodbye.

The trouble is that new partners often don't start out with an attitude of trust, and their expectations often preclude trust from forming. So they are hesitant and cautious with each other, and usually frustrated as well. The way out is to remove the source of frustration and substitute something else. What most sex therapists recommend, where trust is weak and tension (and anxiety) is strong, is that—for a time—intercourse should be eliminated and replaced by nondemand sex.

Nondemand Sex—The End of Anxiety

For new (and sometimes old) partners the absence of trust doesn't show up as suspicion but in anxiety: anxiety about how the other will react to failures, flaws, all the negatives that people can apply to themselves. As we said, anxiety can affect both men and women, but the most severe kind is the performance anxiety of the man: this can lead to impotence or fear of impotence, which can lead only to problems.

The best way of eliminating the problem of performance anxiety is to eliminate the need to perform; and the best way of doing this is to prohibit genital intercourse at a sexual meeting—to arrange beforehand that at least for that night intercourse is out. Holding is in; touching, caressing, everything else may be (and should be) in, but it should be understood that under no circumstances will intercourse take place. Maybe next time or the time after but not this time. The demand for male performance, which the man usually feels whether there's a demand or not, is eliminated. So he can finally stop checking himself to see how he's doing: it makes no difference. (Obviously, the woman shouldn't check him either.) The idea is to have fun—sexual fun—without sexual intercourse, and that's what should be kept in mind. For that night the penis as a thrusting organ might as well not exist.

When the man gets the idea that this is *really* the case, that he is not going to be called upon to perform, a miraculous thing often happens. He gets an erection. It's easy to see why: he's not damming himself up and checking on himself; he's letting himself go with the flow of his own erotic juices. And when there's no physiological impairment—and given, if necessary, some manual stimulation—an erection is more likely to happen.

So the first requirement for relaxation is the removal of anxiety, and this is best done by removing what the anxiety is about: the need to perform, the demand for an erection. Eliminate this and a good part of the battle is won.

Another part of the remedy consists of not adding new sources of anxiety, and this applies to both women and men. We're talking about anxiety about appearance—and about appearances. Many men and women are uncomfortable nude in front of their partner with the lights on, and sometimes the problem is deeply rooted. It's usually based on an exaggerated modesty that is in reality an attempt to deny our interest in sex and sexual intimacy. Sex is something we *do,* and may even enjoy, but it's not something to be acknowledged: we get it over with and then get on to other things. In these circumstances to be open with our body is to be open to sexuality as an idea, as a recreation, as something to talk about, think about, play with. It's to let the sexual self come out, and some people find this very hard to do.

Others are simply afraid of what they look like. Small breasts in a woman, a small penis in a man, big bellies, big bottoms, stretch marks, scars, birthmarks, discolorations, too much hair, too little hair, ugly feet, prominent veins, almost any part of us, we fear, can be a turn-off. There are three things to say about this. First we're probably not as bad as we think; and the chances are that whatever nude bodies your partner has been looking at lately have been about the same. Second, the saying is that appetite is the best sauce, and it's true. When desire gets going, when the erotic comes into play, sometimes the strangest features—a mole on a chest—can become the biggest turn-on. You never can tell. And finally it's your body, and you might as well be comfortable. And let it afford you as much pleasure as possible.

Nondemand sex, nondemand eroticism, means not only not demanding performance but also not demanding adherence to rigid criteria. It means getting pleasure from two bodies, with pleasure being the sole aim of the activities—no ultimate motives, no hidden agendas, no secret goals. There's nothing you can do wrong except take things seriously. And even if one of you becomes somewhat anxious for a time, well . . . don't worry about it.

Prelude to Pleasure: The Witkin Shower

So far we've emphasized the don'ts of intimacy: don't demand (expect, require) sex and don't establish unreasonably high criteria of behavior and appearance for your partner or yourself. But there are also certain "dos" that can help bring about the atmosphere of relaxation and trust that's so important.

One possibility consists of the sensate focus exercises. But there's another activity that seems to help couples relax more completely and more consistently than any other. It's called the Witkin shower, and it can be the simplest and most pleasant experience in the world.

In essence the two of you begin by taking a shower together. (If you're an inveterate bath taker, then take a bath together.) Except for the fact that there are two of you in the tub or enclosure at the same time, the Witkin shower (which is also called the erotic shower) is not much different from an ordinary shower. But there are some differences and a few rules.

Rule 1. You soap each other using your hands alone (and soap, of course). What this means is that you don't use sponges, washcloths, or any such paraphernalia; you just use hands. The idea is to bring skin into contact with skin, and you can't do that with washcloths and sponges.

Rule 2. You dry each other with towels.

Rule 3. You powder or oil (or cologne) each other.

Rule 4. When you follow Rules 1 through 3, *you do it the way your partner likes,* not the way you like. Most of us think that our partner's responses are the same as our own, but we can't count on it.

That's it: what one does the other does; you do it the way your partner prefers, and you use your hands and not some implement.

For starting off any kind of lovemaking, nondemand or otherwise, hardly anything beats the erotic shower. Most couples who try it end up ready for fun, pleasure, spontaneity, affection—in short in a state of beautiful relaxation. So it's more than worth the brief time it takes. And it has one other benefit: it leaves both of you clean. As we said before, one of the most common sexual turn-offs is just plain lack of cleanliness or bad body odors, and the erotic shower takes care of them in the nicest possible way.

One-Night Sex

We're not talking about affairs that you hope and maybe expect will continue and turn into a long-term relationship, but somehow don't last much longer than a night or two. What we're talking about are sexual evenings (or sometimes a few hours) when both partners *know* that that's it: know either by prearrangement or (much more commonly) by the woman being certain, with nothing having been said, that the man is after sex for the night and she will almost surely never see him again.

Most women and the majority of men, for that matter, don't relish one-night sex, would much rather have long-term relationships. But sometimes the need for closeness or sex appears so great that a passing interlude becomes acceptable, even to those who would otherwise reject it.

The important thing is to know whether you can satisfy these needs without hurting yourself, and there are two kinds of hurt to watch out for: psychological hurt, the hurt to the ego; and physiological hurt—in a word—disease.

Damage Control: The Body

Promiscuous people have a greater chance of contracting venereal diseases than nonpromiscuous people; and if the woman has sex before she really knows the man, it's safest to assume that he's had sex with many, many women. So the chances of his being infected are great. The problem is that if he has

contracted diseases they may not be evident; in the words of
Dr. Theresa Larsen Crenshaw, "Infections can be carried by
men asymptomatically and transmitted to women as full-blown
disorders, ranging from vaginal irritations to herpes, yeast infections, syphilis, and gonorrhea. . . . A woman's risk of cervical
cancer is also believed to be heightened if she has many encounters with different men."* AIDS, of course, is the biggest
danger of all. (See Chapter 9 for specific strategies for preventing this deadly killer.)

There's no absolutely safe way of having sex with one-
night specialists, but at least some protection can be provided
by the man wearing a latex condom. This should be insisted
on. If the man doesn't carry them with him, he should buy one
or you should supply it. That is if you feel vulnerable to one-
night interludes, for your own sake make sure you have condoms on hand.

Damage Control: The Ego

The man interested in one-night sex is not interested in relationships; he's interested in sex. He tends not to care for the
woman's feelings except to the extent that it's necessary to get
her into bed. And when he's finished, he doesn't usually display
great tenderness at their parting.

It's very hard for most women to experience this behavior
without feeling crushed. It's very hard to understand that the man
is not making a statement about you but about himself. It's very
difficult for the woman, in other words, to keep her ego intact,
to hold on to her sense of self-worth and self-esteem when
faced with the essential emptiness of most one-night sex.

Some women can sustain it; most cannot. Some women
prefer their own versions of one-night sex, their own tasting of
variety; most women do not. But even women who twenty

*Theresa Larsen Crenshaw, M.D. "A Therapist Looks at Casual Sex," Harper's Ba-
zaar, October 1983, p. 207.

nights out of twenty-one would not dream of it, on the twenty-first night let themselves have sex because it's "better than nothing"—and then castigate themselves for it afterward. Don't do that to yourself. For the woman who accepts sex for a single night, it's best to protect herself with a condom and try not to come down on herself when it's over.

Two women were talking, and this is what the first woman said.

I was at a bar and this man came in . . . Roger. I think he was married—in fact, I know he was married. But it would have been Vic and my twenty-seventh anniversary, and I was lonely. I was so lonely. So Roger bought me a drink, and when I was halfway through he said, "Do you sleep with men?" Except he didn't say "sleep with men," he said other words. One other word.

What I said was yes. Well, he was a gentleman: he didn't rush me through my drink. We took the subway to my place—I have an apartment on the Upper West Side. We walked in and the place was freezing. I phoned the super and he said the boiler was out until morning. Sorry.

I thought of calling it off, but I didn't really want to. So we got into bed, Roger and me, and he never took his shirt off. I didn't take much off either, but I unzipped and unbuttoned and unsnapped—things like that. The whole thing was over in five minutes anyway. Then he got up and left. He did manage to say "So long."

The second woman said: "He used you."

And the first woman thought for a second and said: "No, I used him."

In no way do we recommend one-night sex for women or men: most often it's unsatisfying and wasteful. But for many it's better than nothing, especially when "nothing" is hard to take. When it happens—if it happens—it's important, like the woman with the cold apartment, to know what you want from the transaction, know what it's likely to bring you, and adjust your expectations accordingly—and to do this without maligning yourself. In this way the feeling of control helps eliminate the sense of being a victim.

In the Candy Store

The central fact for a man looking for a partner is that if one woman doesn't work out, he can usually find another without too much trouble. This fact, the general availability of women, often arouses in him the specific intention *not* to be tied down, the specific goal of having as many women as he pleases without establishing long-term relationships—and for some men anything longer than a night or two is long-term.

This attitude is particularly prevalent among men who have only recently become divorced or widowed. Once over the recovery period, the prospects seem so bright, the pickings so ample, the sheer number of women so encouraging, that the man becomes like the little boy set loose in a candy shop. Why limit yourself to jelly beans when you can have chocolates and nougats and fudges and creams and all those other goodies? And why bother at all with something that doesn't seem immediately appetizing when there are so many tempting morsels around that you've never tried before. Why not gobble to your heart's content?

Under the circumstances this is an understandable response. Having been limited for years to one woman (with perhaps one or two brief affairs thrown in), the prospect of having an unlimited number of women seems too great to resist, especially when the man is worrying about his "maleness." So, many men don't resist at all.

For the majority of these men the sampling stage is temporary, partly because it is arduous, partly because it can be expensive, and mostly because it turns out to be unsatisfying. Many men want to wander but most of them want a fixed place to wander from; and more men than not want some element of predictability in their personal lives. It just becomes, for most men, too tiring to keep going out to meet new people, too tiring and ultimately too boring.

More than that sex is better when you get to know each other, and this takes time. First nights, even for people in love, are almost always awkward and clumsy, and sex with strangers is nothing but a series of first nights—usually with a partner you don't even care about, let alone love. So the sex tends to suffer and so does the ego. Unless the man is interested in immediate gratification, one-night sex usually doesn't hold much for him. And this he sooner or later finds out.

He does, at least, unless he's trapped in the image of the young blood, the idea that men are not supposed to be tied down, that commitment is somehow a trap to be avoided, and that while a long-term relationship might be acceptable, it ought to yield to more important things: another attractive woman, for example, a new place to go—or simply moving on, staying free. The man tires of noncommitment, that is, unless he reverts to the mythologies of adolescence.

The myths are caught most arrestingly in the songs of adolescence, especially the songs of the 1960s, when men (and women) just out of adolescence actually were writing the songs. Who does not remember "By the Time I Get to Phoenix": the man (young, it is clear), having left the woman he loves, imagines what she will be doing at different stages of his journey. Why he has left is never made explicit, but the reason is clear: He has left . . . just to leave, just to move on, just to not be tied down.

The same songs are being written today, and they have the same adolescent appeal, the same appeal to the adolescent in all men. The grown-up man will listen (somewhat ruefully, perhaps), appreciate the pull of the message, and know what he really wants: the deeper and more satisfying rewards of a caring, fulfilling relationship. With luck he will also know that in such a relationship he has the freedom he needs to be what he wants to be.

The Intelligent Relationship and Men

A basic problem with many men and the sexual relationship is that they emphasize the sex and not the relationship. But, it's important for a man to realize that full sexual enjoyment means enjoying the relationship as well as the sex. And this means enjoying—valuing warmth and intimacy as the soil from which a good relationship grows.

It is astonishing how many men, usually unconsciously, defend against the slightest sign of warmth and intimacy, no matter how small and unthreatening it may be. The man speaking, Paul, is in his thirties, heavy and short.

> We had just met at a dance, and we had clicked right off—danced the whole last hour together. Now we're going to her place, and I park my car a block or so away. While we're walking to the apartment, she takes my hand and holds it for a few seconds. Then she lets it go and says "Pardon me," as if I had insulted her. I asked her what was the matter, and she said that as soon as she touched me I tightened up as though she had leprosy. What did I think she would do to me? I realized it was true. Here we had spent an hour with practically our whole bodies touching, and here she reaches for my hand and I freeze. It didn't make sense.

Dancing is a social act, although it may have sexual overtones, but holding hands is an intimate act, an act of relationship, and for many men relationship means commitment. Not wanting to feel committed to anyone, they bolt away at the slightest hint of intimacy.

It's true that intimacy, a relationship, means commitment, but it is a commitment that need not mean "forever." It is a commitment to view oneself and the other as more than sexual organs to be exercised and sexual urges to be gratified but as two people engaged together in pleasurable activity, trying to find ways of making it even more pleasurable for them both. Masturbation is not as satisfying as intercourse, and intercourse without relationship is not as satisfying as intercourse with. Given a concern for his own and his partner's pleasure, the entire time together is more enjoyable and the sex itself is usually vastly improved.

Last Word

So the intelligent man—and woman—will not run from intimacy but embrace it, at least for the period of the sexual encounter. The man with performance anxiety would do well to acknowledge what is happening and suggest alternative ways of satisfying the woman—and himself. The man with sexual problems apart from secondary, anxiety-induced impotence should read Chapter 11 of this book.

Above all the intelligent person will foster an atmosphere of communication and relaxation, an atmosphere in which anything can be said and enjoyed. There is no greater guarantee of sexual satisfaction. For the fortunate fact is that while we cannot all be sexual geniuses (whatever that may be), it is always possible to be sexually intelligent. And the rewards are great.

For Maximum Contact and Pleasure

For a relationship to be the joy it's meant to be, you don't have to do a lot of work—you just have to lay some groundwork:

1. Know yourself.
2. Know your partner.

You can do the above with two techniques:

1. Recognizing your feelings.
2. Talking.

Talking is a way for you and your partner to exchange information about yourselves. What turns you on may be very different from what turned on his last girlfriend or her last boyfriend. Gestures, signs, and eyes clenched closed don't convey the message nearly as well as a simple, "I don't really enjoy *that*—how about *this?*" Talking can also, you may be surprised to learn, help you find out what you like. A conversation develops; as you speak, your thoughts may move into areas previously unexplored. And your partner may help draw out your ideas with good questions. By talking about those feelings, you'll be more sensitive to your partner's desires and your own as well.

If you're out of the habit of talking and feeling—because of fear, or fatigue, or just not knowing how—start slowly and build. Your sex life will be better and the rest of your life will be too.

Rate Your Relationships

Knowing who you are is a primary ingredient in a successful relationship. Check off the statements that apply to you now. Knowing why you answered as you did can give you valuable information about your future in a relationship.

_____ 1. I usually feel in touch with my feelings.

_____ 2. I am aware of my hopes and dreams for the future.

_____ 3. I have certain desires that I am working toward.

_____ 4. I know what I like in bed.

_____ Total for questions 1-4

_____ 5. I try to speak up and say what's on my mind in a caring way.

_____ 6. I try not to hold in my feelings or make other people guess what I want.

_____ 7. In bed, I usually share what I like and what I don't with my partner (gently, without demands or disapproval) and ask for my partner's preferences as well.

_____ Total for questions 5-7

_____ 8. Most of the time I'm relaxed, not nervous, around other people.

_____ 9. I'm not uncomfortable when my partner sees me nude.

_____ 10. In bed with a partner, I usually feel relaxed, generous, and playful.

_____ Total for questions 8-10

KEY

Questions 1-4: These four questions measure self-responsibility, one of three elements key to contact and pleasure. Self-responsibility means you've accepted the responsibility for knowing yourself and helping others know you. If you checked three or four items, you know yourself well. If you checked two items or less, ask yourself: What do I want? What do I feel? What are my hopes and dreams? It's your responsibility to know the answers.

Questions 5-7: These three questions measure communication. Knowing yourself is not enough! Can you communicate your needs, feelings, hopes, and dreams to the intimate other? If you checked two or three items, you're a good communicator. If you checked none or only one of these questions, you need to learn how to say more about your inner emotions.

Questions 8-10: These three questions measure relaxation, the third element crucial to contact and pleasure. If you checked two or three items, you're relaxed enough to fully enjoy the pleasure of another person's company. If you checked one item or less, you'll be happy to know that the relaxation techniques in this chapter (such as the Witkin shower) hold much pleasure for you in the future. Try them!

Chapter 9
The Age of AIDS

AIDS has changed the way people meet and mate, possibly forever. In the early 1980s, the epidemic seemed to pose its greatest terror for homosexual men. Then the human immunodeficiency virus (HIV) that causes AIDS raced from one drug user to the next on shared needles. Finally, early in the 1990s, the AIDS virus reached numbers of heterosexual men and women. For the first time, more women contracted AIDS through sex than through drug abuse, and the AIDS death rate in women continues to rise. Nationwide, AIDS is the second most common cause of death in men aged twenty-five to forty-four. Some ninety percent of patients are twenty to forty-nine years old.

Experts suggest that the AIDS virus can be found in all bodily fluids, but it's usually transmitted from person to person by direct contact with blood and semen. The virus can't pass through your skin, but it can enter via mucous membranes like the ones lining the vagina, rectum, and urethra, or through any small cut or sore. This means that vaginal, anal, and oral sex are dangerous for both parties. Kissing and touching probably are not risky, but safest of all are masturbation and talking!

Many other people have acquired AIDS from transfusions of infected blood or through contact with intravenous needles that have tiny amounts of infected blood on them. Finally, HIV

can pass from a mother to her unborn baby, perhaps during pregnancy and definitely during delivery.
    Symptoms of AIDS are:

- lower resistance to infections
- loss of appetite
- weight loss
- low-grade fever
- fatigue
- mouth sores
- diarrhea
- headaches
- blurred vision
- memory loss
- personality changes
- chronic cough and other respiratory symptoms.

The virus itself does not kill; it slowly destroys the white blood cells from our immune system that are key infection fighters. Once these cells are debilitated, deadly cancers, and ordinarily harmless viruses, bacteria, and fungi move in and take over. Death by AIDS is slow and agonizing.

Risky Business

Sexual intercourse no longer can be the unprotected, impulsive, free expression of love (or lust) that it once was. In the movie *Singles,* the character named Janet says, "Casual sex doesn't exist anymore. It's lethal. It's over."
    Everyone should be afraid of AIDS. But in our eternal quest for sexual connection, some of us will continue to cheat on our partners, be promiscuous, engage in unsafe (condomless) sex, and use intravenous drugs, all of which raise our chances of getting AIDS. In spite of the frightening statistics,

one government study found that as many as one in three sexually active heterosexuals had taken a chance in the preceding five years that put him or her at risk of AIDS. Another study found about the same rate of risky behavior in gay men.

If you haven't yet switched to safe sex, ask yourself why. My guess is that you:

- believe AIDS can't happen to you. Believe it! The Centers for Disease Control (CDC) in Atlanta estimates the death toll for just the first 13 years of the epidemic at an astounding 330,000.
- think condoms are too much trouble. Just think how much trouble it will be to get AIDS.
- think condoms cost too much. AIDS treatment costs thousands of times as much.
- end up making passionate love before you even think about a condom. If you and your partner truly loved each other, a condom would be part of lovemaking.
- trust that your partner is disease free. But do you think your new partner is going to confess that he or she shoots up or has ever had sex with a prostitute or has had anonymous sex with someone whose HIV status is unknown? Doubtful. The speaker is a twenty-eight-year-old divorcée from Florida:

> He said I was the only one. He said he would never leave me. So I never gave using a condom a second thought. But after four months it was all over, and I found out from his *other girlfriends* that he had been addicted to heroin, as well as a cheater and a liar.
>
> All of us are in shock, and the worst of it is that he has now vanished and we have no way of finding out if he was HIV positive. We are going for tests as soon as we find a place that will keep our results private.

How will *you* avoid contracting the AIDS virus? Please think about it. You can avoid it with a few strategies.

Prevention Strategies

The New Date

For many people—especially those who came of age in the '60s and '70s—the idea of a date ending with a chaste kiss on the cheek is a novelty. Back in those days it was "love the one you're with" (the words of Stephen Stills from an early '70s song). As one coed recalls:

> After graduating from college in the early '70s, I moved to Boston, got an apartment with some other girls, and entered the singles scene with enthusiasm. Basically, the formula was that you slept with the guy after two or three dates or he dropped you. Most of my relationships ended after about two months. One day a girlfriend and I sat down and counted the lovers we could remember. I had about sixty on my list, and I know I missed a few.
>
> When AIDS came in, around 1982, we paid no attention until we heard of cases of HIV in women. Then we slowed down a little and started hoping the guys would use condoms.
>
> Three years ago I got married and am now in a monogamous relationship. But I still worry about AIDS. I hear that some cases can take years to show up.

The kind of date that ends on the doorstep rather than in bed is the best way to avoid AIDS. A long period of checking each other out is a good idea. The longer you know someone before you get into bed together, the more likely it is that the subject of AIDS will come up in conversation. And the better you know each other, the more likely your partner will want to put you at ease about AIDS. You, presumably, will feel the same way.

The Male Condom

Once you become sexually active, the latex condom is the best way to prevent the spread of AIDS, according to the Centers for Disease Control. The proof is in a three-year test of HIV-negative women whose partners were HIV-positive. Only 3 of 171 couples who used condoms all the time transferred the HIV infection to the HIV-free partner. In inconsistent users, 8 of 55 couples transferred HIV—a much higher percentage.

If you're sexually active and not in a long-term, committed relationship, are you condom-confident? You should:

- Use a condom every time you have sex. Enforce the "No condom, no sex" rule.
- Use a *latex* condom to prevent AIDS. A lambskin condom can stop sperm but not the AIDS virus.
- Store latex condoms in a cool, dry place, not your wallet or the bathroom cabinet.
- Take the condom out of its wrapper only when you're ready to use it, no sooner.
- Don't use hand lotion, baby oil, or petroleum jelly as lubricants. Oil-based products can break down latex.
- Don't stretch or blow up your condom to test it before use. You may break it.
- Never reuse a condom.

The condom forms an impermeable barrier that blocks the AIDS virus —which is carried in semen, vaginal secretions, or blood—from entering the partner's bloodstream through cuts, tears, or sores. The condom does its job whether the sex is vaginal, anal, or oral. According to the U.S. Surgeon General,

"No matter what method you use for birth control, a latex condom—when used correctly and consistently—offers the best protection against HIV and other sexually transmitted diseases."

New Research

One trouble with the condom is that a man has to use it, and a woman has little control over that. The new female condom—a lubricated polyurethane pouch with a ring on each end, one to insert into the vagina while the other remains outside—may sound like a solution, but it's not. Tests suggest that the *first female condom,* called the Reality Vaginal Pouch, *does not protect against sexually transmitted diseases—AIDS, gonorrhea, chlamydia* and all the rest. And *one woman in four* who uses it faithfully *will be pregnant* by the end of a year. So far, the female condom sounds like less-than-perfect protection.

Foams, gels, or chemical-soaked sponges may be the best solution in the future. Scientists are working to develop a vaginal microbicide that will kill the AIDS virus. Some doctors say that the spermicides used with the diaphragm or sponge kill the AIDS virus in lab experiments, but a report from the U.S. Surgeon General's office disagrees: "Birth control pills, sponges, foams, diaphragms, intrauterine devices (IUDs), or being sterilized do not protect you from HIV."*

Status Report

The prevention strategy for long-term committed relationships starts with having your blood tested for antibodies to the AIDS virus. If you and your potential partner haven't talked about AIDS yet, one way to open the door is to wait for the subject of AIDS to come up—it almost always does—and then offer your own HIV status: "Last time I was at the doctor's, I got tested for HIV . . ." Or, if you and your partner are talking about medical

---

*Surgeon General's Report on AIDS, updated 1993.

confidentiality, you can mention that in most parts of the country, free and anonymous HIV tests are available. Couples who are upfront about the fact they are about to begin having sexual relations can agree to be tested together. AIDS testing is even available on some college campuses, and students are taking advantage of it. Says one student who plans to marry, "I would just hate for them to say, 'You're pregnant and you have HIV.' You don't want to enter a marriage like that."(Her test was negative and so was her fiancé's.)

If you think you've been exposed to the virus and your test is negative, have another test in two to six months. Antibodies to the virus can take that long after the original infection to form.

Two negatives or two positives mean you and your partner are compatible. HIV-negative couples need to worry only about birth control, but HIV-positive pairs should think about AIDS control as well. A number of different AIDS strains have been identified, and it may be possible to have two.

The number of people carrying the AIDS virus is on the rise, and so are dating services to help them meet other people with HIV. You've heard the stories and they're real: people who thought their lives were over meet someone who also has HIV, and they go on to have a mutually supportive, caring relationship, thankful to have found each other even if it is only for the time they can help one another.

Other Sexually Transmitted Diseases (STDs)

STD stands for sexually transmitted diseases—genital warts, genital herpes, chlamydia, gonorrhea, syphilis, hepatitis B, and of course, AIDS—and they are linked.

One way they are linked is that people who have unsafe sex expose themselves to any STD that happens to be in the vicinity. Think about it: The person who routinely practices unsafe sex is a target not only for AIDS but for any of the viral and bacterial diseases that pass from one person to another during sex.

The second reason the STDs are linked is that *any STD that causes an open sore provides a convenient port of entry for the AIDS virus.* One such disease, genital herpes, afflicts 31 million Americans! It is caused by the herpes simplex type 2 virus, and many men and women don't even notice the flu-like symptoms that accompany a new infection. But they can't miss its painful sores and blisters, which flare up during times of illness or stress—and which put the herpes sufferer at great risk of AIDS. There is no cure for genital herpes, but the antiviral medicine acyclovir can help control it.

Syphilis, which infects 30,000 Americans each year, is another disease that provides a gateway for AIDS. Ten days to three months after you're infected by the syphilis organism, called a spirochete, you will develop a painless sore that may be so deep inside you, you won't even know it's there. Left untreated, syphilis can cause blindness, deafness, insanity, and damage to the heart and other major organs—and of course, the sore is an open invitation to the AIDS virus. Syphilis is detectable via a blood test, and penicillin is the treatment.

Many other sexually transmitted diseases are less likely to cause open sores, but still, they compromise our immune systems and complicate our lives with pain: genital warts, chlamydia, gonorrhea, and hepatitis B.

Hepatitis B affects 300,000 Americans each year and is on the rise. Its cause is the hepatitis B virus, and it's transmitted in much the same way as AIDS—via body fluids such as blood or semen. It can cause chronic liver disease, which may lead to liver failure, liver cancer, or death.

There's no treatment, but if you're at high risk (which is the case particularly for health-care workers and people with infected family members), you should consider immunization with hepatitis B immune globulin, which can prevent hepatitis B infection.

Chlamydia strikes between three and five million Americans each year—epidemic proportions. Between 25 and 40 percent of the people who have had gonorrhea are likely to get chlamydia as well, since both are bacterial conditions. Symptoms of chlamydia in a man may include painful urination and discharge; in a woman, vaginal discharge. But only 25 percent of women are "lucky" enough to have these symptoms. In the rest, chlamydia goes undetected—and may cause pelvic inflammatory disease, a severe infection of the uterus, Fallopian tubes, and ovaries that can leave a woman infertile. Antibiotics usually can clear up a chlamydia infection.

Each year about a million Americans get gonorrhea, a bacterial disease that can cause a discharge in both men and women. But 20 percent of men and 80 percent of women have no symptoms; in women, gonorrhea can progress into pelvic inflammatory disease. Antibiotics usually take care of a gonorrhea infection.

Genital warts may not seem as serious as the other sexually transmitted diseases, but they're dangerous. These warts can break out all over the genital area, inside and out, and are caused by the human papilloma virus, which has been linked with cervical cancer. The warts themselves can be removed with heat, cold, lasers, surgery, or liquid wart removers. But the risk of cervical cancer cannot be dispensed with as easily! A woman who has had genital warts should be sure to have a yearly Pap test which can detect this cancer.

Last Word

If you have *any* sexually transmitted disease—genital herpes, chlamydia, hepatitis B, and syphilis are the most common—you'd be wise indeed to have it treated. As you can see, STDs are not only unpleasant in themselves but are gateways to AIDS and other infections.

Sexual Safety

For all sexually transmitted diseases—and especially AIDS—prevention is always best. If you can't lock into a safe-sex mindset, think about the other people who would be sad if you got AIDS. Think about the children you may want to have someday. If you have AIDS, you may pass it on to someone very innocent. And do consider yourself. Your life is valuable; AIDS is a tragedy. So take these simple actions:

- DON'T take part in unsafe sex—that is, condomless sexual intercourse with a partner whose HIV status is unknown.
- DO use a *latex* condom.
- DO get tested if you think you've been exposed.
- DO get treatment for any other sexually transmitted diseases you may have.
- DO discuss AIDS with your partner. The more you both know about it and about each other, the better your sex life together will be.

CHAPTER 10
The Thrill Is Gone

I just don't seem to care anymore. Maybe I'm getting too old."
These are the words Barry used to describe his reaction to
what he thought were repeated sexual failures, but these might
also be the words of Evelyn or of hundreds of thousands of
other men and women whose interest in sex seems to be waning, who just don't seem to care anymore.

Before we get into this, we'd like to point out (again) that
in no way does lack of interest in sex have to be abnormal.
Much in life can give pleasure besides sex, and for many people
sexual pleasure is not as strong or gratifying as other kinds of
pleasure. Also there's some evidence that sexual desire diminishes with age, and that this diminution, at least in men, may
be related to hormonal factors. (We'll go into this more in the
next chapter.)

As we grow older, to experience either less sexual desire
or less frequent sexual desire is normal and doesn't mean that
we're sick or strange. But if we have had a reasonably active sex
life, and if we gaze around one day and discover that it's down
to practically nothing, we should take a close look at ourselves
to see what's going on. What we're likely to find is one of two
conditions: a generalized lethargy or indifference toward *initiating* sex; or a specific *avoidance* of sex, a specific sexual problem
(*dysfunction* is the technical term) called inhibited sexual desire. The good news is that both are often resolvable.

Ho-hum

When we're young and just beginning to be active sexually, when we're first married, and even when we're remarried, most of us cannot believe that we will ever become indifferent to sex. We cannot imagine being too preoccupied with other things, ready to relegate sex to something we'll do when we have the time. When we're young, we may occasionally become too tired physically, but mentally we're usually ready.

It's normal for all couples to come down after a time from the peak of sexuality reached during the honeymoon or during early stages of the relationship. Many women and men, of all ages, may come down very far, however, to the point of having either no sex at all or very little compared to what they once enjoyed. There are no physiological reasons; they're not unusually tired, overwhelmed with work, wrestling with major problems: they just have sex a lot less often. And the relationship itself doesn't seem to suffer that much: there's less excitement and more irritability, but that's normal—or so it seems.

Then, unexpectedly, one of them initiates sex. Typically the other partner responds rapidly; the two make love, feel physically refreshed in a way they haven't for some time, feel more optimistic and cheerful, closer to each other, warmer, more caring—in brief, feel as though they're in love again. Typically they tell themselves (or each other) that they have to do this more often. And typically they don't—until another long period of time has passed.

There are dozens of reasons why this condition comes about, but the consequences are clear. For most people the withdrawal from sex brings about a mild level of frustration and at least a mild increase in stress, and these can lead to other conditions: psychosomatic illnesses, mild depression, heightened irritability, compulsive (what others might call eccentric) behavior. For couples the withdrawal from sex tends to widen the distance between the partners, and this allows misunderstandings and resentment to pile up. With frequent sex mild strains between the partners are often swept away in the general releasing flood of sexual expression and closeness; with infrequent sex the areas of strain often become solidified, become obdurate barriers to the easy give-and-take of a flowing relationship.

Intimacy dwindles, tension increases—and the resolution is either a depressive kind of resignation, in which the partners believe that their mildly miserable, mildly disappointed state is normal and not to be helped, or the resolution is a seeking of new excitement, new life, with another partner.

Again we're not saying that minimum sex *must* lead to maximum problems. Sex can be transmuted into many different channels: tenderness and caring for a suddenly disabled partner; intense absorption in outside activities; business, or family concerns; or just plain physical exercise, working it off. But for the majority of couples a decrease in sexual activity to a certain level (which varies for different individuals) complicates their personal lives and their relationship.

The overall answer is to initiate sex more often. It doesn't make much difference who does the initiating: once the invitation is accepted, the sexual urge usually takes over rapidly and the result is a collaboration, not a solo. (If your partner never or rarely accepts an invitation to sex, you may be faced with inhibited sexual desire, discussed next.) Neither does initiating sex mean prodding yourself to it when you don't want to or setting up a formal sex schedule or inventing complicated games to entice or surprise your partner into lovemaking. It's more a question of consciousness-raising, and it involves four steps.

1. *Figure out why your sex life has fallen off so radically.* Serious introspection can sometimes reveal the reason; if it doesn't, then a visit to a sex therapist is in order. If you come to realize that you're disgruntled or annoyed with your partner, talk about it with him or her. If talking seems hard to do, initiate lovemaking—and talk about it afterward, when you're comfortable and relaxed with each other.

2. While you're doing your soul-searching, try to *remember how it feels to make love*—how it feels before, during, and after. (If it feels bad, you're not in the ho-hum category. Read the next section or the next chapter.) Remember the excitement, the pleasure, the playfulness, the renewed vigor, the expansion, the rhythmic dance of your two bodies, the joyful triumph of the orgasm—and the tenderness, the sharing, the intimacy, the openness, the sense of being more fully alive, more fully attuned not just to your partner but to the whole universe. Even if your own experiences fall short of perfection, sex is still (if you're in this category) more good than bad, more positive than negative, in general a desirable place to be. And there's no reason why you shouldn't be there more often.

3. Try to *decide whether your sex life has become routine*—the overtures, the foreplay, intercourse itself, the recovery period. Without putting on a staged performance, all aspects of sex can be varied. Make a date with your partner, the kind of date you made when you were courting. Try quickie sex on occasion: with an indifferent partner it can be terrible, but with a loving partner it can be just plain fun. If there's some aspect of lovemaking you've always wanted to try but have never been able to suggest, don't let it be a deathbed wish: suggest it now. Examine your fantasies about sex and see if any can be implemented with your partner: you might be surprised. If you've never been to a pornographic movie, try one. Even though you might find them objectionable on a conscious level, sometimes they work on the unconscious to arouse real desire. In general try to remember what situations usually stimulated desire in you in the past and then try to recreate them. If your favorite place was a parking lot, try that; if a living room sofa (or floor), try that. In other words recreate the gratifying past to enhance the present, wherever possible.

4. *Remember also that sex, like exercise, is good for you.* It's good for you physically, mentally, emotionally and relationally, and it feels good while you're doing it. The sexual drive is

innate; we are born with it (no doubt to reproduce the human race); and it's a fundamental part of our makeup until we die.

The basic problem with the ho-hum feeling is that it separates us more from life and from our partner than is good for us. For most men and women sex is one of the great fountains of vitality, and many of us would do well to drink there more often.

Inhibited Sexual Desire

Inhibited sexual desire—ISD—is more than simply not moving toward sexual intercourse; it's actively moving away from sexual experiences. It's obviously been around for a long time, but it was first identified and analyzed as a specific sexual dysfunction by Dr. Helen Singer Kaplan.* In summary this is what Dr. Kaplan found:

First, as with impotence, inhibited sexual desire is much harder to treat if sexual desire has always or mostly been absent. If even as a young person you were never (or very seldom) aroused by another person, then psychological counseling is probably needed.

Second, inhibited sexual desire, like secondary impotence in men, results almost entirely from two causes: anxiety and anger. The two can work together or separately: we can be anxious without being angry, angry without being anxious, or both angry and anxious at the same time. Although in our view inhibited sexual desire is most commonly caused by a combination of anger and anxiety, anger seems to operate predominantly in women, anxiety in men.

Third, and most important, desire is not driven away mysteriously by forces beyond our control. *We turn ourselves off.* For various reasons we nip our desire in the bud: as soon as we feel the first faint stirrings of passion, the first thoughts of sex, we deliberately (if unconsciously) squelch them.

Finally, if inhibited sexual desire is under our control, *then the cure is under our control* also: we can learn to leave ourselves alone; and if not turn ourselves on, at least allow desire to come as it may.

Anger and Anxiety

Anger and anxiety appear to have little in common, yet in one respect they're alike: they both can stimulate avoidance behavior. That is they both can lead one away from some person or action; they both can encourage one *not* to get involved. In the case of sex they both impel one to avoid sexual intercourse, and the easy way of doing this, after a time, is to avoid the desire for sexual intercourse.

The motive, however, is different in each case. In anger the emotion is usually directed against a single person—the sexual partner—and the motive is basically punitive. *He keeps ridiculing the way I treat my children? She keeps putting me down for my potbelly? Fine. I'll get him. I'll show her.* And apparently the easiest and most destructive way of getting somebody, of punishing a partner, is to withhold sex. For even if the partner isn't an especially sexual person, to withhold sex completely is to comment adversely on the deepest aspects of the personality; it is to say that in some profound way something is wrong with you, you're sexually a failure.

Lack of desire is at once one of the most effective and safest ways of transmitting this message. It is effective because most people accept it; after a while they do come to feel that they are somehow deficient. Even when they respond by blaming the other—*you're a stick; you're a clod; you're frigid; you're dead; you're an old man (or woman)*—their phrases are mostly defensive, an attempt to stimulate the distanced partner into a sexual reaction. And when they fail, as they almost always do, the conviction of one's own sexual unattractiveness becomes

*Helen Singer Kaplan, M.D., *Disorders of Desire* (New York: Brunner/Mazel, 1979)

more pervasive—and the punishment by the angry partner more successful.

So lack of sexual desire is an effective way of punishing the partner because it works. And it is safe because it doesn't imply sexual failure, as do impotence in the man and lack of orgasm in the woman. If the man is impotent, if the woman has trouble having orgasms, it's their own fault . . . *but you just don't turn me on. How can you blame me if you don't turn me on anymore?*

Anger is typically directed outward, toward a partner, and sexual anxiety is typically directed inward, toward the self. As does male impotence, sexual anxiety results from imagined failure and the fear of failure: for men fear of failure to perform; for women fear of failure to arouse or be aroused; for both fear of failure to have anything like a satisfying sexual relationship.

The role of anxiety in inhibited sexual desire is simple. At first it doesn't keep us from performing the act we fear, it keeps us from succeeding; as we said, it has the nature of a self-fulfilling prophecy. So if we are anxious about sex we tend to fail at it. But this is painful, and after a time we don't want to face that pain again. So we simply avoid having sex, and the easy way to do this is to avoid *wanting* to have sex. In brief we inhibit our sexual desire.

Anger and anxiety often go hand in hand because they can arise from the same situation. When we're widowed or divorced and looking for a new partner, we may become anxious and experience "failure"—and, as we said, this may become a pattern. But while for the most part we blame ourselves for these failures, there is always resentment and anger at the other: for ridiculing us, for not helping, for frustrating us, for not validating our worth. But now, without a permanent partner to focus on, without a clear reason to be angry, we expand our anger to embrace the entire opposite sex. There arises an undertone of anger (and punishment) against all women if you're a man, and against all men if you're a woman. As Evelyn said, "They're all creeps."

Self-Squelching

As we said, inhibited sexual desire doesn't mean that desire doesn't come; it means that as soon as desire appears, we suppress it. How do we do this? There are three basic mechanisms.

1. We focus on our partner's faults. This is what Evelyn does, almost before she starts. "He could hardly open his pants by himself. . . ." What does this mean except that the man was older than Evelyn would have preferred? It certainly doesn't mean that he couldn't be an effective, satisfying lover. But he never had a chance; Evelyn is so *angry* at men in general that she seizes upon every possible negative aspect of a potential lover and *uses it to turn herself off.* She approaches sex with contempt, not desire, for her partner; and most men, sensing this contempt, wither and in fact do "fail."

If we want to, it is very easy to find fault with a potential lover. *He or she is too old, too fat, too short, too ugly, too blotchy, too wrinkled; he or she talks like a clown, acts like a clod, gapes like a fish, looks like a horse, comes on like a cow; his or her legs are too heavy, lips are too thick, nose is too broad, breasts are too small, penis is too shriveled, toenails are discolored, hair is sloppy, clothes are messy—he or she just won't do.* So when desire begins, these are some of the messages we can deliver to ourselves to hold it—and the partner—at bay.

2. *We focus on our own faults.* Generally *anger* impels us to focus on our partner's faults, *anxiety* to focus on our own faults. Thus men may resort to self-blame more than women, but women are by no means immune.

All the turn-offs we apply to others we can, and do, apply also to ourselves. *I'm too old, too fat, too short, too ugly. . . . My breasts are too small, penis too shriveled.* And since we know ourselves better than we know strangers, we can often find more specific, personal things to turn against ourselves. *I'll come too fast; I won't have an orgasm; I'll be impotent; I'll make a fool of myself; I'll be too dry; I'll perspire too much*—we all know what we consider our most unattractive features. And we can all turn them against ourselves to inhibit desire.

3. *We distract ourselves by thinking of something else besides our sexual partner.* Sometimes the easiest way to avoid sexual desire is to avoid anything connected with sex—such as the human body and its sexual activities. And there are so many other things to concentrate on that provide distance from sexual desire. *What time is it? I have to get back home. I have to get up early tomorrow. I need more sleep. I must get some work done tonight. I don't think I've fed the guppies for over a week. How much did this date cost? How much money does she have? What really happened between him and his wife? Is he married? Is she lying? I wonder what the kids are doing now. What would they think about this whole thing? What a weird way to decorate a room. What crazy color combinations this guy wears. Wasn't there a good movie on TV tonight? What time is it?*

The fact is that human beings are endlessly inventive, and if we want to turn ourselves off, we usually have no trouble doing so.

Rekindling

Deep-rooted emotional problems can rarely be solved except with *the help of a professional therapist.* If lack of desire has always been a problem, then, to find a remedy, psychological counseling is almost surely called for.

But the woman or man whose desire seems to be falling off after having been at a fairly high level is in a different situation. The problem is more *superficial, more the result of unfortunate circumstances coupled with unproductive ways of thinking.* And these can be worked on successfully, most successfully with a partner.

Relaxation is one of the keys. Just as it can help cure the impotence caused by anxiety, it can help cure the lack of desire caused by anxiety and eliminate the unconscious anger that can also lie at the root of inhibited sexual desire. The anger—at least with the new partner—may not be very deep to begin with; and anyway it's hard to be angry while you're also being relaxed.

Just as relaxation is a key to overcoming ISD, *nondemanding, nonjudgmental lovemaking is a key to relaxing.* By this we mean any and all of the alternatives discussed in Chapter 8: just holding each other, sensate focus, the Witkin shower, oral or manual stimulation. There are many ways of getting pleasure from two bodies without demanding that either one of them perform to certain standards.

But nondemand lovemaking has a few implications. First it requires a willingness to start *without sexual desire.* If your problem is lack of desire, you can't wait to be cured before you take the curative measures. You have to begin while you're still turned off.

But you can start gradually. You can realize that you're turning yourself off and try to figure out which of the turn-offs you use *before* going out on a date. For Evelyn it's focusing on the partner's faults; for Barry it's focusing on his own faults. *When you know what your turn-off mechanism is, you may be able to catch yourself at it and stop.*

If the evening gets to sex, we recommend starting with the Witkin shower. Why? First because it's not lovemaking: you're not forcing yourself to do anything that's really distasteful to you. Second, it's fun. Third, it's relaxing. Fourth and fifth, it may put you in a sexual mood (stimulate sexual desire), and it gets you and your partner clean enough to follow through.

What the Witkin shower does, what all the nondemand approaches do, is remove the element of performance from lovemaking: of forcing others and/or ourselves to perform—and succeed, or else. And while anger can still express itself, its presence now becomes unmistakable. Usually nondemand lovemaking will remove anger; when it doesn't, a common reason is that the angry person has still not recovered from the loss of the spouse. So sometimes it is necessary to let some time pass, meanwhile trying to work through one's feelings about the former partner. Sometimes psychological counseling, usually on a relatively short-term basis, can help speed the process.

The second implication of nondemand lovemaking is a willingness to minimize the penis as a tool of sex. Both men and women need to understand that sexual desire doesn't always result in an erect penis, and that sexual satisfaction doesn't always demand an erect penis. Once this is clear, many of the turn-offs we use against ourselves and others lose their point. Once we can have desire without disappointment, at ourselves or at the partner, desire is much more free—and likely—to appear.

Last Word

But sometimes desire really does end. Whether it's because the hormones give out or the body changes or some psychological impulse simply winds down, some people, as they grow older, experience less and less desire for sex and sometimes finally none at all.

But it's important that the end of sex not be the end of pleasure. There's no reason for men and women to force themselves into sexual intimacy if they don't want to, but there's every reason for them to be close and warm and loving if they wish. There's also every reason for them to have other interests, other activities, other sources of rewards and gratification. Self-fulfillment, self-development in the artistic, literary, political, business, or in any of at least a dozen different areas can provide great joy; social and intellectual sharing can bring great satisfaction and pleasure. The thrill of sex may be gone or be no longer worth pursuing, but the rewards of living are still available, exciting, and rejuvenating.

Relighting the Fire

When the thrill is gone, when you haven't had a sexual encounter or even a sexual thought for weeks:

- Ask yourself why. Don't dismiss your low desire—you deserve to be fully sexual.
- Know that there's almost always an answer for the suddenly sexless—maybe anger, anxiety, past experiences, health, or a medicine side effect (see Chapter 11). Don't give up till you figure out what's in the way of good sex!
- Remember the joy. Sex can be fun, energizing, an important way for us to express ourselves.
- Start without desire if you can't summon it. Sometimes the act of sex creates the desire.
- Get counseling if you can't relight your sexual fire. If the thrill is truly gone, remember that social and intellectual sharing can be pleasurable, exciting, and rejuvenating.

CHAPTER 11
Sex and Health

M any men and women can continue to have sexual inter-course—genital intercourse—indefinitely, sometimes into their eighties and nineties or beyond. This means that they can also have the gratification and enjoyment that sexual intimacy can bring, the release of tension and emotion. We are not age-bound with regard to sex: we know that we are sexual creatures *before birth* (films of male fetuses in the womb show many of them with erections), and we know that we are sexual creatures from birth on; boys are often born with erections, girls with lu-bricated vaginas. All the evidence suggests that we can be sex-ual creatures as long as we live.

This is not to say that there are no "normal" changes in our sexual lives. We put *normal* in quotes to emphasize the great variations that exist among individuals as they grow older. Normality also seems to imply that changes are based on physiology alone: that our bodies slow down; the production of hormones and other substances decreases, and our sex lives di-minish. It is surely true that hormonal changes are associated with growing older, and that some of these hormones seem to mediate—or be involved in—sexual desire, excitement, po-tency, and orgasm. Age-related diseases (diabetes, heart disease) and the medicines that treat them may affect sexuality. We also know that *at all ages certain psychological situations, such as stress and trauma, can reduce sexuality* as well. Thus the changes in our sex life that "normally" take place as we grow older may be due to psychological as well as physiological causes.

Besides the effect of trauma we do not know how the general attitude of society toward people growing older influences their sex lives. We know what some of these attitudes are: the lack of relevance imputed to older people, the youth orientation of the culture, the identification of attractiveness with youthfulness, the only slightly veiled contempt with which older men and women are treated, the condescension of some political figures, the oversolicitousness or underappreciation of one's children and family—to name a few. Also as we grow older real losses occur: the death of a spouse, friend, or sibling; the loss of jobs or income; the more frequent, more serious illnesses. We do not *know* how these attitudes, these events affect us; but we suspect that they drive many older people into a state of chronic depression.

And we do know something about depression: that it can account for many of the physical and psychological symptoms of aging and that *at any age* it reduces sexual desire. In both sexes, then, mental *and* physical health can change our sexuality.

Sex and Health in Men

As men grow older, they may notice several changes in the way they and their penises respond to sex.

Less frequent desire. Of all the effects of aging this is the most controversial. To summarize: it does appear that the desire for intercourse decreases with age and that the decrease is associated with a decline in the production of the hormone testosterone. There is also some evidence that taking doses of testosterone increases desire for a while and may possibly increase potency as well.

How often should a "normal" man have sexual intercourse? No numerical goal can be set; there is none. Some men don't need sex at all; others strongly need sex. But if there has been a diminishment of desire as explained in Chapter 10, or if there are still occasional stirrings of desire (or fantasies, or sexual dreams), then sex should be attempted again. For the fearful or hesitant man who has abstained from sex for some time, a few counseling sessions could be helpful.

Longer refractory period. The refractory period is the time between one ejaculation and the next erection: how soon after having an orgasm can a man have an erection again? At the peak of male sexuality (seventeen to nineteen years of age or so), the refractory period can be as short as ten to fifteen minutes. It lengthens very gradually as men grow older, and in some elderly men a refractory period of a few days or longer is usual. In addition some men (not many) seem to have a refractory period without having orgasm. That is they'll become stimulated and have an erection; the stimulation will stop without orgasm or ejaculation; the penis will relax—and then the man has to wait several hours (or days) to have another erection.

Women do not have a refractory period, and many can have multiple orgasms—one orgasm right after another with practically no interval between them, as long as there's adequate stimulation. What if the woman desires sex again after a few hours and the man is still in his refractory period? He can use manual and oral methods, which can work just as well as the penis in helping a woman have an orgasm. In brief, length of refractory period need not be a bar to enjoyable sex. (It's also true that the vaginal area of many women is extremely sensitive after orgasm, so that additional stimulation becomes actually painful—and so do multiple orgasms.)

Softer penis. As men grow older, the hardness of the penis during an erection seems to diminish: the erection can still be

perfectly good, but the penis is somewhat softer than it used to
be. This is caused, usually, by loss of tone in the arterial walls,
so that they do not engorge as fully with blood as they used to.
Erections are caused by the filling of the blood vessels in a part
of the penis called the corpora cavernosa. The more blood, the
harder the penis; so as less blood gets into the corpora cavernosa, the penis stays softer. Now it's not as easy as before for
the penis to enter the vagina, and this often creates anxiety for
the man and his partner. The answer, of course, is adequate lubrication and mutual assistance.

Less ejaculate. As men grow older, the quantity of the
ejaculate decreases. This seems to be inevitable. Moreover, after
a prostate operation there is no ejaculate at all, since the semen
is redirected to empty into the bladder and is then expelled
with the urine. On the other hand, except for the man's worrying about it, the effect of less (or no) ejaculate on the sexual
satisfaction of the man or his partner is infinitesimal.

Less forceful ejaculation. Not only is there less ejaculate,
but also during orgasm the ejaculate doesn't go as far as it
did when the man was younger. (Neither does his urine stream,
for that matter; and for some men this is another thing to
worry about.) The cause may be a reduction in the tone of
the muscles that squeeze the ejaculate through the penis; as
before, except for the man's worrying, less forceful ejaculation
has no real effect on the sexual satisfaction of the woman or
man.

Need for manual stimulation of the penis. With the loss of
tone in the arterial walls and the reduced flow of blood to the
penis, the man sometimes has more difficulty than before in
having erections spontaneously. Psychological factors—expectations of problems, worry, mild spectatoring, mild anger, generalized depression—may also play a role here, and perhaps a
large role. Be that as it may, the result is that, as men grow

older, they may no longer have erections simply by thinking about (or planning) sex or being with a sexually exciting partner or even while engaging in foreplay that does not involve direct stimulation of the genitals.

So the man worries. Many women worry also, women for whom, as we said, the proof of their desirability as sexual partners lies in the behavior of the man's penis. The truth is, however, that in no way does the need for direct manual or oral stimulation of the penis mean loss of attractiveness for the woman or the power to satisfy for the man; in no way need it diminish satisfaction in the sexual act. In fact a great many couples report that once they can relax and accept the need for direct stimulation, their sex is more fun, more intimate, and more rewarding than ever.

To sum up: in a purely mechanical sense as men grow older, their penises do not react with all the spring, vigor, and firmness that they did when they were younger. But given reasonably good health and a relaxed, loving attitude on the part of both partners, the penis can still afford both of them as much pleasure as ever. A major requirement, however, is that the man understands what is happening and responds not with panic but with acceptance. And if his partner doesn't know that the changes he may be experiencing are normal and need not interfere with sexual enjoyment, then it's his responsibility to tell her—at least if he wants sex (and the relationship as a whole) to be as good as it can be.

Sex and Health in Women

As women grow older, their sexuality hardly changes at all, at least in physiological terms. If they had orgasms before, they will have them now; if they were multiply orgasmic yesterday, they will remain so today. The only area in which some change may be noticed is vaginal lubrication. It may take longer for the vagina to lubricate itself and there may be less vaginal fluid available. In some cases the vaginal fluid disappears completely, and external lubrication is required.

In addition women as well as men may experience some loss of sexual desire. As with men, this appears to have some physiological, hormonal basis; and—oddly enough—as with men, the hormone involved appears to be testosterone, the male sexual hormone. Women also produce testosterone, and as they grow older, the production diminishes. This may be a contributing factor toward less frequent desire for sex.

There's one other fact, associated with sex but not directly related to it, we want to mention here. Based on our clinical experience* it appears that some women past menopause still experience the combination of stresses termed the premenstrual syndrome. (The premenstrual syndrome is a constellation of symptoms—cramps, nausea, a feeling of bloatedness, tension, irritability, depression, any or all of which may attack a woman usually a week or so before her period begins.) Women who before menopause had premenstrual symptoms may have the same symptoms after menopause, at roughly the same times as if they were still menstruating. This is not true of all women, but it appears to be true of many women. The cause is still unknown.

So what? So if you've stopped menstruating, you would think that you would stop having premenstrual symptoms—but it may not be the case. You may still encounter those monthly bouts with stress, though usually they're weaker than before. And these new ones leave just as surely as those earlier ones left and sometimes more rapidly. They're nothing really to worry about, but the point is this: if you happen to be a postmenopausal woman with premenstrual symptoms, tell your partner what's going on; it will make life much easier for both of you. And the same thing applies if you're a man and you have reason to think your partner may be in this category.

*Specifically on the clinical experience of Dr. Mildred Witkin.

Looked at broadly, however, the woman's sexual being is less vulnerable to the effects of aging than is the man's. But this does not mean that she cannot find a man who can satisfy her sexually. For both women and men the main sexual organ is the brain, the human mind. And the woman who knows the physiological changes that occur in men as a normal part of growing older, and the anxiety that often accompanies those changes, can help her partner do what he would most like to do—satisfy her sexually. In fact couples who can accommodate creatively to changes in the man's sexual powers can find in their older years the best sex they have ever had. This is not just a wish or a fantasy; it is a fact that has been confirmed by many sex and marital counselors. But first you have to know what's going on.

Problems, Problems

In the normal process of growing from infancy to youth and from youth to maturity, there's a natural rhythm to sexual frequency and capabilities. Given fairly good health, as we said, sex can be enjoyable throughout one's life. But as we grow older, *physiological problems become more common.* They may have psychological components having to do with mental attitudes (stress and ulcers, for example), but our bodies are actually affected. And some of these physiological effects can have a drastic influence on sexual capabilities.

Mastectomies and Sex

Although a mastectomy is usually one of the most devastating experiences a woman can have—a traumatic blow to her self-concept and femininity—it *in no way affects the physiological, sexual functioning of the woman.* Once the initial stress, trauma, and sheer physical exhaustion are over, once her emotional and physical stability return, physiologically the woman is sexually intact. She can still experience desire and excitement; she still has the ability to lubricate, have orgasms, in fact, do anything.

Then why include mastectomy as a problem? Because the psychological consequences can be so shattering that many women perceive themselves as sexually undesirable and tend to withdraw from sex.

The problem is that in our breast-oriented culture it is not only important for women to have breasts, it is important that the breasts be firm, round, and of decent size. To be flat-chested is somehow to be deficient; to be missing a breast completely is to be "half a woman." So the self-image of the woman with a mastectomy is often that of someone deeply impaired, grotesquely disfigured, an object of scorn and disgust, unlovable and undesirable.

We must emphasize that, with very few exceptions, this is not how most other people, men and women, feel about the woman who has had a mastectomy; this is how she feels about herself. And thus she basically feels like an unsuitable sexual partner.

But organically her sexuality is whole. And so, in large degree, is her attractiveness. It is true that a few men recoil at the thought of a mastectomy, and some few do divorce or leave their women. Most married men do not have these problems, however. Most married men have little trouble adapting to the idea of making love to a wife without a breast, and many, if not most, nonmarried men, at any age, have little trouble making love with a new woman without a breast. Further there are many men who are expressly attracted to mastectomy women, who in fact prefer them to others. One important reason is that it helps men feel strong and protective. Sex is often better for both the woman and the man than it ever was: the woman, feeling that she has something to make up for, is usually more willing to experiment; the man is often more gentle, loving, and tender.

If a man is attracted to a woman he knows has had a mastectomy, how does he approach her? The answer is the same as with any other woman. When he is ready to invite her to bed he can tell her that he knows about it and doesn't care, that she turns him on anyway.

What of the man who approaches a woman and then finds out that she's had a mastectomy? If he's still attracted to her, there's no reason to behave differently than he ordinarily would. ("If it makes no difference to you, it makes no difference to me" is all that's needed.) If he's one of the relatively few men who are turned off by mastectomies, then it's best to explain his feelings as early (and considerately) as possible. ("You're really attractive, but I don't think I can handle that.") Clearly he should not abandon her then and there or call the evening to a sudden halt; if he leaves the initiative to the woman, she will probably move away soon enough.

How should the woman behave? Basically she is still a complete woman; the absence of a breast—or both breasts—doesn't make her less so; her need is to recognize that fact and that her life need not be controlled by the missing breast.

When should she tell her date about the mastectomy? Circumstances vary, but the best time is probably when the "chemistry" or "turn-on" has done its job: the man has invited her to bed and she's inclined to accept. This gives the man time to adjust, ask questions, check his own attitudes, and decide what to do. It also has given the two partners a chance to get to know each other before sex, at least to some extent, and to decide whether there's some kind of minimal compatibility between them.

What about artificial or rebuilt breasts? If the new breast is visually and functionally like any breast—that is, if it looks the same and can be kissed and caressed—then there's no need to mention the mastectomy at all. If it can be looked at but not touched, then that fact ought to be mentioned. If, exposed, it doesn't look like a real breast, if it's basically an evening-gown and swimsuit breast, then it should be mentioned at the beginning.

Should she have her breasts rebuilt? It's a question that's often asked, and the answer depends on the woman. The reconstructed breast is not only a physical restorative, it may also restore the woman's self-image and self-confidence and help heal a badly damaged ego. If she has a long-term partner she should certainly check with him first, since many men object to the artificial look and feel of the reconstruction. Of course she should certainly talk to a competent surgeon first and would probably also do well to have some exploratory meetings (together with a long-term partner, if there is one) with a trusted family doctor, psychological counselor, or sex therapist.

The scarred area. During sex, if the woman wants to keep covered at first, she should do so; and if the man feels the same way, he should tell her. Later in the relationship, when they are more relaxed and trusting with each other, they may both want the woman to be completely nude, since physically she's usually more comfortable that way.

Sexual positions. Any position with which the mastectomy woman feels comfortable is fine. Any practice with which the woman feels comfortable—manual stimulation, oral sex, whatever—is also fine. On the other hand some women tend to avoid the female superior position (woman on top): in that position the woman's breast area is very prominent, and some women missing a breast are sensitive about flaunting their loss.

Prostate Problems

Many men over forty have some trouble with their prostate gland (usually an enlargement), and a number of them ultimately develop prostate cancer. In a sense it's usually a relatively benign form of cancer, in that it typically develops late in life, grows very slowly, and tends not to metastasize, or travel to other parts of the body. The first symptom of prostate problems is urine dribble, both after urination and without urinating at all. The usual remedy is surgical removal of the prostate. In most cases this does not impair erection, but certain procedures do result in impotence. It's wise for the man facing a prostatectomy to check—and see if there are alternatives if he's one of the unlucky ones.

The main function of the prostate gland is to produce a fluid that's added to the semen. It does *not* produce testosterone, the hormone involved with sexual desire, nor does it produce sperm cells. Thus removal of the prostate has no effect, in and of itself, on desire or the ability to have children. It does reduce the amount of fluid discharged during ejaculation; but as we mentioned earlier, this has little to do with the sexual satisfaction of the man or his partner.

One complication, however, may arise. In some cases estrogen-like drugs may be prescribed for men with prostate cancer, to inhibit the development of new tumors. Estrogen is one of the female reproductive hormones, and in men *may* decrease desire and potency, as well as cause a delay in ejaculation. On the other hand the vast majority of men whose prostate has been removed report no sexual problems at all.

Diabetes Mellitus

Diabetes mellitus is the common form of diabetes (*mellitus* means sweet and refers to the sugar-laden urine of diabetic people) and is known to afflict some 13 million men and women in the United States.* It is by now a fairly manageable illness, but it *may* have two side effects with regard to sexuality. It *may*

---

*Figures are from the American Diabetes Association. Some 12.7 million Americans have Type II diabetes (non-insulin dependent, formerly called adult-onset), the most common form of the disease. An additional 300,000 Americans have Type 1 (insulin dependent) diabetes.

cause impotence in men, as well as ejaculation problems; and it *may* cause orgasm problems in women. That is about half of the men with diabetes do have problems with impotence, and many diabetic women do seem to have orgasm problems. In fact diabetes is the leading medical, physiological cause of impotence in men.

The illness creates these conditions primarily through its effect on the nerve fibers that lead to such organs as the penis and the clitoris. The effects are different, however. In the penis, sensation is not affected but erection is; in the clitoris, sensation itself may be affected. Men with diabetes can still feel all the penile excitement and pleasure they always felt, but they may not be able to have an erection and they may have problems with ejaculation. There may also be other effects on the penis and its auxiliary organs, but damage to the nerve fibers is the main factor.

The diabetic man. Many textbooks note that, for men, the onset of diabetes is signaled by increasing impotence. This may be true, but we must emphasize three points. First, impotence can be caused by many factors other than diabetes, most of them temporary. So an awareness of impotence should not be a cause for alarm, although it should be a cause of a visit to the doctor if it persists. Second, at least half of diabetic men don't seem to have problems with impotence or ejaculation at all. And third, of those that do have problems, many are not wholly impotent. That is they are not totally limp; the penis grows somewhat larger and harder and more erect, and the degree of size, hardness, and erection can vary considerably.

Most men with diabetes, therefore, will not experience total impotence. But for many men it's all or nothing; partial potency is as bad as no potency at all. Do these men, and the fully impotent men, have to give up sex? More specifically do single diabetic men have to give up the search for new sexual partners? The answer to both questions is generally no. As we stated earlier, in terms of physiology the woman can be satisfied by manual and oral means; and in terms of overall satisfaction with sex as a relationship, the mechanics of intercourse are not the only important factors. Concern, caring, enthusiasm, sharing, enjoyment, fun, all contribute as much to the experience as the penis and the vagina. For the man's part, with unaltered sensations in the penis, and usually with the ability to ejaculate (although it may feel different), he can still get a great deal of pleasure out of the plain physiology of sex—plus the same pleasures of closeness and intimacy as the woman.

But can a really impotent man approach a woman for sex? Is he being fair to her? And how would he go about it?

The answer to the first two questions is yes. And the answer to the third question is that he can approach women the way he always has. There is certainly no need to reveal his impotence until they are both interested in making love. At that point he might explain that he has diabetes and has trouble with erections, but that his penis still has all the feeling it always had and not only enjoys being caressed, it still enjoys being in vaginas.

For although a penis is limp, it need not be permanently exiled from vaginas. There is a technique known as stuffing, which is performed, as the name implies, by stuffing the soft penis into the lubricated vagina. (Generally this works better with the woman on top.) Some moderate thrusting may be done, and although the sensations are not exactly like those of an erect penis in a vagina, many women and men find it an enjoyable interlude or climax to the sexual experience. For note: the clitoris, which is the woman's main organ of sexual excitement, is located fairly close to the entrance of the vagina and can often be stimulated by the pressure and rubbing of the man's pubic bone against the vagina during thrusting. Many women can be brought to orgasm by this means. And if it doesn't work, manual and oral stimulation remain available.

Finally, as with men and mastectomy women, women with diabetic men often find their lovers better than "normal" men—again, because they tend to be more considerate, more concerned, more eager to please.

The diabetic woman. The woman with diabetes may have lowered sensation in the clitoris. This does not affect desire, which is almost entirely mental, but it may affect orgasm. Since of all women's organs the clitoris is by far the most sensitive to sexual stimulation, loss of feeling there can lead to difficulty in reaching the peak of sensation needed to bring about an orgasm. And so the woman may lose that ability.

She does not lose her enjoyment of sex, however, nor of specific sexual, genital contact, nor of holding, touching, and caressing, nor of warmth, tenderness, and fun. So what is she to do?

She should tell her new partner just before intercourse, that she may not have an orgasm, but it's not his fault; it's what sometimes happens with diabetic women. She might go on to say that she would still love to see him having an orgasm, would enjoy helping him along, loves the physical contact and sexual caresses, and would get an enormous amount of satisfaction out of just being with him. Many men have no trouble at all with this situation, and some men (including many premature ejaculators), doubtful of their ability to give a woman orgasms in the first place, are relieved to be free of the responsibility. So their own enjoyment and creativity increase, and the relationship can be satisfying indeed.

Hypertension

Hypertension—high blood pressure—affects an estimated 63.64 million Americans.* In itself it has no effect on sexual capabilities, but it's a dangerous illness to be walking around with, and medication is the usual remedy. The antihypertensive drugs are effective but some of them cause sexual problems, almost entirely among men. The principal problem is impotence, although a few men experience less desire or have trouble having orgasms. Some newer drugs have very little effect on impo-

*Based on current statistics provided by the American Heart Association.

tence but may have undesirable side effects for some men or may not work against the hypertension per se.

If the hypertensive man does have medication-induced impotence, what should he do about it?

Some men stop taking the drug a few days before they expect to have sex and take their chances. This poses one problem: it could kill them. Other men give up sex completely; but this kills an important part of their lives.

Without resorting to either alternative, one answer is to emphasize manual and oral sex and de-emphasize—without abandoning—penile-vaginal sex.

After all medication-induced impotence is not much different from diabetes-induced impotence, and the same considerations apply. The single man can still look for new partners or keep with a current partner; he need give up neither sex nor genital pleasure. The penis still has sensation and can provide great pleasure when caressed; the stuffing technique can still be used; and women can still be approached in the full knowledge that the man can still give her a wholly satisfying sexual experience, orgasm included.

Male Impotence and the Woman

But male impotence can cause problems for the woman. One we have spoken of at length: the need of some women to experience the man's erection as a validation of their own desirability. But many women, secure in their own sexuality, encounter another problem when faced with an impotent man, even a man impotent for purely physiological reasons, for reasons that can in no way be imputed to the woman's lack of desirability. This problem has to do with *lack of perceived effectiveness*.

Many women with "normal" sexual partners are not especially happy with those men or with their own sexual gratification. But they often do get one satisfaction from sex: the sense of being effective, of having an impact. They do not need a man to have an erection simply by looking at them, but they need to feel that they are *doing* something, that by their manual or oral stimulation, the maneuvering of their bodies, the man is growing excited, becoming erect, having an orgasm, ejaculating. This knowledge, this sense of *mattering,* of making a difference, is very important.

Many men also feel this same need, which underlies much of their desire that the woman have an orgasm; her failure to do so is not just a reflection on his sexual prowess but also on his effectiveness as a sexual human being.

To some extent the impotent man deprives a woman of this feeling, and if the man also has ejaculation problems, as happens sometimes, she is denied all evidence of effectiveness. And so sex becomes different for her, not only because the penis is no longer a clear determinant of her effectiveness but also because she is missing an important kind of feedback. Sex for this woman often grows to be less satisfying, more anxiety-provoking; it is as though she herself were impotent and ineffective.

The answer (again) is relaxation, trust, nonidealization of the penis, and enjoyment: enjoyment of sex, enjoyment of the relationship.

Colostomies

The man or woman with a colostomy bag to explain may be more embarrassed than any other physically impaired person. Sexuality is untouched, however, and there is no reason at all for the operation to spell the end of sex.

As with mastectomies, there is a need to tell the partner about the operation before making love. And again partners may be accepting or rejecting, with more partners inclined to accept than reject. (If your partner's colostomy is too much for you, the advice given to troubled mastectomy partners holds: tell that person that you find him or her very attractive but that you can't handle the situation.) Once lovemaking actually begins, or even when it's only imminent, desire and excitement are usually enough to carry both partners past the colostomy apparatus with no real problems.

Backaches, Arthritis, Heart Problems, and Other Physical Impediments

Question: What do you do when you can't get your body around in the agile way you used to—because your bones and muscles are giving you a hard time or because the doctor has told you to take it easy? Answer: you do the same as you've always done but less strenuously. If sex is not a matter of genital performance, it's not a matter of athletic performance either. It's a matter (to repeat) of physical pleasure in a rewarding relationship.

In an extreme case the kind of pleasure that is possible was exemplified in the film *Coming Home*. A veteran of Vietnam completely paralyzed from the waist down was unable to move. He and the wife of an Army officer (still in Vietnam) fell in love, and in one memorable scene they actually made love. The film was not explicit, but it was clear that oral sex was involved and that the woman was totally satisfied. And the veteran, who couldn't feel anything below his waist, at least knew what was happening and derived pleasure from that and from his ability to please his beloved.

The film was a fiction but the reality is not. Sex really does begin in the brain; it really is possible to be paralyzed and experience—give and enjoy—sexual pleasure. It is certainly possible to have back problems, hip problems, neck problems, joint problems, and enjoy good sex. Speed is unnecessary and neither is great effort; slow is as good as fast; easy is as good as agitated. It isn't necessary for the man to do most of the thrusting from the male superior (man on top) position; sex can be just as good, and is preferred by many couples, when the woman does much of the thrusting in the female superior position.

Or the couple can enjoy genital intercourse in the lateral (side-to-side) position, with neither of them straining too hard. The fact is that for most older people and many younger people, easygoing gliding sex is just as pleasurable as bucking-bronco rodeo sex and carries its own unique rewards.

Last Word

In sexual terms we human beings are rather lucky. Women and men are capable of giving each other sensual, sexual pleasure in so many different ways that none of us need feel deficient if some of those ways seem barred to us. And men and women are capable of receiving pleasure in so many different ways that none of us need feel cheated if we cannot experience every one of those ways with our partner. With knowledge, sensitivity, and creativity there is enough for all.

For Peak Sexual Health

A healthy body is a main requirement for a healthy sexual response. We all know that even when we're just a little bit under the weather—say, with a cold—rolling around in a passionate embrace is the last thing on our mind. A more serious health condition can sap your sex drive even more. To be the lusty, robust sexual creature you know you are:

- DO stay physically fit. Keeping in good shape gives you energy for sex, makes you more willing (and less embarrassed) to shed your clothes, and helps ward off health problems.
- DO treat any health conditions early. The longer you let a disease run untreated, the harder it will be to reverse.
- DO expect changes—but not losses—in your sexuality as the years pass.
- DO remember that with understanding, sensitivity, and creativity, you can enjoy sexual pleasure even if there are real physiological problems.

Part Three
Living in the World

CHAPTER 12

The Trouble with Children

When we have a family and suddenly find ourselves single again, generally nobody is more important to us than our children. It is they in whom we pour our dreams for the future and our hopes for a vindication of our past; and in time of stress they are usually the ones who matter most, whose love, support, and understanding we most need, and whose lack of support is most devastating.

On two occasions especially do we need their support: during the separating experience, when we are going through a divorce or the early stages of bereavement; and again during the period of reemergence and reconnection, when we are looking for—and think we may have found—a new partner. Our expectations of our children are different in both cases and so may their responses be different and possibly disconcerting.

Children During Divorce

Divorce and the Younger Child

However well we think we're hiding the breakdown of our relationship, children do tune in. Studies that measure psychological well-being in the year before a divorce have turned up symptoms of distress in girls and distancing from the family in boys which acts as a shield against the stress involved in a parental breakup. After the actual divorce, the girls' distress level stays the same and the boys' level rises to meet it. This distress can show up in a variety of behaviors, ranging from reclusiveness, to physical problems such as headaches and stomachaches, to delinquency.

You may think that a child of divorce would get over the event quickly, but a child's bond with parents is permanent and the loss of the parental partnership is felt deeply. You can help by not dumping on the departed spouse; remember your criticism will only make the child feel uncomfortable or angry with you. And this is a time to listen closely to your child's feelings, provide many opportunities for feelings to come out, and offer encouragement for him or her to act out grief or anger in appropriate ways.

Older children are equally uncomfortable with choosing sides—but if they do, it's often with the father.

The Woman—Choosing Up Sides

Sarah is in her late forties, with faded blond hair and a small, wiry body. She smokes almost continuously.

> We had been married close to twenty-five years when my husband left me—no word, no warning, no nothing. Just left. He had found himself another woman—younger than me—and that was the end. She had money and Ed has money, and I guess they figured if they put their money together they could have a great life with each other. Maybe I'm being a little bitter.
>
> I was about forty-five at the time, working for the past three years for a furniture chain. Not that we needed the money—Ed is a very successful stockbroker—but the kids were out of the house, and I

wanted something to do. And it was nice to have my own supply of cash.

Ed had worked it all out. Broke the news to me at dinner, took a cab that night to his girlfriend's place, began moving his stuff out the next day. He's a good planner.

So the first thing that happened, my ulcers flared up again. Not many women have ulcers, but I'm one of the lucky ones. The next thing we had to tell the kids.

Actually *I* had to tell them. It was one other little chore Ed left for me. "You're better at it than I am"—that's how he put it. That's how he gets along—everybody does things for him, because they're better at it.

I thought, thank God for the kids. We have three—two girls, Laura and Valerie, and a son, Mark. The girls were twenty-one and twenty-three, then, and Mark was twenty-four. Valerie was in Texas with her husband; Laura and her husband lived near me—in the same city. Mark had a small place near Laura.

So I asked Laura and Mark over for dinner and I told them. I figured it wouldn't be easy, but it would be okay. They were grown-ups, and they could handle it. And I wanted some people I could count on, some people who would be on my side. I needed them to tell me I was all right; they would stand by me. I needed them to tell me they loved me.

So this is what they did. First they didn't believe it. So I convinced them. So they just sat there for a while, and then Mark said, "That's tough." And then Laura said, "Why do you think Daddy left?"

I'll never forget those words. She wasn't asking why Ed left; she was asking what I did wrong. She wasn't even asking; she *knew* what I did wrong. She just wanted me to face it; that's all. She wanted me to examine my life and find out where I was guilty.

Of course that's not what she said. And of course first I tried to explain: he had found this other woman; he didn't love me anymore—and if she really wanted to know why he left, why didn't she ask *him*. And then tell me the answer, because I was goddamn curious myself.

Everything went downhill after that. It had started pretty low, and it got worse and worse. They were not going to commit themselves; they were not going to give an *inch* of sympathy; they were not going to understand how I felt. They were going to *analyze* the whole thing.

"Why do you think Daddy left?" *They* thought he left because I was too hot-tempered. I've been that way all my life—I blow up in a minute and I get over it in a minute. Ed used to joke about it. They also thought he left because I didn't pay enough attention to him. Not true. Because I didn't care what he thought. Not true. Because I was never home. Not true.

I see now that I expected them to take my side, to be for me and against Ed. He had left me for no reason, without giving me a chance. Not that I would have known what to do. But I wasn't young anymore and not especially beautiful. And I had a job but not such a great job. I could support myself but that's about all. And I had this goddamn ulcer. And I smoked too much. And I thought, it was so clear that Ed was wrong, that Ed had hurt me: how could they not see that? But they couldn't see it. They wouldn't. They would absolutely not choose between me and Ed. They met Ed's girlfriend—he took them all to this super restaurant—and they said she was really very nice. Impartial, you know?

So they were no help at all. No: they hurt. For those first few months all I got from them was pain. After a while I didn't even want to talk to them, and I know they avoided me when they could.

Things are better now. Once the divorce was final, and once I got on my feet again, things got better. I stopped expecting them to love me and hate Ed, and that's what did it.

For parents like Sarah, the first problem with children, grown children, is that most often they will not take sides. They do not want to be forced to choose between their mother and their father and will resist attempts to "coerce" them. Even when one of the parents is clearly the injured party, as was Sarah, most children will not side with that parent against the other, but will do their best to remain neutral and treat both parents alike.

Blaming Mom

In fact, regardless of the reason for the breakup of the marriage, many children will paradoxically tend to gravitate, at least in the early stages, to the father. There are many reasons. First there is still a deep cultural bias that it's the woman, not the man, who holds the family together. Even when the children have grown, she is responsible for keeping it going; and *if the family breaks up by the man leaving, it is her fault. She has somehow failed.*

Another reason is that there is often some uncertainty about how the mother will support herself, and the children fear that they will have to do the supporting. And who takes care of her if she gets sick? So they begin to resent the one they may have to take care of and support—*even if* the woman has a job or an income and is self-supporting, *even if* it is the father who has left the mother. Many loving children, caring children, in today's world, with their own careers to make, their own family to care for, do not like the prospect of having to care for their mother also. It is a burden that seems unfair.

Nor is the burden seen to be only that of financial support or prospective financial support. Children often fear the need to give excessive emotional support to the mother. The father can take care of himself, they feel, but the mother needs help. Notwithstanding considerable evidence that women are stronger emotionally than men, better able to bear emotional stress, the children feel that the father can "take it like a man" but the mother will "collapse like a woman." To some extent this notion arises from the fact that women are more emotionally open than men, especially where weakness is concerned: the woman will tend to reveal her bitterness and hurt, while the man will tend to conceal his. And so to the children the mother appears to be constantly demanding attention and support, to represent a constant drain on their emotional resources. And this they begin to resent.

Finally (with many exceptions) *many children tend to be unconsciously more hostile toward their mothers than toward their fathers.* The main reason is that children of both sexes almost always begin closer to the mother: it is almost always the mother (or some other woman—grandmother, aunt, schoolteacher) who cares for the infant, the toddler, and the preschooler, and usually the schoolchild as well. Even when both parents work, the mother is usually the one who comes home in time to meet the children (if either parent comes home), prepares the meals, sees after their needs, is more involved in their personal lives. For the average child from birth into the teen years the mother is usually more *present* than the father.

So if the child experiences a sense of being wronged, it is usually the mother to whom the wrong is attributed. Even if the father is clearly the villain of the household, and has done major damage to the children and the family, very often *the mother is blamed for not having protected the children better, for*

not having magically transformed the father into a better man.
She tends to be placed at the center of the family, and if the
center is perceived to be inadequate, she is blamed for its inadequacy.

Further, a necessary condition for becoming adults is to
separate from the parents, not necessarily physically, by moving
away, but always psychologically: by being one's own self, living
according to one's own standards. *Because of the initial closeness, it is harder for children of both sexes to separate from the
mother than from the father;* although it is hardest for girls, being of the same sex. But feeling an absolute psychological imperative to separate, *children also feel angry at the parent from
whom separation is difficult.* This anger is almost always unconscious, and it is almost always directed at the mother.

In other words: whether the woman is the active or passive partner in a divorce, whether she is suing or being sued,
she cannot count on the immediate sympathy and understanding of her children. This is not to say that there are not
many exceptions; but they do remain exceptions, not the general rule.

Faced with this situation, what should the woman do?
The most important thing is not to complain to the children
about her husband. Her husband is their father, and they do
not want to hear their father denigrated. (They would feel the
same way about the father denigrating the mother.) No matter
how much the children feel that the father may be at fault, no
matter how much justification the mother may have in expecting them to take her side, *children do not want to see their parents break up and will resent any attempt to involve them in an
indictment of a parent.* This they almost always find hard to
tolerate.

It's not easy for the woman deserted by her husband to
conceal her resentment against him. Nevertheless, even in this
time of trauma, the best (and most difficult) approach is to
consider herself first as the mother of her children, concerned
with their needs, and second as a deeply wounded woman with

needs of her own. *The divorce is a traumatic event for the children also, even grown children, adult children—and for the grandchildren.* It is a psychological hint that something was wrong between their creators and that, therefore, something may be wrong with them. Children may also take their parents' divorce as a prediction of their own future; if it happened to my mother and father, it could happen to me. Too often these "predictions" turn into self-fulfilling prophecies.

Society recognizes the trauma to younger children but does not yet realize the effect of a divorce on older children (and grandchildren). But nevertheless the effects are there. The axis of their world, which they have known as a unit all their lives, has split; they don't know what to do about it and *they don't know what to do about the emotions it generates.* Thus many adult children suppress their emotions, and defend themselves by distancing themselves from what's happening. They don't want to be involved. They wish the whole thing hadn't happened; there's nothing they can do about it; and they're angry, shocked, scared—and stuck. That's why they won't take sides. Even though a sense of common justice tells the woman that she has a *right* to a greater share of their sympathy, the *reality* is that children have two parents and will not split them.

The Woman Carries On

Besides respecting the neutrality of the children, it's important for the woman to reassure them of her ability to cope. This may be difficult, for sometimes the one thing the woman (or man) feels she or he cannot do is cope: the hurt is too great; the trauma is too severe. But perhaps you recall: when they were small, the most intolerable situation for children was one in which the parent seemed unable to cope, seemed to display a sudden, unexpected weakness. One woman remembered her young son, about five years old, who suffered from the usual bruises and bangs common to boys his age, and the usual misunderstandings and disappointments; but what generated the greatest anxiety for the child, an anxiety bordering on hysteria, was when she herself tripped over a crack in the sidewalk and fell to the ground. The child was terrified, began screaming and crying, and would not be quieted until some time had passed enough for the reassurance that his mother, and thus the solidity of the world, were both restored to him. The parents are the center of their children's lives, the shield and the haven; and if that protective function cannot be counted on, the universe becomes totally threatening.

This feeling lingers long in children at an unconscious level. Like many childhood dependency needs, it tends to be reactivated in trauma; and so the grown children do not want to see their parents being helpless; they want to see them being competent. And the reason that it's important for the mother at this stage to grit her teeth and appear competent is not just because that's what the kids want; it's because if they cannot see her as competent, they will tend to treat her as an inferior, and that's even worse.

With the mother acting like a mother, the children will eventually provide the kind of support the mother needs. They may never side with her against her spouse, but they will begin to understand that she is sometimes lonely and overwhelmed and that they can help without being overwhelmed themselves. And then she and they are on a sound footing again.

The Man: Steady as It Goes

During a divorce men generally have an easier time with their children than do women, for the same reasons that give women a harder time. Usually they are not as emotionally involved with their children, and usually they are less demonstrative. Thus they seem less entrapping than the mother, less apt to represent an emotional and financial drain. The father seems more self-sufficient, and this makes it easier for the children to draw close—or rather, not to separate too far.

Again this tends to be the case as long as the father has been a tolerably acceptable parent; and it usually makes little difference whether he is the one suing for a divorce or being

sued. Even if the father should behave "emotionally," break
into tears, have spells of depression, the children tend not to be
driven away, as they may be with the mother. When the mother
bursts into tears, the children worry about being responsible
for getting her back into shape again; when the father bursts
into tears, the children tend to blame the mother for driving
him to such extremes.

So the father typically starts out with an advantage,
and his main job is not to alienate the children. As with the
woman, *the key is to remember that especially in this situation
he is a parent first and a hard-pressed man second.* Thus he will
not attack the mother, place any onus for the separation on
her, complain about alimony settlements—in brief, he, like
the woman, will *absolutely avoid inviting the children to take
sides.*

Some children do resent the father for leaving the mother
or allowing the mother to leave him. These children often become angry, sometimes actively hostile. It is important for the
man in these cases to understand their reactions: the children
are behaving like children. Time may help: the time it takes for
the children to see that the mother is not destroyed and that
the family is still a family, even if a fragmented one. Confront-
ing hostile children, the father does best to try to accept their
anger, hurt, and pain, and to continue to offer all the warmth
and love he can. Certainly he should maintain contact with his
grandchildren; and if his children oppose this (some do), he
must make very clear to them the harm they are doing by de-
priving their children of a grandfather's love. In this case family
counseling is often helpful.

Summing It Up

Divorce is not an easy time for anybody in the immediate or ex-
tended family. It has long been known that it is especially hard
on younger children, but it appears to be harder in general than
we once believed. It is hard on older children as well.

What are parents to do—especially what are they to do with their rage and anger—if they do not share these feelings with their children? It's important to let the feelings out, but to friends or adult relatives they count on as friends. If none is available, a counselor is a good person with whom to unburden oneself. The uncritical perspective of the counselor can encourage the expression of emotions that might be hard to reveal to others, no matter how sympathetic, and this unburdening can be a significant cathartic experience. The parents do best to behave as parents toward the children, and especially to refrain from criticizing or blaming the other parent. With this approach the children will often come to offer the love and understanding each parent may want.

Children of the Widowed

The widowed parent of older children has an easier time than the divorced parent, because more can be shared—including the entire mourning period, with all its emotions.

A problem that sometimes arises, often after the first shock is over, is that the surviving spouse feels the need to reveal some secrets about the spouse (or about himself or herself) that the children never knew. If these secrets contain positive information about the parent, then of course there's no harm. But occasionally the parent wishes to unburden herself or himself of a feeling of guilt for some past misdeed and confesses that "sin" to the children. Or, in the sweep of emotions, as well as what is often an unexpected closeness with the children, the parent will talk about the deceased spouse's faults or weaknesses—or "sins"—about which the children knew nothing.

This is usually a mistake. As we said much earlier, anger at the departed spouse is very common, because the death is experienced unconsciously as an abandonment. The best way of working through the anger, it has long been known, is to recognize it and express it. But the expression should not take the form of invective, because children do not want to hear ill of their parents, dead or alive. The surviving spouse may express anger that the deceased parent didn't take better care of himself or herself, didn't allow himself or herself to enjoy life more, may even express anger at fate. Anger so expressed can be helpful to the children, who are also angry with the parent for abandoning them. Thus the surviving parent's anger can help the children get in touch with their own anger and express it with caring and love. But as far as negative secrets are concerned, whether their own or their deceased spouse's, if they feel they have to talk to someone, let it be a trusted friend or a counselor.

Children and Remarriage

If you think your children objected to your dating someone new, wait till you announce you want to marry that someone! It's not unusual for children to oppose a remarriage—they don't want a "replacement parent." They don't want to think of you as someone with sexual needs. And during your time without a spouse, you may have turned your daughter into a confidante and your son into the man of the house; now those special relationships are threatened.

Difficult as it may be, when you start to think about remarriage, subtract the children from the equation. Then add up the remaining pluses and minuses of the relationship, such as whether the man or woman you're considering is a good partner for *you* (see the end of Chapter 14, on remarriage). If he or she loves the children too, you end up with a bonus, but it shouldn't be the deciding factor. It's a mistake to marry someone *because* he likes the kids, or not marry *because* the kids don't like him. The speaker is twenty-nine-year-old Maria:

> I was ecstatic about the way Roberto got along with
> my three girls—sometimes I thought they liked him

better than their real father. They begged me and begged me to marry him. I liked him and he wanted to get married, so I said yes. It didn't take long to find out he and I were a pleasant but boring match, and I began to feel I had to get out. Now I'm twice divorced, and the girls are having a hard time with it. The older one is withdrawn, the middle one seems distant, and the little one is very clingy.

The moral of the story (as I saw on a T-shirt): "When Momma ain't happy, ain't *nobody* happy." Just as your distress before the divorce spread through the family, your emotional well-being also affects their happiness. You owe it to yourself and your family to make the right choice for you.

Frank is eighty years old, still vigorous, a little hard of hearing but usually too vain to wear his hearing aid. He lives in a hotel for older people.

I don't go with anybody now—any special woman. There's one woman here I see every so often, but I don't talk about it. The boys don't know about her. She and I were talking a few weeks ago about leaving this place and setting up our own apartment, but nothing's going to come of it.

I almost got married again, about seven years ago. That was about four years after my wife died. She had been sick a long time, but it was still a shock. You never expect it.

I stayed in the old place for a while, then I moved down to Florida, to a senior citizens' hotel. My younger son, Eddie, has a business there and also a wife, Clara, and I thought I could do without winters for a long time.

For a year or so everything was fine. Eddie visited me; I visited him. There were more women than men at the hotel, and I was one of the younger ones. And I was in good shape then. So I was very popular with the ladies. But it didn't amount to anything.

One day a new woman came in; her name was Isabel. We hit it off right away. We went out a couple of times. And then when Eddie and Clara came for a visit, I introduced her. They were very polite but strained. Then, when we were alone, they began to make jokes about how she was after me, and I had better watch my step or she'd hook me. Well, maybe she was after me, but I liked her.

I took it as a joke though; they were just kidding. Meantime Isabel and I were going together. Every time the kids phoned they asked about Isabel, and they would make some remarks. They were always supposed to be funny, but I began to get tired of them. I didn't even want to mention Isabel anymore.

One day Isabel started talking about getting married. It seemed like a good idea. We liked each other I had a little money and she had a little money, and if we put it together, we could have a nice place of our own. And there would still be enough to leave the children—we were living off the interest, you know, and not touching the principal. We wanted to have money left for the kids after we died.

I went to tell Eddie and Clara about me and Isabel getting married—thinking about marriage. I had a feeling they wouldn't be crazy about the idea, but I thought it would be okay. Isabel and I were both going to sign prenuptial agreements leaving our own money to our own children—there was no problem with that.

So I told them. As I said, I didn't expect a great reaction. But I didn't expect what I got either. First they attacked Isabel. She was loud; she was pushy; she was bossy; she was a mental case; nobody could

live with her. How could I think of her? What was
the matter with me? That got them started on me. I
was crazy; I was stupid; I didn't know what I was
doing; I couldn't be trusted to tie my own shoelaces.
I was an imbecile. If I married somebody like Isabel,
it would serve me right. I was so dumb.

You can't imagine what it was like. I wasn't prepared for it. I was punch-drunk. I didn't know what
to say. Eddie drove me back to the hotel, and he
didn't even stop talking in the car. He kept right on
with how bad Isabel was and what a jerk I was. It
was a nightmare.

Naturally I told Isabel. She still wanted to get
married, but I wasn't so sure. I didn't know what to
do. I called my older son, Ian, and he said I should
do whatever I thought was best. But if he were my
age he would think a lot before he got married
again. So I knew Eddie had spoken to him.

I talked to Eddie and Clara a few more times. I
wanted them to change their minds—at least, soften
up a little. They didn't change their minds at all. As I
said, I didn't know what to do. Then one day Isabel
said she was going to California. Her daughter lived
in San Diego and had been trying to get her to move
there for a long time. And if we weren't going to be
married, what was the use of hanging around?

Eddie and Clara thought it was a trick to get me
to marry her. They don't know a thing. I wanted to
marry her, but I didn't know what to do. It's hard to
fight your own children. So I didn't do anything.
And Isabel went to California, and that was the end
of it. Except I still miss her. We were really good for
each other.

So now what? So now I'm a lot older and a lot
more tired. There's this nice lady, but it doesn't
amount to anything. I'm back in the North. Eddie

phones once a week, and every so often I see Ian
and his wife. We don't talk about much. Nothing
new happens to me—more aches and pains, that's
all. And I worry a lot about getting really sick. But I
wouldn't talk to the kids about that. I don't want to
depress them: I'm depressed enough myself.

By no means do all men and women who want to remarry
come up against this reaction from their children, but a surprising number do. It is one of the most painful experiences a parent can go through. And more often than not, the parent
decides not to remarry.

But that's not usually the end of it. When children prevail
against their parent, especially against the parent's wish for a
new life, there's often a fallout: depression. The parent feels that
a chance for happiness has been thwarted, that the possibility
for having a new, warm, loving, deeply fulfilling life has been
arrested. Unwilling, typically, to express anger against the children, he or she tends to become depressed; and too often this
depression can take a very long time to lift.

Why is the opinion of their children so important to parents? For one thing we put more of ourselves into our children
than into anyone else. Their approval validates our effectiveness as parents; their opinion carries more weight because it
comes more heavily laden with our own emotions, the emotions we have poured into them. And while this is generally
true, it is less true in those areas of our lives in which we are
the experts, in which we feel confident. The details of our business, cooking, clothes, friendships, those aspects of our lives
that we know better than anyone else, are relatively immune to
the children's opinions. They have their ideas; we have ours.
But where *opinion* is more a factor, many parents begin to defer
to their children, to give the children's opinion more weight
than their own. In effect the child becomes the parent and the
parent becomes the child.

In brief: the less secure we are, the more the opinion of others becomes important. And people thinking of remarrying are almost always full of deep insecurity.

First they wonder whether remarrying is a wise decision. They cannot obliterate the knowledge and experience life has brought them; they cannot suddenly not remember what they know of the illusions of love, and that loving couples seem to change after the excitement of courtship begins to fade. So there is a rational component to their hesitation: they know their own and their partner's capacity—the human capacity—for making mistakes and harboring illusions more certainly than their children do.

More important is the emotional insecurity that results from a decision to marry. Nobody is immune to this. The most loving two people at any age, contemplating marriage, have innumerable sudden spurts of doubt. They question themselves about the sense of the whole business: Am I making a mistake? Do I really love this other person? What is she or he really like? Will I satisfy this other person? How will we get along?

These are difficult questions for all people; for the previously married—more insecure, more uncertain—they can be paralyzing. To help them over their insecurity and uncertainty they depend on their children for the care, concern, and approval they need to move ahead into this new life. And all too often the children respond with a full-scale, humiliating attack on the whole idea—including the parent's mental competence.

Why should so many children be so adamantly opposed to a parent's remarriage?

Money Is the Root . . .

For some it's a question of money. The parent's money was supposed to go to them; now it will go to the spouse or the spouse's family. Even prenuptial agreements, in which each partner renounces a claim on the other's estate, have little effect; the children may feel that in the meantime the parent will spend more on the new partner and on joint activities, and there will be less left for the original family: less today, less in the estate. And less means not only for them but for their children, the parent's grandchildren. Don't think of us, the children seem to say, don't even think of yourself; but for God's sake, how can you do that to your own grandchildren?

When children object on the grounds of money, the objection usually has two parts. One we have just described: the fear that the parents will squander money that "rightfully" should go to the children. The other objection is directed at the prospective partner: he (she) is only after the parent's money. "It wouldn't be so bad if he [she] really loved you," the child says, "but can't you see what he [she] wants? It's just your money."

In a way parents of children who voice these objections are lucky: at least the problem is out in the open. Sometimes a child might fear losing the parent's money but understand that to come right out and say so might be to appear selfish. So he or she finds other reasons, one or a dozen, to oppose the marriage. No matter how those reasons are debated, the parent cannot satisfy the child, because the real issues, the real fears, are not discussed.

There's another fear related to the fear of not being left enough money, and it applies mostly to the remarriage of a divorced father: he will no longer support the mother, and the children will have to do so. This is a double blow: the children will get less from the father, and they will have to lay out their own money (or time) on behalf of the mother. And while most children don't mind doing this occasionally, they usually don't relish the prospect of perpetual responsibility for a parent. But this is the prospect they see if the father remarries while the mother remains single.

Further for many people there is a deep relationship between money and love, between the means to satisfy material needs and desires and the means to satisfy nurturant needs and desires. Sometimes the two seem to be one: give me money and you give me love; take away money and you take away love. (And many parents *do* use money to demonstrate love.) For these children a parent's remarriage is not just a threatened loss of money; it is a withdrawal of love. For the child in us all almost nothing is harder to accept, and almost nothing is more vehemently opposed.

Say It Isn't Sex

And some children of parents who plan to remarry have a lot of trouble with sex—that is with acknowledging the parents as sexual beings.

With most of these children it's not the parents' age that counts as much as the fact that they are parents. The children *never* accepted their parents' sexuality, never believed it, never acknowledged it. Even when common sense told them that their parents must have had sex at least every so often, they never took the thought seriously. It was not that they denied it; they just totally ignored it. For these children the parents' sexuality—*while they were all living together*—wore a cloak of invisibility: the children just didn't see it. And they don't want to see it now.

Why are some children disturbed by their parents' sexuality? Sometimes it's because sex is supposed to be "dirty" while the parents are idealized as being superior: my mother and father could never do such a thing. Even when they grow older and are sexual themselves, these children often cannot see their parents actually "doing it."

But sometimes the problem has deeper roots. It brings back a time when the parents were the child's sexual objects: the time described by Freud as the Oedipal stage, when the child desires the parents. One way of coping with this stage is to deny finally that the parent is a sexual object of any kind: how can you desire someone who knows nothing of desire? So the problem is papered over—as long as the parents are seen as being asexual.

This fantasy can be maintained as long as the parents are together. Even when a newly single parent starts dating, the dates can be explained on other grounds: the parent needs companionship; it gives him something to do; it keeps her from being lonely. To some extent these fictions—for that is what they almost always are—are applied to a remarriage also: she's not remarrying for sex; he's remarrying for companionship.

But the fiction becomes harder to maintain with marriage, because the question must arise: if they're not going to have sex, why should they get married? Unwilling to supply the obvious answer—they *are* going to have sex—the child typically finds a reason to oppose the marriage and provide an alternative: his or her own companionship, companionship of friends, companionship of grandchildren. So everything becomes companionship and nothing becomes sex, because sex stirs up some long-sleeping dragons. And when the dragons start to stir—when the remarriage of a parent becomes probable—the child unconsciously mobilizes all of his or her resources to fight it.

Pride of Place

As long as the family is a unit, the children should come second, the spouse first, in a parent's estimation. (When one parent does put the children first, as often happens, the other parent may resent it powerfully, and this can be a major source of marital difficulties.) Even though children would rather be first, somewhere inside them they acknowledge the justice of the parents being first for each other.

With a divorce or death the situation changes completely. Now the children come first. Their old dream becomes a reality: they become the most important people in their parent's life. And if not they themselves, then *their* children, the parent's grandchildren. Few parents have trouble letting their own children take the lion's share of the grandparent's affection; for in this case the grandchildren are their proxies, and what is given to the grandchildren is given to the children also.

All this is threatened by the parent's remarriage. There will be less time for the children and grandchildren, less attention, less day-to-day concern; they will simply be less important to the remarried parent. The dream of being first, finally realized, will be dead again. And so the marriage is opposed.

The Child in the Children

Whether children who object blindly to a parent's remarriage are young or old, their *unconscious motives* are those of the young child. This is one reason why parents have so much difficulty with them. The parents want to sit down with their children and reason with them. The *young, emotionally needy child does not listen to reason;* reason is not what he or she is after. The parents try to work out compromises; *the young child cannot conceive of compromises,* must either lose or win. The parents want to be understood, but *the young child is not understanding;* in fact the reverse is true. *The child wants to be understood,* because he or she is sure that, once understood, his or her nurturant needs will be fulfilled.

What Is the Parent to Do?

There are no easy answers. You, the parent, may know all the reasons that your children are against your remarriage, know exactly where they're wrong and why—but what difference does it make? What can you actually do if they threaten to withhold their emotional support, withhold your grandchildren, stop visiting or asking you to visit them, or simply keep up a storm of vituperation that never ends, so that every occasion with them becomes an occasion of hurt and anger? How can you subject yourself to that, especially to start a life with a person you don't know very well, with prospects that are usually cloudy at best, with the knowledge that there isn't much time ahead especially time to make mistakes—with the worry that perhaps you *are* making a mistake in even thinking of marrying again? How can you sustain the constant hammering of the children's disapproval? And why should you, when the solution is so easy—simply don't get married?

Often this is the solution the parent chooses: he or she doesn't remarry. Sometimes it's the right decision; sometimes the marriage really would be unsuitable and the parent knows it and uses the children's objections as an excuse for breaking off. But often, also, marriages that would work, which would be fruitful for both partners, are frustrated because one or both sets of children oppose it.

There's another solution. If the children are acting childishly, the parent can continue to act like an adult, remaining calm and rational, making independent decisions. (A marriage counselor might be of real value at this time.) But as long as the opposition of the children is expressed as opposition only and not as threats, it need not be a barrier to remarriage. And once that decision is made, there's every reason to behave as a parent would with balky young children who *know* they're being balky: that is with the assurance that they will ultimately acquiesce. Children do not want a rupture between themselves and their parents; and if the parent seems self-assured and has legitimate expectations of the children (such as being at the wedding ceremony, for example), much more often than not the children will come around.

The situation becomes truly agonizing if the children threaten to withhold their own or the grandchildren's love. The threat can be to end all communication between grandparent and grandchild—visiting, excursions, even telephone conversations.

To remarry in these circumstances is to risk losing much for an uncertain future. But remarrying promises rewards that the children cannot give. The link to the children is a link to life in the past: *it keeps us going.* The link to a new partner is, or can be, a link to the future: *it rejuvenates us*. We are more effective than we were, more important; someone cares for and about us. And we are no longer alone.

Remarrying means more than the security that a person will be there for us if we are sick. We are now the center of each other's lives, as we cannot be the center of our children's lives. No matter how loving grown children may be, they lead their own lives, and, to some extent, parents are an "extra." Moreover we and our new spouse now form our own unit, no longer dependent on others for nurturance, no longer "extras" or appendages, but a couple to be taken into account, people to be reckoned with.

Remarrying, of course, is also a link to sex, to the erotic life. The reawakening or renewal of sex can work seeming miracles not just on the emotions and attitudes but on the body itself. And by sex we don't mean only genital sex, although we certainly don't exclude it; we mean the full range of sexual pleasures, from simply holding each other to engaging all the organs one can think of. Sex can be a part of a living marriage at any age—again, even if it's only holding each other. Children and grandchildren can't supply it and you can't give it to yourself, and if you find a loving partner who can share life and sex with you, your life can be immeasurably enriched.

Not all children are difficult with regard to the parent's remarriage. Many are supporting, helpful, and encouraging; many are genuinely pleased to see their mother or father established again with a spouse of her or his own. This tends to happen most readily when the parent is remarrying in the same class, social and economic. (In our clinical experience it appears that religion does not seem to weigh very much in older marriages.) Further, where there is more than one child, it is not at all uncommon for the children to divide on the issue, with some being for the remarriage and some against. And of course there are many, many children who are delighted at their parent's new happiness.

Last Word

In highly charged emotional issues with children, the best thing a wise parent can do is act like a wise parent. Just as wise younger parents, in the midst of divorcing, will not force young children to choose between them, so wise older parents will not try to influence older children to take sides. Just as wise younger parents will not allow the young child's unreasonable demands to influence their decisions, so wise older parents will resist cutting their actions to the measure of the children's threats. If basically reasonable parents have raised basically reasonable children, the situation resolves itself and the family is a family again—not as it was before but still a family and often enough a happy one.

What Children Are and Aren't

Divorce puts a spotlight on children. Here's what you can expect:

- Children are childish (even grown children).
- Children are not a reason to date or not date someone. Nor are they a reason to marry someone or not marry someone. You don't need their approval to make a move.
- Children—at least some of them—are unlikely to like anyone you choose.
- Children are not duty-bound to take sides in a divorce.
- Children are entitled to their own opinions and feelings—but so are you.

CHAPTER 13
The Economics of Being Single

The economics of being single divides into two parts: how to have enough income to meet your survival needs (including health insurance) with something left over, and what to do with that something left over. There are many books and institutions (banks, brokerages, insurance companies) that can offer help in money and insurance matters; the question is how to spend what's left.

Beyond Survival: A Buyers' Guide

The Man Goes Shopping

If you're a rich man, you can skip this section; in fact you can skip this whole chapter. If you're not a rich man, but you still have extra income, discretionary income, what should you buy with it?

If you're not interested in women, then you are free to buy anything you please. If you are interested in women, then your most important possession, it turns out, will be a car. This holds true whether you live in a city with good public transportation or in the suburbs (or beyond) where public transportation may be virtually nonexistent. As a man your basic pattern will be to meet somebody, take her someplace else, bring her back to her home, and get yourself home again. If you're in the suburbs, it may be impossible to do any of these things without a car.

It would seem different in the city, with its buses and taxis and sometimes subways and trolleys. But these may involve long waits, especially during the hours you're likely to be out. There's also something unromantic about standing with your lady on a street corner at eleven P.M. waiting for a bus to come—and it's very disheartening to stand alone on a different street corner some time after midnight wondering which will arrive first: a taxi, a bus, or daylight.

More than that, you don't want to be a slave to bus routes, destinations, or schedules; you want to be free to wing it sometimes. Nothing offers this kind of freedom better than an automobile. Further, there's something image-enhancing about owning a car. You become active, not passive; you're in control. In a figurative as well as literal sense, it puts you in the driver's seat. This doesn't mean that you can parlay a car into a conquest with no effort; it does mean that men tend to own cars, and having a car is a great advantage. And the more expensive—or prestigious, or glamorous—the car, the more impressive the driver becomes.

After a car your next investment is a *wardrobe*. It may not be quite true that "clothes make the man," but it is true that the wrong kind of clothes can help unmake him, as far as women are concerned. What are the wrong kind of clothes? Those that are worn, unbecoming, or grossly out of style.

It is also helpful when meeting new women to know how to *dance* at least reasonably well. A few basic steps in a few dances are important. (What are the basic dances? Fox-trot and almost any Latin dance—they're all played sooner or later. It doesn't hurt to know a little disco either.) Remember: dancing is a good way to have physical contact with a woman in a casual, enjoyable manner.

On a less important level are furnishings for the *apartment*, which need be no more than serviceable and fairly clean.

If you meet someone, you'll probably spend more time in her apartment than in yours, and if you choose to live together, it also is more likely to be in her apartment. If the two of you decide that your apartment is better for both of you, you'll both want to change it together. The point is that as a man you are not expected to have great taste in furniture, so it's not something you have to live up to. On the other hand there's no reason to deprive yourself of fine furnishings if that's what you like.

In all it really isn't that hard to be a man and single. Once your survival needs are met, and assuming that you can support yourself, you'll probably be able to meet lots of new people. Without a car life is easier if you live in a metropolitan area; if you don't have a car you may be able to find a friend who does. Or once you get to a meeting place, you may be able to find a woman with her own automobile.

The Woman Goes Shopping

It's harder for the woman, because the woman needs everything.* For initially attracting a man on a limited income, probably the most important factor is *appearance*. This comes down to cosmetics, "beauty services," clothes—and for some women cosmetic surgery.

Cosmetics and cosmetic surgery do many things for women and men. They can make them look younger, and thereby open up a wider range of potential partners for them. At least of equal importance they help them feel better about themselves—so much better, in many cases, that some patients will undergo uncomfortable and expensive cosmetic surgery procedures again and again. Thus more and more women and men are opting for cosmetic surgery, the classic face-lifting operations.

*For a discussion of the unique stresses to which women are subjected, see *The Female Stress Syndrome* by Georgia Witkin-Lanoil (New York: Newmarket Press, 1984).

Cosmetic surgery (and cosmetics) aside, probably the single most important factor for a woman looking for a man is *dressing well*. This doesn't necessarily mean dressing expensively, but unless you make your own clothes, you'll probably spend more than you want to. Is it worth it? There's no way of knowing; but you will be comparing yourself to women who do spend more on clothes and on beauty treatments—and that can make a difference in your own mind especially.

How much should you spend? The answer is, enough to help you feel comfortable. The attractiveness of a woman by no means lies in her gown or her hairstyle but in something more inherent: in the way she meets the world. The woman who meets the world with a sense of confidence meets the world in an attractive way, and men will tend to be attracted to her. If you can have that confidence in an old pair of jeans and a sweatshirt, then they may be enough. However most women (and men) do not feel confident unless they are dressed in what the culture declares is "appropriate"; and unfortunately for "dating" men can do with one suit and a few neckties, but women need dress after dress.

Women will also probably be spending more on their *apartments* than men do. One reason is that the apartment is home to a woman and tends to be more important to women than to men. Another reason is that entertaining—either of a single man or a group of men and women—is usually done in the woman's home. Lavishness in the home is not crucial, but comfort and attractiveness are.

For attracting a partner cars are less useful for the woman than for the man. But it helps if you're not in a city to have a friend who has a car. And if you can afford it, a car offers a great sense of freedom and that can make up for a lot of frustration and irritation—whether related to a man or not. Further, having a car enhances the attractiveness of a woman to the man who doesn't have a car of his own.

Finally a new source of manpower for a woman might be in travel abroad. Apparently many foreign men find American women uniquely attractive, different—more exotic—from the women they know and therefore more alluring. So the over-forty-five American woman looking for romance can often find it abroad where she would not at home. An example is a woman who attended a gourmet cooking course in Switzerland and who left Switzerland married to an Italian man of her age who also liked gourmet cooking. And we know of others like her. It's not exactly a *common* occurrence, but it can happen.

The Picking Order

"Power," said Henry Kissinger, "is the best aphrodisiac." To some extent this is true, but the reasons aren't necessarily the obvious ones. Women are attracted to powerful men (and men to powerful women) not, primarily, because of what that person can do *for* them but because of what that person does *to* them on a deep level. Power over external forces is perceived as an *internal* condition: the powerful person seems to have internal power, not just external power, and this has a magnetic pull. The same is true of money. The person with money is admired *not just* because of what the money can buy but also because the power of money is assimilated to the owner. The wealthy man or woman is actually perceived as being more intelligent and attractive than he or she otherwise might be. Further the possession of wealth or power tends to increase one's self-confidence; and this, as we have said, leads to a universally perceived air of attractiveness.

The Rich

Since rich is desirable, very rich is very desirable, and extremely rich is practically divine. This applies to both sexes. The best way of getting a partner, male or female, is to have a lot of money.

Obviously "a lot" is relative: what is a substantial sum to a divorcée making nineteen thousand dollars per year may be trivial to a widow clipping seven thousand dollars' worth of bond coupons per month. But the point remains: in the search for a partner the rich have an advantage.

Not only do the rich have an advantage over the non-rich, they also have an advantage over the young. The ability of older men with money to attract much younger women is well-known; a more recent phenomenon is the ability of older women with money to attract younger men. This has always been true, but it's happening more often these days and more openly.

The age gaps, however, do differ somewhat. Wealthy older men may choose partners thirty to fifty years younger than they; whereas the age difference between the wealthy older woman and the younger male partner doesn't usually exceed twenty years or so; in effect the woman in her fifties or sixties marries (or relates to) a man in his thirties or forties. This seems to be happening because both women and men are giving themselves permission to do it. What helps obtain this permission is one of the things money can buy—a younger appearance. Cosmetic surgery can do a lot toward making women and men look younger than they are; health spas and beauty treatments can also play a role; and the right wardrobe can do still more. Many a man in his thirties today would feel awkward and defensive about going out with a woman in her fifties who looks "old." But to be seen with a glamorous, radiantly healthy, elegant woman who appears to be in the ageless forties—that's a different matter. In turn the younger-looking older man has a better chance of attracting younger women.

The Dependable

The next best thing to being rich—again, a relative matter—is to have a dependable source of income: *current income* and *retirement income*. Though a steady job is not exactly an aphrodisiac, unemployment can be a positive turn-off to all but the most flexible, adventurous woman. The unemployed man will be subject to extra scrutiny: Why did he lose his job? Why can't he decide what he wants to do? Will his indecision affect other areas of our life? We define ourselves by our jobs; anyone without one is an unknown quantity to everyone else (possibly even to himself!). Likewise, it's assumed, if you're of preretirement age, that you're self-supporting, that your current income is adequate for your needs. But your potential partner may be worried about what happens when you retire. He or she wants to retire also and does not want to have to go on working to support you. And he or she also knows that for the two of you to live on one basic retirement income alone is to live with more anxiety and concern than may be desirable.

What is an adequate retirement income? Again it varies with expectations: for some people seventy thousand dollars per year is barely enough; for others seven hundred dollars per month is princely. In general Social Security income is the minimum. Pension plans, whether government or private, are a good bonus; so are individual investments, IRA funds, Keogh accounts, and annuities; and just plain stocks and bonds, just plain money in the bank (if of a sufficient amount), can help considerably.

The Well-Connected

If you can't be rich yourself, it's good to have a rich relative or two. Children are the best kind, but brothers and sisters will do also. Again rich depends on the context; and in any context it means "able to help in an emergency." What any person fears, and the older one gets the greater the fear, is to take on an emotional commitment and see it turn into a crushing financial burden. A reliable retirement income is one form of insurance against this; another form, less reliable but still useful, is rich relatives.

Of course the relatives must cooperate. They need not make explicit or implicit guarantees, but they must at least let your partner (or potential partner) see that they have money. An invitation to their home is the easiest way.

Sometimes relatives can do more. A fifty-year-old widow, without any income at all, was totally supported by her son. And not just supported: supported elegantly and lavishly—so much so that she appeared to be well-to-do herself. And appearing so, she was attractive to well-to-do men; one of whom eventually married her. By then her partner knew the truth, but he was already in love. And he also had good reason to believe that the son would not abandon his mother if she and her new husband really needed money desperately; his earlier behavior had shown that.

The Professional

Money isn't everything; occupation, status, and physical beauty still count for something. But they count most with people who have money themselves. A man or woman without much money *must* look for a partner who can contribute something financially; the person with money, however, can look for other things. Often this is prestige or status, occupations or positions that seem glamorous, exciting, "superior." What are some of the occupations that many economically secure people are drawn to? Doctors and lawyers of course, some politicians, college professors, architects, writers (if you've been published), psychologists, editors, and acclaimed artists and performers— are a few examples.

Who Picks Whom?

The general trend is that poorer people want to marry up in wealth and richer people want to marry down in age. The rich have a good chance of getting what they want: if not the exact person, at least the desired age bracket. The attractive poorer man has a fairly good chance of marrying a wealthier woman, especially if he marries someone older than he is. The poorer woman with no (or little) retirement income, no rich relatives, no glamorous profession has the hardest time finding a partner, and the difficulty becomes almost insuperable if, ironically, she will only consider a well-to-do man.

Hints on Money and Dating

On a first date: if you're a woman, unless you and he have made previous arrangements, usually the man pays for the whole thing. Increasingly expenses are being shared, but this is by prior discussion and mutual agreement.

On a first date: if you're a man, expect to pay for the evening. If you can't or won't, discuss the arrangements with the woman before you make a definite date.

If you don't have a car, find someone who does. But bear in mind the "rule of the road": if the car owner finds someone to go off with, he or she is *not* honor bound to get you back to your place.

Most dates are made for Saturday night, but that's when entertainment is most expensive. Other nights may be better and so may Sunday afternoon. You know about *museums;* how about *art galleries?* In the suburbs many *libraries* offer free entertainment on Sunday afternoons, ranging from small concert orchestras to jazz groups and baritone soloists. Often they'll sponsor *art exhibitions* and so will schools and other public institutions. Look for the exhibition openings: they're fun to go to; the artists being exhibited are almost always interesting people, delighted to talk to the public; and often there are wine and snacks on hand. If your taste runs to *sports,* small local colleges can provide the excitement (if not the skills) of the major college and professional teams at only a fraction of the cost. The events are listed in local (neighborhood) newspapers, library bulletins, and similar publications; and the telephone is always available.

Last Word

Dates and dating opportunities won't come looking for you. You have to do some exploring yourself, open yourself to new experiences, new ways of thinking. You have to adapt, adjust, begin to find new pleasure in being with new people, doing new things.

Dollar Signs

Money counts for a lot, but it isn't everything. "Crying poverty" on a date—talking about how much things cost and how little money you have to buy them—will not bring you anything of value. If you're short on cash, be good-natured and quiet about it. Even the wealthiest people run short sometimes, but they create a feeling that more money will soon flow into the account, so meanwhile, let's *enjoy* this concert or that glass of wine. To borrow some wise words from the business world:

- **Don't complain.** Constantly moaning about expenses will make you a dreary choice for a companion. Stretch your funds as best you can to cover your needs—apartment, clothing, grooming, entertainment. Then relax and enjoy.
- **Don't explain.** No need to deliver a blow-by-blow account of who got what in the divorce or how upset you are about the dwindling savings account. Who would *you* rather date, a poor pitiful boardinghouse mouse or someone so resourceful that he or she is actually enjoying the challenges of limited finances?

  Besides, you yourself are more valuable than anything money can buy. That's the real bottom line.

CHAPTER 14
Before Remarrying

Many single-again men and women swear that they will never remarry. Why give up freedom for servitude? Why should the man, having practically his pick of women, able to taste all the pleasures of variety and none of the flatness of predictability, why should he decide to cleave to one woman again—and not just live with her but make it legal, make not just an oral commitment but actually put it in writing? And why should a woman escaped from a painful situation, supporting herself, free to do as she pleases, why should she decide to take on again the obligations not of a free companion but a "fettered" wife, expected once more, perhaps, to place the wishes and preferences of another ahead of her own? Why get married at all when you can enjoy many of the benefits and pleasures of marriage without much of the hassling and entangling?

There are many intermediate answers to these questions, but the final answer is that marriage represents a commitment that cannot be duplicated any other way. The marriage certificate is not only a legal document, but it is also an emotional fact, a sign that two people are serious about each other. And it is this fact, the fact that it is a commitment and is felt to be one, that makes remarriage such a problem for many men and women.

And so, faced with the prospect of marrying, faced with the desire to be with one person for the rest of their lives, faced with the fact of being in love and the contrary fact of the pain of their last experience, many men and women react in a very simple way. They become terrified.

Terror, Panic, Fear, Apprehension, and Just Plain Reluctance

Where does this terror come from? The fact is a mixture of factors can be involved, and a man or woman can be influenced by any or all of them.

The Pain of the Past

Men and women whose spouses left them generally view their original marriages as painful, even if up to the point of dissolution the marriage appeared idyllic. Actually such marriages are never idyllic; there's always some radical discontent working, usually on the part of both partners. But there's also a tacit, unspoken agreement to deny the discontent, not to speak of it nor recognize its existence, until finally the whole package becomes too heavy for one partner to bear, and she or he leaves. So the injured party, the one who has been deserted, always has bad memories of the first marriage.

So does the person asking for the divorce—for if the marriage had been good, why would he or she want a divorce in the first place?

On the other hand, widows and widowers with good memories of their marriage have the fewest remarrying problems once the mourning period has been worked through. But unhappily married widows are as reluctant as divorced people to remarry and sometimes even more so. So the first reaction is what if I make the same mistakes I did last time? What if the same thing happens?

The Loss of Autonomy

The loss of a spouse means the loss, at least for a time, of company (and possibly sex), of somebody to depend on during emergencies, of someone to fill at least part of the empty spaces in a life and a home. These losses are hard to take, are in fact traumatic. But once they are absorbed, they also represent a freedom from external restraints, external demands, external responsibilities. The single-again woman and man are on their own, on a mountain by themselves; and when they get past the terror of the loneliness, they begin to enjoy the freedom and the view. Not only a partner is gone; a critic is gone; a demander is gone; a frequent intruder into one's own personal space is gone. And it's incredible how simultaneously bracing and relaxing this newfound feeling of freedom can be.

For some women, those who married fairly young and have not been independent, this feeling of autonomy can be especially energizing. Typically these women have spent most of their adult lives taking care of their husbands and children and never taking care of themselves, never putting themselves first. They've never tested their strength and capacities, except their capacity to be wives and mothers.

There are many useful, interesting, relevant things such women can do; but for the widow or divorcée without much income there is only one thing to do, and that is to go out, get a job, and become at least partially self-supporting. This often has its own terrors, but once they are overcome and the step is taken, the rewards are often immeasurable. And while the monetary rewards are often skimpy and unfair, the reward in self-esteem, self-value is well worth it: she is taking care of herself. She never was really sure that she could do it, but now she is and is doing well. The ability to make money has never been reckoned one of the major virtues of any religion or code of ethics, but the realization that we have the ability does wonders for our spirits.

Facing remarriage, the woman in this position of late-gained, hard-won autonomy fears that she is not only assuming a burden she had been free of but is also giving up an autonomy more precious for being so long doubted and delayed. Panic and terror are natural results.

Sharing the Wealth

For the man the question of newfound economic autonomy rarely arises, since he has usually spent his adult life earning money and trying to earn more of it. But the prospect of marriage now adds to his economic uncertainty: unless his new wife can support herself absolutely, he may have to support them both, and he'd rather not—not necessarily because he's selfish, but because it wouldn't leave enough left over from the necessities to enjoy some of the amenities. Even if the wife intends to go on working—what if something happens to her? Who pays all the bills from that time on? *He* does, and the thought can be a panicky one.

For her part the woman, especially the newly independent woman, worries about losing control of her own money. She has just begun to make some and spend it on herself; is she now supposed to share it? How much will she have left? Is she now supposed to start asking her new husband for money, put herself again in the position of a supplicant? She never knew how uncomfortable that position was until she got out of it; is she now supposed to resume it all over again?

Remembering the double role that money often plays—as a means for buying things and as a symbol for love—it's not hard to see how hesitation about marriage can arise from unresolved problems with money.

The Smarts

People of any age who have been married know that it can be one of the most rewarding of human institutions and it can also be one of the most difficult. They know that marriage involves sharing; they know that they are willing to share, but they also know that they may not get a fair share in return. They are willing to give up independence for interdependence, but they would still like a little bit of the independence balance tipped their way. They know that there will have to be compromises, and not just compromises but also capitulations where they will "have" to do something they would rather not do—visit an in-law or children, for example—because the new spouse expects it of them, expects it perhaps to the point of demanding it.

And they don't know if they can make it. They know much more about marriage than when they were young and married the first time; they know much more than they really *want* to know, and they know (or fear) that they may be a little too stiff to bend the way they used to, a little too rigid to rebound as well, a little too tired to bring the same energy to the marriage as before. They wonder, in other words, whether they can measure up, knowing, many of them, that apparently they didn't measure up the first time. And this doubt feeds other doubts and fears.

The Couple Doesn't Belong Together

Some people marry when they shouldn't or whom they shouldn't, and then regret it. But usually there's plenty of evidence beforehand that the marriage won't work out; the couple simply prefers to ignore it. And there's no doubt that older people also can talk themselves into marriages that simply shouldn't be, ignoring all the warning signals. One of those signals may be panic, which is not so easy to ignore.

The basic answer here is not to try to foresee the future, but to consult the past in a very specific way. That way is to ask, how does it feel to be with that person? The last time together and the time before that, and the time before that—regardless of what the two of you were doing—what were your feelings? Were you happy or discontented? Were you frank or concealing? Were the two of you sharing or withholding? Did you feel then that you wanted to be there more than any other place, that this was the one person you wanted most to be with? Given affirmative answers, it's more likely than not that the marriage will work out; given negative answers, it's more likely that it won't. Given ambiguous answers, it may be best either to wait or see a marriage counselor.

Down with Terror

There are two good things about terror and panic: they don't last forever, and they do let you know that something is going on and give you time to do something about it.

What to do? It depends on the kind of person you are, and whether both of you are in a panic or only one of you. Generally there are three types of advice, all of them good under certain circumstances: Don't just stand there, talk; don't just talk, do something; and get yourself to a counselor.

Don't Just Stand There, Talk

Talking is the first thing anybody should do, and you may as well start by yourselves before you see a counselor. It's probably best to begin with money, because that's a very clear-cut subject. If both of you are working, will both of you continue? If one of you is working and the other has an independent income, will the worker keep on working? If so, for how long? If one of you has money and the other doesn't, how will the non-earner get money? Get it all settled.

If both of you have money, what's the best way of handling it? The best way seems to be the his, hers, and ours approach. In brief: both of you contribute to a general fund out of which common expenses are paid, and each of you keeps the rest of your income for individual expenses. Settle the actual contributions of each, make a start toward settling what expenses are common and what are not, and you're practically done.

But this business of individual expenses does have pitfalls. It's crucial that she or he spends individually, *without fear of censure* from the partner. In this way each partner can retain some of the independence and autonomy that are important in any marriage.

Once money matters are settled, it's important to go on to other matters. But how do you do this; how do you talk about pain remembered, about fears, doubts, hesitations, despairs? How can these be settled the way money problems can be settled? They can't, and that's not what the talk is about. You're not talking now to settle something; you're talking to share—to share precisely those fears, doubts, and hesitations that are so hard to handle.

Often this seems almost impossible to do: first because we're not used to doing it; second because we're afraid it will drive our partner away. But if this does happen, if talk before marriage, talk during courtship, does cause a partner to flee, imagine what would happen after marriage, when the conflicts that inevitably arise will never be resolved because they will never be discussed. In fact, however, the kind of talking we're describing almost always is helpful.

Why? Because the operative word is *sharing,* which is really the giving of a gift, the gift of yourself, of some of the deepest parts of yourself. You're not trying to get anything *done;* you're not asking for anything except attention and understanding; you're sharing an important part of your life. When your partner understands this, which is generally the case, most often she or he offers two gifts in return. One is the gift of love. The other is the expression of some of the same fears, doubts, and hesitations that you've been expressing, coming from the same deep places, arousing in you the same deep response. So you understand each other, have experienced each other in an entirely new way, and the consequences may be enormous. Even if nothing specific has been settled, everything seems better, easier, more manageable; the doubts seem more insubstantial and vague, the strengths and love more sturdy and solid.

Not all partners feel terror; some are quite sure of what they want. But talking to them of your anxieties and fears usually has the same overall effect. They too recognize the talk as a sharing and a gift; they too tend to respond with love. They also tend to respond with cheerfulness and optimism, and this can help greatly. And again: if your talk does frighten them off, it's almost certainly because they've got some deep-rooted problems that they're not facing—and when a person can neither talk about nor listen to real emotions openly expressed, he or she may not be the most desirable mate.

It's not that talk solves all problems. Not everybody can reveal her or his deepest feelings; men especially, full of despair and anxiety, may be unable to share them, may still play the macho male, pretending to a confidence they do not have, fooling the woman (but not completely), fooling themselves (but not completely). So some severe difficulties may remain. But talking, sharing emotions, can only help, and even if some residue of doubt remains, often it helps to remove at least some of the obstacles to what can be a happy, successful marriage.

Don't Just Talk; Do Something

Jerry is in his late forties: tall, broad, a little heavy, hair thinning but still dark. He's been a salesman, moderately successful, of heavy industrial equipment most of his working life.

> As soon as I met Emma that was it. I knew immediately she was the one I wanted. I met her in the lobby of a movie house. She was going one way; I was going the other. I looked; she looked. I said hello, and that was it.
>
> She's gorgeous, a couple of years younger than me. Great figure. Great sense of humor, real quick wit. Always upbeat, always a lot of fun.
>
> I was a widower—my wife had died a few years before. She was a divorcée. Her husband had left her: met a rich older woman and left. Now he's alone and doing lousy, and sometimes it bothers Emma. But not much; he really hurt her. That was about the same time I lost my wife.

Well, we hit it off right away. From that time on, we stayed with each other whenever we could. Her place or my place. Her place was nicer, so we usually met there. It didn't make much difference.

I always figured we'd get married, and I thought Emma did too. I figured a year or so of playing around, and then make it legal. God knows, I couldn't think of another woman, and I was sure she felt the same way.

That was in Chicago. What happened was all of a sudden I had a big opportunity in New York City. A construction supply place was up for sale, and my brother heard about it. Between the two of us we could manage the down payment and the work, and the business was a good one. But we had to take over in three months. So right away I spoke to Emma, and she got all excited. It really was a good deal. I asked her to marry me, and she said sure. And I thought that was that.

Next day I began talking about arrangements—when and where, who to invite, everything. And she began to hem and haw. And I said what's the matter? And she said maybe we're making a mistake. And I said what mistake. And she said I don't know.

So this went on and on, week after week. She tells me she loves me. She tells me she wants to marry me. She just doesn't want to do anything to get married. All right: we took a blood test and got the license, but that was it. Meanwhile time is passing by and we're not getting married, and I'm getting confused and also a little angry.

A week or so before we were supposed to take over, my brother and I had to fly down to make some final arrangements. On the plane I'm thinking of Emma. And I decide that things have gone on long enough.

We fly back a few days later—that was about a week or so before the final move—and I go to see Emma that night. She's nervous, and I don't say a thing.

Next morning I sit her down in a chair, and I sit opposite her. I ask her if she loves me, and she says yes. I ask her if she's sure, and she says yes. So I stand up and say let's go, and she says where. And I say we're getting married.

There's a dead stop, and Emma says when. And I say now. And she doesn't say anything, but she turns white. I say, you love me, right? She says yes. And you want to marry me, right? Yes. So let's go. What can she say? She's stuck.

We get in my car and drive to a small place outside of Chicago to find a J.P. All the time Emma's not saying a word. But as soon as we come near the J.P.'s office, she says something. She wants breakfast.

So we stop and have breakfast, and the truth is she's eating like a horse. Which I take to be a good sign, because if she's really upset she won't be able to eat. And meantime she's still white, and I'll tell you what we're talking about. We're talking about the Chicago Cubs.

And then we went to the J.P., without Emma saying a word, and his secretary came in, and he married us. It wasn't a bad ceremony at all. And then I kissed the bride, and all of a sudden she started to smile. It was the biggest, broadest, most beautiful smile you'll ever see. I asked her how she felt and she said terrific. So we called up our kids and some of our friends and family, and told them to come to Emma's place that night. We brought champagne and cold cuts and cake and tons of other stuff, and we had the best wedding party anybody ever had. A few days later we came to New York, and everything's been great ever since.

We'll never know what was bothering Emma, although it was probably a combination of all the things we mentioned earlier. What's clear is that in this case talking didn't help: Emma's problem was too deep and hurt too much. What's also clear is that Jerry did the right thing.

How do we know? Didn't he coerce her in a way? The answer is no. According to Jerry, once Emma had admitted that she wanted to marry him, she had to go through with it. But that wasn't true, as they both knew. If there were any real basis to Emma's fears, she would never have married Jerry no matter what she had admitted.

What she needed was an optimistic, cheerful partner; and had they had the year or so Jerry had envisaged, she would probably have come around by herself. But they didn't have a year; they had only a few months—which finally came down to a few days. What Emma needed then was a concentrated dose, a year's worth of optimism and hope packed into a few hours, and that's what Jerry gave her.

Obviously not all partners of reluctant, yes-no spouses can do what Jerry did, nor is it always necessary. But if the man or woman is certain of his or her own feelings, and just about as certain of the partner's, then he or she might very well take a strong initiative. It need not be threatening—marry me or we're through—but matter-of-fact: I'm making arrangements, buying invitations, setting a date . . . taking all the steps, including reserving a car for the drive to the clergyman or J.P. (Justice of the Peace). Most often the reluctant partner will go along (if not, then counseling is necessary), and if the signs have been read properly, more often than not the results will be more or less terrific.

Get Yourself to a Counselor

Couples having trouble remarrying are appearing in marriage counselors' offices more and more often. What do they find there? Basically a chance to talk and a chance to listen: to talk about real things, deeply felt things, to listen with sympathy and understanding. There's no magic in it and usually no real strain; it's not usually a matter of digging deep into one's childhood and uncovering long hidden neurotic conflicts. It's more a question of exploring current feelings under the guidance of a person who will tend to keep you and your partner on track, who will encourage the expression of emotions and their acceptance by the partners, who will work toward a resolution of problems, and who, finally, if the partners are really not well suited to each other will help them recognize it. It doesn't usually take much time; once a week for one, two, or three months is usually enough.

Old problems. Besides helping a couple overcome the fear of remarriage, counselors can perform the crucial function of helping them explore what was wrong with their first marriage.

Unhappy marriages don't just happen; they happen because something has gone wrong: the initial choice of a partner or something along the way. Some attitudes may have been brought to that first marriage that had to spell trouble sooner or later; some expectations may have been so unrealistic as to constitute a virtual time bomb; some habits of thought or behavior may have been so irritating as to become unbearable after a time. Something went wrong that was never set right, and ultimately the marriage broke down.

Men and women unhappy in their previous marriages know this or strongly suspect it. That's one reason that they're so apprehensive about remarrying: they don't want to make the same mistake twice; and they're not always sure what that first mistake was. (Was it putting the children first? Was it visiting my parents so often—but I thought he liked them! Was it sex? Was I too fussy? Did I neglect my home life—but she never seemed to mind. . . .)

Most people in this predicament do considerable soul-searching, even those who feel themselves the injured party, who feel that the other is to blame for the breakup. For there is always the nagging suspicion that some of the blame must be theirs, that even if they hadn't done anything wrong, they could at least have done something to make things better, have seen more clearly, behaved more intelligently. And most people resolve that this time it will be different, they won't make the same mistake twice.

Communication. The crucial resolution is to communicate. There's a theory that all marital problems can be traced to a failure of communication—not of name calling and sarcasm but of genuine communication. Whether or not this is true, there's not the slightest doubt that the quality of a marriage is practically synonymous with the quality of communication, and that poor communication can only mean trouble.

The other habits that undermined the first marriage can also mean trouble, especially where there's apprehension. In brief when there has been an unhappy first marriage and now another marriage is in the making, it is imperative that the couple talk to each other about what they expect, what they fear, what they'd like, what they're prepared to do; and if they have trouble talking, then they should go where they're encouraged to talk, and listen, in the friendly, encouraging atmosphere of a counseling office.

Sex. There's no way of knowing how many people don't marry because they have sexual problems. We're not talking about physiological problems, such as we discussed in Chapter 11; we're talking about the sexual problems of healthy people. One was mentioned in Chapter 10: inhibited sexual desire. There are six others, three that apply to women and three that apply to men. The women's problems are lack of arousal (excitement stage), problems in having orgasms, and vaginismus, where the vagina closes involuntarily when something comes into contact with it, effectively barring intercourse. The man's problems include impotence, especially secondary impotence, where the man cannot hold an erection; premature ejaculation, where the man cannot control his orgasm but comes too

quickly for both his own and his partner's pleasure; and retarded ejaculation, where the man cannot ejaculate at all, at
least while having intercourse with his partner. (Contrary to
what many people think, retarded ejaculation is not a boon to
intercourse but deeply troubling to the woman and extremely
frustrating for the man.) These are the sexual dysfunctions.

The good news is that the most common dysfunctions
are highly curable, which means that the symptoms disappear
and the dysfunction vanishes. The other good news is that in
some cases self-cure is possible—*but not self-prescription* without knowledge. What may seem to be a common-sense remedy
may not work at all; and the most striking example is premature ejaculation. Men with this problem typically try to cure by
distraction—thinking of something other than sex, and this is
almost guaranteed to fail. On the other hand given the right approach premature ejaculation, which is probably the most common of male sexual dysfunctions, is also probably the most
curable.

Do-it-yourself sex therapy has been presented in some
books; they may or may not be helpful, depending on your
problem and what you bring to it. If you do read the books and
still have the problem, don't let that be the end of it. Counseling with a well-trained sex therapist can usually be effective
where books cannot and can make a striking improvement not
only in one's sex life but also in one's outlook in general. In
brief: before giving up on sex or marriage because of a sexual
dysfunction, consult a trained, skilled sex therapist.

Prenuptial Agreements

One way of resolving tensions about money is the prenuptial
agreement. This is exactly what it sounds like: a legal agreement fashioned by attorneys and entered into before marriage,
concerning the disposition of each partner's assets. Generally
the documents describe the circumstances under which one

partner does and does not have access to the other's assets—
and to how much.

Most people have heard of prenuptial agreements, but to
our knowledge they're still fairly uncommon. Why? Because
they introduce an element of cold calculation that may not be
very pleasant. The speaker is a thirty-eight-year-old woman
named Helen.

Ralph left me a lot of money when he died—at least,
it seemed a lot to me. He also left me a stockbroker
he had confidence in, and with good reason. He had
done very well for Ralph, and he kept on doing very
well for me.

I started dating again a few years after Ralph died,
but nothing serious. I was thirty-five or so. Then I
met Jonathan and we fell in love. It was almost in-
stantaneous. A few months later we decided to
marry.

That's when I began having money worries. I had
a feeling that Jonathan had about as much money as
I had, but I wasn't sure. What I was sure of was that
I didn't want to give up control of what I had. It
wasn't that I thought he was marrying me for my
money, it was . . . something else. Jonathan is a few
years older than me but he looks five years
younger—he's absolutely handsome, gorgeous smile,
great physical shape. A real head-turner with the ladies. So I guess I thought it couldn't possibly last—
he'd grow tired of me one of these days. I said I
wanted a prenuptial agreement.

Jonathan said sure, whatever I wanted was fine.
So we got together with our lawyers for the first
meeting, and the questions began: assets, stocks,
bonds, bank accounts, the whole thing.

I started to get depressed. We had another meeting with the lawyers scheduled for the week after,

and I spent the whole time moping around. Something was wrong. I didn't know whether I wanted to
marry Jonathan after all. I wasn't sure he was right
for me. I wasn't sure things would work out. I just
didn't know.

The morning of that second meeting I woke up
and I knew immediately what was wrong. It was the
agreement. It was taking all the romance out of the
marriage. I don't know if romance is the right word.
I think I mean spontaneity or commitment. Or love.
Whatever it was, it was spoiling everything.

I phoned Jonathan and said let's forget about the
prenuptial business. He agreed, and we phoned the
lawyers and called the whole thing off.

I felt much better, scared, but better—certainly
better about marrying Jonathan. We were married
two years ago, and so far everything's been fine. I'm
still a little worried about money, but at least I'm
feeling good about me and Jonathan, and that's the
main thing.

There's no doubt that prenuptial agreements can have this effect, the effect of dampening a marriage, of bringing a sour note
into what ought to be a harmonious situation. There's no doubt
that it implies a certain reserve, a withholding of full commitment; and even though the emotional commitment may be
fully there, the apparent questioning of it can cause some discomfort. Again what's often involved is not giving up money
but giving up control—when the last time we gave up control
was during the trauma of the event that left us single.

For people who need this sense of control, the prenuptial
agreement may be helpful. It settles a matter they find deeply
disturbing and lets them go into more important things, such
as being together. In other words, and this is worth repeating,
the wish to have a prenuptial agreement is not a reflection on the
love or commitment one partner feels toward the other, but re-
flects a deep need to retain some feeling of self-determination.

So therefore: do what feels best. If you opt for romance and your partner opts for a legal document, it's worth remembering that he or she is probably acting from a deeply wounded part of the self. If you're the one who wants the agreement, understand that your partner may feel hurt, and that the best remedy for both of you is to sit down together and talk as openly as possible about what's on your minds.

Commitment

What can be done to make the remarriage a good one, a lasting one? Some ideas have been touched on already. Find out, as well as you can, how you contributed to the problems of the first marriage and try to correct it. Learn to communicate—another way of saying learn to talk about the things that are important to you and that you're afraid your partner may take the wrong way—whatever the wrong way might be. Try to have reasonable expectations of what the marriage might entail. If you're a man, try to understand how strongly your new wife may cherish her newfound sense of autonomy and treat this as something to be valued, not as a threat to your masculinity. If you're a woman, and your partner is worried about his sexuality, try to understand how devastating the waning of sexual prowess can be to a man, how he may withdraw from sex as a result—and how you can provide reassurance better than anyone else. For both of you understand that as you grow older, sex may be slightly different from what it was before but can even be better. Try to free sex from its symbolic values—of submission for the woman, of machismo for the man—and enjoy it for its own sake. And try also to remember where the other is coming from: a trauma has been experienced and recovered from, but there may still be scars and residual pain; and this calls for concern and caring, not for recriminations and anger. In short tell your partner to read this book.

That brings us to here; what comes after? Beyond the "normal" problems, there's one problem that affects remarrying men and women more than any other group. It's the problem of divided loyalties, of distributed commitments.

Married the first time, we're expected to commit ourselves to our new partners above everybody else, especially parents and friends. Even possessive parents, who find it almost impossible to let their children go, usually give at least lip service to the idea that the spouse comes first. (And deep within themselves these parents know that this is as it should be; that while parents should not be simply abandoned, they can no longer have first claim on their children's affections, time, and attention.) Siblings, friends, and more distant relatives, of course, have a much easier time. In fact, when a young couple today argues about commitment, it is more common for the conflict to be career versus spouse rather than parents versus spouse.

But though we can dissolve the marriage commitment, we can't dissolve our commitment to grandchildren or children who may need money, time, and help. We can't dissolve the emotional investments in other people that we have been building for years. And this can cause real problems.

Bea is about fifty-five years old, small and slender, dark and reserved. She is an airline reservation clerk.

When I met Marty, it seemed like a perfect match. We were both about fifty-two, both widowed a few years earlier, and we both liked the same things. We were married six months later.

For the first year everything went fine. We did things together; visited my daughter Barbara and her husband every so often, had Marty's two sons over from college whenever they could make it. I didn't think there would be any problems. I thought we were both reasonable people.

Then something exciting happened: Barbara told us she was having a baby. Naturally we were delighted. It was my first grandchild—Barbara is an only child—and it was just thrilling. We talked about it all the time, Barbara and I. She wanted to keep working to the last minute, so we used to go shopping together on Saturdays. There are so many things to buy for a new baby, and it's so much fun to look. Marty made jokes about never seeing me, but he didn't really mind. Besides, it wasn't true.

When the baby came—it was a boy, Charles David—we were all at the hospital. It was a long labor, but the baby was beautiful. We visited Barbara every day at the hospital, and drove her and Charles back to their place when she was discharged— Frank, my son-in-law, was getting some last-minute things ready in the baby's room.

You know what babies are like. They're adorable, but they need so much time and attention. And you never get enough sleep. Barbara was just exhausted, so I used to go there after work to help out. I told Marty I would fix dinner for him in the morning, but he said not to bother. He's a pretty good cook himself. He said he would have some hot meals ready for me when I came home, but most of the time I was too tired to eat.

It took a few weeks for Barbara to get her strength back, and for her and Frank to get into the baby routine. I wanted them to have a little fun, so I said I would baby-sit for them. You can't imagine how grateful they were. Marty and I would go over on Saturday and give them the night off, and sometimes they would come over on Sunday, drop Charles David off, and visit their friends. It was a perfect arrangement. The baby was such a good baby and so beautiful.

Then Marty and I had a bad fight. His lodge was having a big picnic one Sunday, and he wanted us to go. I happened to know that that was a day when

Barbara and Frank were planning to bring the baby over—and I'm not too crazy about picnics anyway, or his lodge brothers. I told him to go without me. He got very angry. He made a big fuss about not going if I wouldn't go. I was his wife; I was supposed to go, that kind of thing. I just let it pass. I didn't see any reason why he couldn't go by himself, and I told him so. P.S.: He didn't go. He stayed home and sulked.

A few days later he said he wanted to go to the movies that Saturday. There was this picture he had to see. And he wanted to go out to eat. Well, he knows that on Saturday night we baby-sit for Barbara and Frank, and it was out of the question. I was surprised he even thought of it.

For a few weeks everything was quiet, and then one Thursday night Frank says he wants to talk to me. I have to choose. I have to choose between him and the baby, between being his wife or everybody else's mother. And I had to choose right away, because he couldn't take it much longer.

I never heard anything so ridiculous. Of course I didn't tell him that. But he was jealous of a baby! A grown man, fifty-four years old, and he can't understand why I might want to spend some time with my children and grandchildren. Anyway I told him I didn't like ultimatums, and he blew up.

He left that weekend, and we've been divorced for three or four months now. The truth is I didn't think he'd go through with it. I thought he was more grown-up. I didn't mind when his sons came over, why should he mind my spending time with my grandchild?

I still see them a lot, but not as much as I used to because they're starting to take the baby with them when they go places. I get lonely when I'm not with

them. I miss Marty a little; he was nice to be with
when he was reasonable, and I guess one of these
days I'll start looking for someone else again. But
I'm feeling depressed. Barbara and Frank are thinking of moving out of state, and I'm not sure what I'll
do if that happens.

It's not easy to spend less time with the children than before;
it's not easy to spend time with a new spouse's children when
your own need you so much more; it's not easy to spend less
than you'd like for a grandson's birthday present because you
and your spouse are saving for a trip abroad (or he gave less to
his grandchild). In brief: it's not easy to give first commitment
to your new spouse, not to your families, children, and grandchildren.

This is not to say that nothing is important except the
spouse, or that the spouse must inevitably come first in all
things. It's simply not true that a lock of the loved one's hair is
worth more than all the gold in Araby, or that the spouse's desire to see a movie always takes precedence over the need to get
some work done at home. Inherently their needs are no more
important than our own.

But they're no less important than everybody else's; and
the habitual flouting of those needs, the habitual placing of the
spouse somewhere in the background, to be attended to *after*
the "important" things are done (such as spending an hour on
the telephone with a daughter)—*always to be attended to
later*—this is where trouble enters. And it's the kind of trouble
that can eventually destroy a marriage.

Last Word

It's true that many people hesitate about remarrying because
they're afraid of repeating the mistakes of the past. But the past
is not only to be feared; it's to be learned from. Even now

you've learned a lot, if only that you, like everybody else, can make mistakes. But you've also become sensitized to problem situations; you know what it feels like when deep discord sets in. And hopefully you have some ideas about how to handle it now: talk, discuss, share, if you can; and if you can't, or if the talk seems to be making things worse, see a counselor.

So if that person does come along, that man or woman you want to spend the rest of your life with, marry. Marry and enjoy each other; marry and enjoy the world; marry and enjoy life. We are a bonding species, pulled apart by the need for autonomy, drawn together, drawn close, by the need for intimacy. Marry for love; find autonomy in that marriage, and have the best of all worlds.

Living Together—True or False?

So your daughter says she's moving in with her fiancé, your son says he's trying a "trial marriage" with his girlfriend, your boyfriend has invited you to rent a beach house with him, and your widowed mother announces she's sharing an apartment with a POSSLQ (person of the opposite sex sharing living quarters) rather than remarrying. . . . Many people who are nervous about marriage think of living together as a good way station.

Does practice make perfect? Does it make any difference at all? Since the number of people trying cohabitation (living together) is double what it was ten years ago, the answer is worth finding out. Learn the surprising facts by taking our quiz.

True or false?

_____ 1. Living together usually leads to marriage.
_____ 2. Cohabitation first makes for a happier marriage later.

_____ 3. Trial marriage lowers the risk of divorce.
_____ 4. Men report greater satisfaction from cohabitation than women.
_____ 5. Living together can speed up the wedding date.

Answers:

1. False. Only one in three couples who live together end up married. One of three cohabiting couples break up within two years. In general, women hope it will lead to marriage; men think of it as the equivalent of going steady—they get companionship and sex in one terrific package deal. A word to the wise: If you have your sights set on engagement, get a ring, not an apartment.
2. False. Those who live together first and then marry still fight about money, autonomy, adultery, and sexual problems. The good news is that they handle problems with less bickering; they handle divorce with less acrimony.
3. False. In fact, most researchers report that risk of divorce among cohabs is slightly higher. A University of Wisconsin study indicates that within ten years of the wedding,thirty-eight percent of cohabitors split up, as opposed to twenty-seven percent who never lived together. One reason may be that cohabiting couples have already practiced thinking of the relationship as something they can get out of. A second reason is that people open to cohabitation may be more open to divorce.
4. True. Though both men and women agree that living together, as opposed to dating, means less phoniness and getting to know each other better, cohabitation involves more money and more work for women, even if the couple has decided on a fifty-fifty split. Women care more about pretty towels in the bathroom, special party foods, and art on the walls than men—so they

end up paying for it out of their own purses. This tends to be less true in marriage: she feels more comfortable asking for the money, or bills are more likely to be shared.

5. True. Couples who live together do marry more quickly, usually within two years. Non-cohabiting couples average a three-year wait. On the other hand, the cohabiting couple also tends to break up more quickly, within the same two years! Living together speeds up the rate of getting to know each other and coming to a conclusion.

My advice is to look at living together as an alternative to marriage, not a trial marriage. If it turns into marriage and that's what you wanted, that's a plus. If not, you found out what you needed to know about your partner.

Remarriage: Is It Right?

People who have divorced often are skittish about remarriage, and their fears often obscure the relationship. Here's a checklist—not necessarily foolproof but certainly helpful—to guide you in separating green-light situations from the red. Check the statements that apply to your situation:

_____ 1. The spouse-to-be is threatened by your strength and freedom and seems likely to try to take it away.

_____ 2. You can't agree on how to handle your money. (I recommend three separate accounts: his, hers, ours. A spouse who wants to control all the money wants to control you too.)

_____ 3. The new spouse is abusive, either verbally or physically.

_____ 4. The new spouse has many of the same unattractive qualities of the old one. (We gravitate toward the familiar, and that's not always best.)

_____ 5. You can communicate—that means talk!—openly with each other about any subject.

_____ 6. You're committed to staying married. (Studies show that people who divorce and people who stay married have the same number and same types of problems! But the married ones stay married because they promised to.)

_____ 7. You feel your spouse-to-be cares for *you*, not just your money, sexuality, or status.

_____ 8. You enjoy being with him or her. (Eighty percent of couples who are happily married say that being each other's best friend is the reason for their success.)

_____ 9. You feel deeply connected; you feel you understand each other's desires and dreams.

Total for questions 1 through 4: _____ **Red light!** DON'T go ahead if you checked any question from 1 through 4. You're about to enter a dangerous situation that would take work to make it work.

Total for questions 5 through 9: _____ **Green light.** Go ahead with wedding plans if you checked any of the items in this group *and* no items in questions 1-4. Though no one can guarantee the success of a marriage, it seems you have the basics for a good relationship in place.

CHAPTER 15
Security

Security means different things to different people, but as we grow older, it increasingly comes to mean two specific things: having enough money to get along on (and fall back on in an emergency) and not being alone. Insecurity is the reverse: not having enough money and being alone. The amount of money each person "needs" varies enormously; as was mentioned in Chapter 13, these are matters best taken up with financial experts.

Sometimes it seems too late to expect substantial improvement in income, but loneliness is something else. It is never too late to stop being lonely. But there's one basic rule. If we find ourselves without a partner, we cannot afford to put all our hopes in one basket: that soon a partner will come along.

Because society teaches women and men that to be unmarried is to be incomplete, a partner becomes more central. But the woman or man who can be happy *only* with that certain special someone and sees no point in developing other relationships may never find that partner and never find a way out of loneliness. Because of the favorable sex ratio for men, they usually have a better chance than women of finding a partner; and as they grow older, men tend to take advantage of those odds, to end their casual sleeping-around ways and settle down seriously.

But security doesn't have to depend at all on having a permanent, long-term, sleep-in partner. We have one totally practical alternative: to join or establish a network of people with interests similar to our own and a desire to help in emergencies, to be there when needed—we for them; they for us.

There are many such networks, and we'll talk about some of them shortly. But the basic need is to be where those networks exist, and the first question may be: is your present dwelling place the right place to be?

Moving Out: The Younger Single

One of the big shocks of sudden singlehood is the rise in living expenses, especially housing. If you were each contributing $500 a month for a $1,000 apartment and your roommate leaves, suddenly you're lease-bound to pay it all. The stakes are even higher in a house or condo: you won the place in the divorce but you can't afford the upkeep. Moving out may be so expensive you don't want to do that either.

For younger singles, cost considerations drive their search for a place to live. The good news is that you may have more choices than you thought.

Find a less expensive place. A move may be expensive, but perhaps not as expensive as a long-term drain on your finances. You may want to consider moving to a smaller place— after all, one less person will be living with you—or one farther away from expensive suburbs and cities. Your consolation, especially if your spouse has been fussy about his surroundings, is that you can now decorate exactly as you please.

Find more money. Try to get a better-paying job. If you can't, invest your money in a safe fund that will pay dividends, or do some moonlighting if you have the energy—keeping busy helps. Another way to find money: slow down your spending.

Get a roommate. If you interview carefully, a roommate can not only help relieve some of the financial pressure but stave off loneliness and be a friend.

Going Home

Another option is going home to live with your parents or other relatives. But unless your parents are phenomenally understanding, this can be a very complex arrangement! Even if you're thirty years old, your parents will always see you as their child and may treat you that way. They may even impose house rules and curfews. If you must return home, choose a room that's as apartment-like as possible to give you the most privacy. Look for one with its own entrance to the outdoors—this way you can come and go as you please (and have guests in). It also helps if you can do some of your own cooking and have access to your own refrigerator, so every meal is not a replay of your childhood. Pay rent, and clean and care for the rooms you use—this will help your "landlord" see that you can stand on your own two feet.

Moving Out: The Retired Single

Your wife or husband has died or left; your children are no longer with you, and suddenly your home or apartment seems too big, holds too many painful memories. It's time to get out, go someplace else. Or is it?

If it's less than a year after the divorce or death, then it's not time enough. Counselors, psychotherapists, psychologists agree almost unanimously that after a trauma it's unwise to make *any* major change in your life until *at least* a year has passed. It takes at least that long for the shock to be integrated and the real self to re-emerge. It's even better to wait two years, but one year is the minimum—not only for a new home but also for a new job.

And then what? If possible, stay where you are, at least as regards your home. Uprooting is hard on everybody, and it gets harder as we grow older and have to uproot ourselves from places where we have sunk our roots deep. As we live in a neighborhood, we evolve our own sort of network—people who, if they do not actively care for us, at least know us, are at least nominally interested in us and aware of our habits, will greet us, will probably help us in an emergency. They form part of a familiar milieu, and there is no inherent reason to give them up. There is especially no reason to give up people with whom we have established good relationships.

This doesn't mean that there are *no* reasons. Sometimes they arrive in the form of opportunities: a better job, a new marriage, a new goal or career. Sometimes there are financial constraints: for the divorced especially, the old place may be too hard to maintain on a new, lower income. And sometimes, as we grow older, a more poignant reason presents itself; our human milieu, the friends who helped form the fabric of our lives, die or move away.

In that case it may be time to think of moving. It may be when we can't make friends with the new people in our old neighborhood, or when, along with the old friends who left, the old institutions went also—the churches, temples, meeting places we used to gather in. If the people we value and the places we value have left us, and if we cannot reach new places because of transportation problems—*and if we cannot find new people to take us there*—then it's probably time to move. Where to?

Broadly speaking, there are four basic choices: moving in with your children (discussed soon), moving to an ordinary apartment, perhaps smaller than your present place, moving to a retirement apartment, and moving to a retirement hotel. Each has advantages and disadvantages, but for deciding among

254 Living in the World

them in a specific area there is one helpful criterion: a mixed environment, consisting of people of different ages, at different stages in the life cycle, is the healthiest psychologically, and therefore physiologically as well.

Standard Apartment

If you can afford it, if you are now and intend to remain active for some time, and especially if you're employed (or self-employed) full-time, a standard apartment is usually the best choice. Generally located more centrally than the retirement hotel or apartment complex, they help keep you closer to the heart of things, the places you want to be. And they usually do provide a mixed environment: single people just starting out, couples of all ages with children of all ages, older single people, some of whom may be very much like yourself. In our view it's worth spending a little more (without straining yourself), or renting a smaller space than you'd really prefer, to enjoy the stimulating variety of the ordinary, standard apartment.

Retirement Hotels and Apartments

Retirement hotels are found in every state, and although they're all different, they share some common features. The fee usually includes not only housekeeping services but also meals—two or three—communally eaten in the dining room. (In some hotels you may be asked to share a room with another person of the same sex.) Nursing care is usually available, as is a physician making daily visits.

One advantage of the senior hotel is that you can almost always find people there in your age bracket. Another advantage is that your routine needs are looked after; and a third is that medical care is available.

There are also disadvantages. One is that, since everybody knows each other, the average hotel is not unlike a college dormitory, buzzing with rumors and gossip; and if you don't like being talked about or hearing others talked about, you may not be comfortable there. Second, there are usually many more women around than men, so if you're a woman hoping to find a new man, you'll probably be disappointed. Also interests and outlooks tend to be narrow—children and health are the main topics of conversation—and transportation is often limited to one bus leaving the place in the morning and returning at night.

Since seventy-year-olds tend to be the "youngsters" there, the first consideration is to make sure you're in the right age category. If you are, and if you need—or want—a little help in doing your daily chores, and if you don't mind (or actually enjoy) living in an essentially closed environment, then the retirement hotel may be just what you're looking for. But investigate them carefully; there are great variations in quality among them.

Most states by now offer retirement apartments, apartment buildings or complexes devoted wholly to retired people, usually over the age of fifty-five. Typically they're subsidized by government and/or private agencies, and typically rents are low. In some cases means tests are required. They're available for both single and married people.

Retirement apartments are something of a cross between standard apartments and retirement hotels. Like the hotels, medical care is usually available, and usually many group activities are planned aimed specifically for the tenants. So some of the turned-in atmosphere of the hotel is there. Also, without families, without couples with young children, the environment isn't as mixed as it is in standard apartments.

On the other hand retirement apartments usually offer a more varied mix than the hotels. First there are *couples* there; second the age bracket usually goes down to the mid-fifties (and up into the seventies), so there's a broader group of people to meet. Also many of these "retired" people hold steady jobs and have interests other than health and children to talk about; and finally, with a generally younger group of people, there will be more automobile owners and drivers there, who may be able to get you away from the place more often. Of course you do have to see after your own housekeeping, cooking, and shopping needs.

It may be for you if you can't afford your own apartment and/or consider the presence of children more a hassle than a pleasure. It may also be for you if (1) you can find them, since they're not really common yet; and (2) if you can pass the means test that may be required. Because of the availability of medical care, and because of the rather more stimulating environment than that of the typical retirement hotel, a good retirement apartment becomes very attractive for the sixty-and-over single person. As usual you have to check each one carefully to make sure it meets your needs.

Living with Children

If you love your children, why not move in with them, especially if they ask you to?

Some older single parents do this with no trouble, some who move in together fight all the time, and some turn into children themselves. In other words it's also something to think about very carefully. Problems can arise, even if you consider yourself to be an independent, reasonably self-reliant person.

Basically it's hard for you to stop being a parent and planning your children's lives ("giving advice" is what you might call it; "interfering" is what they might call it), because you've been their parent all their lives. And basically it's hard for the children not to be *your* parent because in the first place they're parents already and in the second place it's *their* house. There's nothing like running a house to make a person assume the prerogatives of parenthood.

So the possibility of clashes is built into the situation, and sometimes clashes are hard to avoid. But the danger (and many older people feel this) is that to avoid clashes, to give up and simply acquiesce to the children's "demands," is to take the first step toward dependence and, finally, senility. What to do?

The answer is to clarify as many issues as you can think of *before you make any move*. Some of these issues might be money, grandchildren, and the daily routine.

Money. We said in Chapter 13 that when older people remarry the best financial arrangement is his/hers/theirs: each contributes to a general fund and also keeps a portion for her or his own use. The same thing applies here. If you have an income you must insist that some of it go into the general household fund and some of it you keep. As far as is possible, don't shortchange yourself or them. Don't give the lion's share to them and keep a trifle for yourself (because they "can use it more" than you can), and don't withhold from them because they don't need it. You need to know that you are paying your fair share, and they need to know it also.

Grandchildren. Your grandchildren are your children's children, not yours. This is hard to remember sometimes, because you love them so, but you must understand it to be true. What it means is that on your part you do not raise their children, they do. What it means on their part is that you are not a built-in baby-sitter; baby-sitting is a service you perform for them. And what *that* means is that when you do baby-sit for them you expect recognition. One way is for them to provide you with transportation, if you don't have your own car or can't drive; another possibility is for them to hire another baby-sitter and take you out for a family "date."

You need transportation because you *must* meet people with your specific interests, and you *must* socialize with them. If you can get there by yourself, fine; if not, they must drive or arrange to get you there. This cannot be at their discretion, because of their good nature; it has to be because they are reciprocating for your efforts on their behalf.

Routines and responsibilities. It's helpful to all when you're flexible enough to fit into any reasonable routine and discreet enough not to interfere with theirs. What's also important is that you insist on discharging your responsibilities: housework, yardwork, repairs, cooking, whatever.

There are a few possible danger areas here: that you'll do things your way, not their way, and that you may not do things well enough. Here it's reasonable for you to be the one to concede. It's their house, though you contribute to it, and they have a right to prescribe how things should be done and what standards should be met. Best thing is to grin and agree.

Networks

In the end where you live is less important than being able to get from there to where you want to go: the working places, the shopping places, the visiting places, the recreation and/or cultural places that witness your life's activities.

To these you might want to add the networking places. A network is considered a group of people with similar, active interests, actively in touch with each other. Sometimes the keeping in touch is done mostly by mail, but that's not your goal. Your goal in networking is personal contact, personal meeting, touching, embracing, handshaking, people you can visit and be visited by, so that if some unexpected trouble (or good fortune) happens to any member, everybody knows about it quickly and can do the appropriate thing.

This means meeting new people *with no prospect of marriage in mind or of a marriagelike situation.* It's important not to forget this, because if your main purpose is to find another partner, you'll probably be disappointed, but if your purpose is to make new friends, you'll almost certainly succeed. (Of course, this doesn't mean rejecting any potential partners who may appear!)

But why make new friends? Aren't old friends enough? They may be if there are enough of them and you get to see each other regularly. They're not enough if you see them only rarely. Also you may not be getting much stimulation from them, much exposure to new things, unless they too are actively involved in life.

A good way of meeting new people is to join an existing organization. This is where groups such as singles clubs can be rewarding, especially if they're sponsored by a religious or civic organization. Ironically, as discussed in Chapter 5, a singles club is not necessarily a good place to meet a permanent partner, but it's a very good place to meet other people, people interested in the same things you are.

You might also join the religious institution that sponsors the club or some other religious organization. They do help extend your web of relationships. Also if you haven't been inside a church or temple for a while you may be surprised: many types of services have changed dramatically in the past ten years or so, and some of the changes may be to your liking. If you can't see joining a religious organization, you might join a fraternal or service organization. In fact why not join both?

In addition to joining general-purpose groups, think of joining special-interest groups. There are enormous numbers of them around; in fact there's hardly anything one person enjoys doing that doesn't already have an organization attached to it. Walkers have walking groups and dancers have dancing groups; music lovers have music groups and word lovers have poetry groups; and sports lovers have a thousand different groups they can belong to.

If none of these applies to you, think of political parties and amateur acting companies. Political parties always need volunteers for a dozen different tasks; and usually, whatever you're doing, you're doing it with other people. Amateur acting companies can be great fun; and if you can't act (and don't want to try), there's always something useful you can do with scenery, costumes, makeup. Best of all, you're doing it in an atmosphere of excitement and exuberance—and you're involved with a lot of other people.

That's the whole idea—not to swamp yourself with a million things to do, so that you scarcely have time to change from your hiking boots to your dance costume, and not, certainly, to lose track of yourself in a never-ending storm of activities. But to keep yourself engaged with other people in a variety of ways: by telephone talking over plans for the future; in a library to hear a great plays discussion; in a church meeting room to work on a bazaar; in a friend's home to say hello, how are you, I'm glad you're feeling better. The activities should be enjoyable on two levels: for their own sake and for the sake of the people you do them with, the people they keep you in contact with. For from that kind of contact—human contact, involved contact, mutually caring contact—arises usually the greatest security for all of us.

How to Belong to a Group

Misunderstandings, quarrels, and problems do tend to arise when people get together in groups, and the main thing is to keep them from escalating. That is, most problems start as misunderstandings, and if they can be stopped at that stage, there's no problem.

To nip a problem in the bud of a misunderstanding, *the first rule is to not store things up*. If something bothers you, don't hold it in one minute longer than necessary. Soon it gets added to other things that bother you, and others, and others . . . and now you've got an explosion or a real problem. So when something bothers you, speak to the person who did the "something." And then speak your own feelings, not how the other person feels.

So here comes Joan, and she had some people over to discuss opera and you weren't invited—and you *know* she knows you're an opera lover. You have two ways of approaching her.

1. How come you didn't invite me? You know my phone number. You never ask me to anything. What do you have against me?
2. Joan, I really felt bad when I wasn't included in that opera discussion you had. I certainly would have come if I'd been asked.

In approach 2 you're talking about your feelings, not Joan's behavior. Thus you give her a chance—actually encourage her—to apologize, explain that she tried to phone you and ran out of time, and promise next time to keep on trying until she reaches you. Approach 1 ("You didn't . . . you never . . . you're against me") encourages Joan to become defensive; "I tried to reach you; how come you're never at home? What do you think I am your personal secretary or something?"

The overall idea is not to be an injustice collector or become defensive but instead to state your feelings about the facts (as you understand them) in a way that allows the other person the fullest scope to respond. And then go back and enjoy the group.

How To Leave a Network

Generally you won't leave a network unless it stops serving its purpose or the activity becomes too much for you—or if you remarry. Two things often change then: the group's activities may not really be oriented toward couples; or your partner may prefer another way of spending time, and you prefer to spend your time with him or her.

So there's usually a separation. All separations are painful, and so are separations from people one has grown to like and

sometimes to love. But a few things might make it easier: to remember that separations don't have to be sudden but can be
gradual, and that they don't have to be complete but can be
partial. You can still be there—want to be there, ask to be
there—for special occasions or emergencies; they can still be
with you for your own special occasions or emergencies. Keeping in touch, by telephone and an occasional meeting, doesn't
take much time. And knowing that these people, these networks, are in place, ready to use your strengths or minister to
your weaknesses, can provide deep satisfaction.

Last Word

Security—you have it already, but you may not know it yet.
You've read this book and *you know where you stand*—that's security. You have security even if you know you need hours of
practice being with other people, need to make new friends,
need to spruce up your appearance a bit, because *you know.*
That's the security.

If you've conquered your loneliness and now have a circle
of friends; if you've made a move to a house or apartment that
suits your needs better; if you've done some quality work lately
and been paid or recognized for it . . . if you've done any of
these things, you've added to your store of security with some
solid personal votes of confidence.

If you're lonely, living in the wrong place, or unrecog-
nized in talent or intelligence, these matters can be remedied.
What it takes is some understanding and belief in yourself.

1. **You're not so different from other people.** Though you may
   feel lonely, you are not alone; I can assure you that thousands or even millions of other people feel the same way
   you do.
2. **You can make changes in your life.** Many of us fear change.
   But you can take the fear out of change by making its ele-

ments more familiar. You're afraid to move to a new apartment? Just answer some ads and view a few places—you need not buy or rent now. Go see what people are doing at the Y, at the village meeting, at the concert—make no contact or commitment if you prefer. A slow adjustment to new situations takes the fear away. Eventually, even the most timid person will be able to make beneficial changes. In my practice, I've seen it happen many times, and it can happen to you.

3. **You have control over your own life.** In fact, you have more control than anyone else. If you feel you cannot make the changes you want, see a therapist or counselor and start the process.

Personal Security

Many of us have felt insecure—financially and emotionally—sometimes all our lives. Yet how wonderful it feels to know we can take care of our every need, in full, the way a perfect parent or spiritual guide would.

If we cannot have this perfect caregiver, let's try to help ourselves. We can try to provide for ourselves, calm ourselves and find our place in the world. Here are some key elements of self-security:

1. **You support yourself.** Make living arrangements you can afford. Take steps to begin working if you haven't done so yet.

2. **You are socially comfortable.** Feeling at ease in social situations—parties, religious gatherings, special-interest groups—takes practice. The more you do it, the easier it becomes. Make your appearance the best it can be, so you'll stop checking yourself in the mirror so often. Read, so you have something to discuss. Look for the

humor in any situation, and don't suppress your wit. If you make a serious gaffe—one single woman we know was serving herself at a buffet when her napkin caught fire from the chafing dish!—laugh it off. She did, and ended up sitting with the person on the line who had helped her extinguish the blaze.

3. **You are considerate.** If you're not naturally thoughtful of others, read a good etiquette book so you're up on the social conventions. Most etiquette is about making life pleasant for others.

4. **You leave time for yourself.** You can find out who you are, what you like, and what you believe by talking with other people—but you also can learn much by sitting quietly in a chair, completely alone with yourself. Tuning in to how you're feeling and learning who you are can bring a great sense of understanding and security.

CHAPTER 16

Passion

People looking for new relationships may feel they can never trust again or love again as they did the first time.

That may be so, even for the younger person who may seem to have more resilience and flexibility than someone older. The naive, beautiful innocence of first love—imagining all the perfection in the partner that we can fantasize—is bound to be a nostalgic memory as the partner becomes more human and real and quite imperfect. Although feelings of despair, rage, or guilt may be part of becoming single again, after a while we can learn how to enhance our capacity for love and survive the emotions that give us pain. For the younger single, the most recent statistics show that younger women are most likely to remarry and renew their commitments again: start families, adopt children, and build relationships. According to the U.S. Census Bureau's 1990 figures, thirty-eight percent of younger women who divorced in their teens or early twenties were remarried by age twenty to twenty-four; with each passing year, however, fewer women remarried. As for men, age seems to make less of a difference: Traditionally, a man remains "attractive" as he passes through his forties, fifties, sixties and beyond, while a woman is seen as somehow losing her beauty during those years.

But all this may be changing. The trend is for both men *and* women to remarry in their thirties—the aftermath, perhaps, of a youthful bad decision. And these men and women are not necessarily remarrying each other. One remarkable relationship is the May-December marriage, where the man (or the woman) thinks he's young again—and starts acting it. Most of these relationships fail: the initial spurt of vigor subsides, and the man realizes that he's not younger at all; the older woman realizes that she tires so much more easily. So it's important to be very cautious in entering these relationships, in expecting much to happen.

And yet . . . something does happen. The man's potency, in eclipse for perhaps a score of years, seems to return almost to the full; his energy and vitality surge forward again; his senses seem to grow sharper, more acute. And the woman begins to radiate a true allure, a true erotic presence. The potency, the strength of the presence, are real. Powers and capacities long thought to be vanished return, and our very bodies, the muscles, cells, blood, tissues and bone that make us as we are, play a role. Our ardor and our passion make us young again, if only for a while: make us feel young and make us capable of exercising again some of the abilities of youth.

Something happens. What happens? And how, *even without a lover* or partner, or very much money, or a very interesting life, can we make it happen to us? The answer is *passion.*

The Passionate Mind

There's one essential thing we can learn from passion, and it's this: the way not to grow old any faster than we must, the way not to grow ill, or sour, or dependent, or fearful, or resentful, or disparaging, or sarcastic, or isolated, or despairing before our time, the way to remain our own person as long as we can, is to keep our sense of passion alive, to "be in love." There are two crucial points that relate to this.

The first point is that *passion is not limited to sexual passion, and is not even limited to people.* We can grow passionate about objects, causes, and activities that to other people might seem odd indeed. A few years ago practically the entire population of Costa Rica took to the streets because their soccer team lost in the world finals. People can grow passionate about the theater or their political party, about reading a book or riding a bike, about getting their work done or making their voice heard, about saving a tree or keeping a building from being demolished.

We all feel these pulls at times; usually we ignore them. We tell ourselves we do not *want* to become engaged; it's not worth it; there are more important things to do; the cause is silly; the other people involved don't amount to much; the enterprise has no real meaning and can have no real effect. Or we turn on ourselves and tell ourselves that *we* are not important enough to make a difference; *we* don't amount to much; the other people won't think very highly of us; our contribution is trivial; our assistance is not required.

In brief—and this is the second crucial point—*we turn ourselves off* and draw back from engaging the outside world. We do this by disparaging the object (the partner, the group, the cause, the activity) or by disparaging ourselves. There's a strong parallel here to the sexual dysfunction discussed in Chapter 10, inhibited sexual desire; and in both cases the result for many people is the same: a withdrawal from life and an unhealthy, inhibiting, corrosive concentration on ourselves and our shortcomings.

If the turning away from the world is essentially the same as the turning away from pleasure with the opposite sex, then the relief is essentially the same. The first step is to become aware of what we're doing to turn ourselves off. Chances are we're using both approaches: putting down the outside world and putting down ourselves. The next step is to make a decision, take control, and to get involved anyway, to find something (somebody) we're interested in and move in that direction in spite of all the negatives that ring in our minds. And the third step is to let passion or excitement or engagement happen and not allow old fears and anger to control our lives.

What is the end of passion? Passion cannot last forever, at peak intensity always. The end of passion need not be ashes and despair but can be love and commitment. At any age we humans need an "other" to relate to. We want the flow of our own energy to be outward—reaching, creating, engaging, pulling our fears with it. In turn we receive a flow inward, a gift from the world of its own energy, its own stimulation, its own invitation to rejoin the dance of life.

The Objects of Desire

The good thing about committing ourselves is that it doesn't have to be to something or someone stupendous. We start out waiting for Mr. Fantastic Prince Charming or Ms. Incredible Dream Girl, and we fall in love with somebody . . . well, somebody rather more like us than not. And we know we're in love not by what that person is but by how we feel: we want to be with that person as much as possible, want to make that person a part of our lives.

What we're talking about is the *feeling of connection,* and you can *connect with anything you want,* with anything you find yourself moving out to. We offered some ideas in the last chapter; we could have added a hundred others.

Getting Started

For the person who has retreated far into the self, who may have lost a second spouse after the first, who may be more beaten down by circumstances than most people are, moving out may be hard to contemplate. (If a new traumatic event has occurred, it may still take two or three years to get over it.) But when the time comes, if one simply cannot summon the will or energy to meet new people, even in a noncompetitive, nonjudgmental context, what then?

In such cases a preparatory step may be needed, and it's this: if you can't get yourself to move out, try getting yourself to move—one step at a time. We're talking about things you can do by yourself. Our list of resources, for example (see page 273) could be a starting point. Choose a book that interests you, and look for it at the library. While you're there, see if anything else attracts you—other books, records, courses, movies, special programs. Make a day of it. You may even meet someone at the library; at the very least, you'll have something interesting to talk about by day's end.

Another way to get yourself moving is by taking walks: just getting out of the house regularly, on specified days at specified times, and walking—and more than a block or two. Or buying new kinds of clothing, a new style that you haven't tried before. Change your hairstyle if you're a woman; grow a moustache (or shave one off) if you're a man. Buy new furniture, or one piece of furniture, one you've admired, even if it's not typically "you." In brief do something constructive, even if it's "different."

Starting to Get Started

For some people even essentially solo activities are hard to get into. Or if not unapproachable, then they seem pointless or silly: what's the good, what difference will they make? Or some psychologically aware people may shrug knowingly: it's a trick you're playing on yourself, a way of psyching yourself up, as artificial as a rubber nose.

This may be true, but it doesn't matter. If you can't get out of yourself and make a commitment to life in one of its myriad forms, the first step is to do something *whether you want to or not, whether you're in the mood or not,* no matter what experience or common sense tells you. This is a case where *everything that keeps you from moving,* everything that tells you to stay where you are, every voice of gloom and doom, *is wrong.*

Moving out to other people is usually best because it helps keep you from falling into a depression. But if you can't move out to others you're probably in a depression already and *any kind of change, any kind of movement,* is often the best way to start to get over it.

There are many things wrong with being in a depression, at least the kind you're likely to encounter. (Clinical depression, in which the person is essentially incapacitated, is another matter and requires professional help.) The first problem is that, although depression may not keep you from your daily round of activities, it keeps you from enjoying them. Second, and maybe more important, *it leads you to believe that that's the way things really are; in a depression you're absolutely convinced that the best that can be said about life is "who cares?"* So your incentive for change vanishes, and you proceed along a self-perpetuating cycle of misery and meaninglessness. That's why—like it or not, ready or not—you have to get yourself going again.

What if you're bedridden or housebound? What if, literally, you can't get out and take walks, and you can't afford to buy new clothing or furniture? What then?

Then you can try moving out by telephone and mail. Most parts of the country are served by talk-radio, where listeners speak by telephone to the host and his guests. Listen to them, pick the ones you like, and when you have something to say, say it. And don't limit yourself to the telephone: start using the mail to reach people. If certain books say something special to you, write to the author; he or she will be delighted to hear from you. The same is true of television and radio shows, magazine and newspaper articles—all the forms of information, entertainment, life itself that can come into your home. You can contact the people who create them; and again most of them will be happy to hear from you. Even if you don't hear from them, you've expressed yourself, and that's all to the good.

Finally (this suggestion may be easier for the retired person than for the person working full-time), start to write your autobiography. This doesn't contradict the idea of getting out of yourself. When you write about your own life, you begin to think about yourself objectively, from a psychological distance. Then, if you're in a state of gloom and misery, instead of being the victim you *become the master. It's a way of taking control of your life, of doing something nobody else in the world can do, because nobody else knows what you know about yourself and your life.* That's not the only reason to write your autobiography. The fact is your life has been unique in many ways, and there are many people who will be eager to know about it.

We're not talking about the mass of readers who turn books into best-sellers; realistically it's not likely that your work will actually be published. We're talking about the people in your family: children especially, grandchildren even more so, nieces, nephews, cousins, even brothers and sisters, even childhood and adult friends. They are interested because your life touches on their lives, is part of their history. Your life helps fill in their background, makes their lives more vivid, extends their own lives backwards in time and outward in space. As they read your autobiography, they acquire more than new information, new facts; they actually seem to themselves to have lived longer, and in some psychological sense they have.

So an autobiography is not just a way of mastering your current circumstances (which may, in fact, be fine), nor is it an ego trip. It's a way of touching other people: yourself and the people you knew when young, yourself and the people around you today. And even if some of the touching is only in your imagination and memory, it can still be helpful. It's being involved with your past, making it alive again.

Last Word: Moving out with Passion

To be single again is to experience trauma. Moving out with passion is the final stage in recovering from trauma. It can't be rushed and it shouldn't be rushed: there's much to work through. But some time between one and three years after the trauma, you'll begin to explore the world again, making new contacts or picking up old ones, connecting again with the stream of life.

What does that mean? It means courage to act out with passion: the courage to speak when it's important to speak, to say yes to something desirable even if you've never said yes to it before, to say no to hurt or humiliation even if you've said yes a thousand times in the past. It's making the connections and adjustments to others that you have to make because you're a human being and being yourself and expressing yourself as the best that you are. And it's not being afraid of rebuffs or ridicule, of the easy insulters, the casually sarcastic, the people whose first reaction to anything good is to put it down. It also means the courage to reach for more for yourself because you deserve it, even though reaching for yourself is hard to do . . . and the courage to stand and walk—and *skip*—and not curl up and lie down.

We have not tried to paint the world as pink and glowing, but we hope we have shown that it offers pleasures as well as trials and pain. We have not tried to minimize the personal problems you may have, but we have tried to help you overcome them, or work through them, or just ignore them. The world you move into, the world you live in, is, after all, the only one around, the only one that may have treasures waiting for you. We hope you summon up your courage and find those treasures.

Resources

Passionate Attachments: Thinking About Love, by Willard Gaylin, M.D., and Ethel Person, M.D., Macmillan Publishers.

Sexual Violence: Our War Against Rape, by Linda A. Fairstein, William Morrow & Co, Inc.

Men Are From Mars, Women Are From Venus, by John Grayh, Ph.D., HarperCollins.

Love Codes: How to Decipher Men's Secret Signals About Romance, by Elayne J. Kahn, Ph.D. and David Rudnitsky, Signet Books.

Miss Manners' Guide for the Turn-of-the-Millennium, by Judith Martin, Pharos Books.

The Morning After: Sex, Fear, and Feminism on Campus, by Katie Roiphe, Little Brown.

A Fine Romance: The Passage of Courtship from Meeting to Marriage, by Judith Sills, Ph.D., Ballantine Books.

You Just Don't Understand, by Deborah Tannen, Ballantine Books.

Passions, by Georgia Witkin-Lanoil, Ph.D., Newmarket Press.

The Female Stress Syndrome, by Georgia Witkin-Lanoil, Ph.D., Newmarket Press.

The Male Stress Syndrome, by Georgia Witkin-Lanoil, Ph.D., Newmarket Press.

For more information about AIDS

The Centers for Disease Control National AIDS Hotline, (800) 342-2437 (in Spanish, (800) 344-7432). The CDC National AIDS Clearinghouse, (800) 458-5231, or send your name and address to P.O. Box 6003, Rockville, MD 20849-6003 (free information).

Early Care for HIV Diseases, by Ronald A. Baker, Ph.D., Jeffrey M. Moulton, Ph.D., and John Charles Tighe, San Francisco AIDS Foundation.

The Guide to Living with HIV Infection, by John G. Bartlett, M.D. and Ann K. Finkbeiner, Johns Hopkins University Press.

The Plague Years, by David Black, Simon & Schuster.

And the Band Played On, by Randy Shilts, St. Martin's Press.

Index

Additional copies of *Single Again* may be ordered by sending a check for $12.95 (please add the following for postage and handling: $2.00 for the first copy, $1.00 for each additional copy) to:

MasterMedia Limited
17 East 89th Street
New York, NY 10128
(212) 260-5600
(800) 334-8232 *please use Mastercard or Visa on*
    1-800 orders
(212) 546-7638 (fax)

OTHER MASTERMEDIA BOOKS

THE PREGNANCY AND MOTHERHOOD DIARY: Planning the First Year of Your Second Career, by Susan Schiffer Stautberg, is the first and only undated appointment diary that shows how to manage pregnancy and career. ($12.95 spiralbound)

CITIES OF OPPORTUNITY: Finding the Best Place to Work, Live and Prosper in the 1990's and Beyond, by Dr. John Tepper Marlin, explores the job and living options for the next decade and into the next century. This consumer guide and handbook, written by one of the world's experts on cities, selects and features forty-six American cities and metropolitan areas. ($13.95 paper, $24.95 cloth)

THE DOLLARS AND SENSE OF DIVORCE, by Dr. Judith Briles, is the first book to combine practical tips on overcoming the legal hurdles by planning finances before, during, and after divorce. ($10.95 paper)

OUT THE ORGANIZATION: New Career Opportunities for the 1990's, by Robert and Madeleine Swain, is written for the millions of Americans whose jobs are no longer safe, whose companies are not loyal, and who face futures of uncertainty. It gives advice on finding a new job or starting your own business. ($12.95 paper)

AGING PARENTS AND YOU: A Complete Handbook to Help You Help Your Elders Maintain a Healthy, Productive and Independent Life, by Eugenia Anderson-Ellis, is a complete guide to providing care to aging relatives. It gives practical advice and resources to the adults who are helping their elders lead productive and independent lives. Revised and updated. ($9.95 paper)

CRITICISM IN YOUR LIFE: How to Give It, How to Take It, How to Make It Work for You, by Dr. Deborah Bright, offers practical advice, in an upbeat, readable, and realistic fashion, for turning criticism into control. Charts and diagrams guide the reader into managing criticism from bosses, spouses, children, friends, neighbors, in-laws, and business relations. ($17.95 cloth)

BEYOND SUCCESS: How Volunteer Service Can Help You Begin Making a Life Instead of Just a Living, by John F. Raynolds III and Eleanor Raynolds, C.B.E., is a unique how-to book targeted at business and professional people considering volunteer work, senior citizens who wish to fill leisure time meaningfully, and students trying out various career options. The book is filled with interviews with celebrities, CEOs, and average citizens who talk about the benefits of service work. ($19.95 cloth)

MANAGING IT ALL: Time-Saving Ideas for Career, Family, Relationships, and Self, by Beverly Benz Treuille and Susan Schiffer Stautberg, is written for women who are juggling careers and families. Over two hundred career women (ranging from a TV anchorwoman to an investment banker) were interviewed. The book contains many humorous anecdotes on saving time and improving the quality of life for self and family. ($9.95 paper)

YOUR HEALTHY BODY, YOUR HEALTHY LIFE: How to Take Control of Your Medical Destiny, by Donald B. Louria, M.D., provides precise advice and strategies that will help you to live a long and healthy life. Learn also about nutrition, exercise, vitamins, and medication, as well as how to control risk factors for major diseases. Revised and updated. ($12.95 paper)

THE CONFIDENCE FACTOR: How Self-Esteem Can Change Your Life, by Dr. Judith Briles, is based on a nationwide survey of six thousand men and women. Briles explores why women so often feel a lack of self-confidence and have a poor opinion of themselves. She offers step-by-step advice on becoming the person you want to be. ($9.95 paper, $18.95 cloth)

THE SOLUTION TO POLLUTION: 101 Things You Can Do to Clean Up Your Environment, by Laurence Sombke, offers step-by-step techniques on how to conserve more energy, start a recycling center, choose biodegradable products, and even proceed with individual environmental cleanup projects. ($7.95 paper)

TAKING CONTROL OF YOUR LIFE: The Secrets of Successful Enterprising Women, by Gail Blanke and Kathleen Walas, is based on the authors' professional experience with Avon Products' Women of Enterprise Awards, given each year to outstanding women entrepreneurs. The authors offer a specific plan to help you gain control over your life, and include business tips and quizzes as well as beauty and lifestyle information. ($17.95 cloth)

SIDE-BY-SIDE STRATEGIES: How Two-Career Couples Can Thrive in the Nineties, by Jane Hershey Cuozzo and S. Diane Graham, describes how two-career couples can learn the difference between competing with a spouse and becoming a supportive power partner. Published in hardcover as *Power Partners*. ($10.95 paper, $19.95 cloth)

DARE TO CONFRONT! How to Intervene When Someone You Care About Has an Alcohol or Drug Problem, by Bob Wright and Deborah George Wright, shows the reader how to use the step-by-step methods of professional interventionists to motivate drug-dependent people to accept the help they need. ($17.95 cloth)

WORK WITH ME! How to Make the Most of Office Support Staff, by Betsy Lazary, shows you how to find, train, and nurture the "perfect" assistant and how to best utilize your support staff professionals. ($9.95 paper)

MANN FOR ALL SEASONS: Wit and Wisdom from The Washington Post's *Judy Mann*, by Judy Mann, shows the columnist at her best as she writes about women, families, and the impact and politics of the women's revolution. ($9.95 paper, $19.95 cloth)

THE SOLUTION TO POLLUTION IN THE WORKPLACE, by Laurence Sombke, Terry M. Robertson and Elliot M. Kaplan, supplies employees with everything they need to know about cleaning up their workspace, including recycling, using energy efficiently, conserving water and buying recycled products and nontoxic supplies. ($9.95 paper)

THE ENVIRONMENTAL GARDENER: The Solution to Pollution for Lawns and Gardens, by Laurence Sombke, focuses on what each of us can do to protect our endangered plant life. A practical sourcebook and shopping guide. ($8.95 paper)

THE LOYALTY FACTOR: Building Trust in Today's Workplace, by Carol Kinsey Goman, Ph.D., offers techniques for restoring commitment and loyalty in the workplace. ($9.95 paper)

DARE TO CHANGE YOUR JOB—AND YOUR LIFE, by Carole Kanchier, Ph.D., provides a look at career growth and development throughout the life cycle. ($9.95 paper)

MISS AMERICA: In Pursuit of the Crown, by Ann-Marie Bivans, is an authorized guidebook to the Pageant, containing eyewitness accounts, complete historical data, and a realistic look at the trials and triumphs of the potential Miss Americas. ($19.95 paper, $27.50 cloth)

POSITIVELY OUTRAGEOUS SERVICE: New and Easy Ways to Win Customers for Life, by T. Scott Gross, identifies what the consumers of the nineties really want and how businesses can develop effective marketing strategies to answer those needs. ($14.95 paper)

BREATHING SPACE: Living and Working at a Comfortable Pace in a Sped-Up Society, by Jeff Davidson, helps readers to handle information and activity overload, and gain greater control over their lives. ($10.95 paper)

TWENTYSOMETHING: Managing and Motivating Today's New Work Force, by Lawrence J. Bradford, Ph.D., and Claire Raines, M.A., examines the work orientation of the younger generation, offering managers in businesses of all kinds a practical guide to better understand and supervise their young employees. ($22.95 cloth)

REAL LIFE 101: The Graduate's Guide to Survival, by Susan Kleinman, supplies welcome advice to those facing "real life" for the first time, focusing on work, money, health, and how to deal with freedom and responsibility. ($9.95 paper)

BALANCING ACTS! Juggling Love, Work, Family, and Recreation, by Susan Schiffer Stautberg and Marcia L. Worthing, provides strategies to achieve a balanced life by reordering priorities and setting realistic goals. ($12.95 paper)

REAL BEAUTY . . . REAL WOMEN: A Handbook for Making the Best of Your Own Good Looks, by Kathleen Walas, International Beauty and Fashion Director of Avon Products, offers expert advice on beauty and fashion to women of all ages and ethnic backgrounds. ($19.50 paper)

THE LIVING HEART BRAND NAME SHOPPER'S GUIDE, by Michael E. DeBakey, M.D., Antonio M. Gotto, Jr., M.D., D.Phil., Lynne W. Scott, M.A., R.D./L.D., and John P. Foreyt, Ph.D., lists brand-name supermarket products that are low in fat, saturated fatty acids, and cholesterol. ($12.50 paper)

MANAGING YOUR CHILD'S DIABETES, by Robert Wood Johnson IV, Sale Johnson, Casey Johnson, and Susan Kleinman, brings help to families trying to understand diabetes and control its effects. ($10.95 paper)

STEP FORWARD: Sexual Harassment in the Workplace, What You Need to Know, by Susan L. Webb, presents the facts for identifying the tell-tale signs of sexual harassment on the job, and how to deal with it. ($9.95 paper)

A TEEN'S GUIDE TO BUSINESS: The Secrets to a Successful Enterprise, by Linda Menzies, Oren S. Jenkins, and Rickell R. Fisher, provides solid information about starting your own business or working for one. ($7.95 paper)

GLORIOUS ROOTS: Recipes for Healthy, Tasty Vegetables, by Laurence Sombke, celebrates the taste, texture, and versatility of root vegetables. Contains recipes for appetizers, soups, stews, and baked, boiled, and stir-fried dishes—even desserts. ($12.95 paper)

THE OUTDOOR WOMAN: A Handbook to Adventure, by Patricia Hubbard and Stan Wass, details the lives of adventurous outdoor women and offers their ideas on how you can incorporate exciting outdoor experiences into your life. ($14.95 paper)

FLIGHT PLAN FOR LIVING: The Art of Self-Encouragement, by Patrick O'Dooley, is a life guide organized like a pilot's flight checklist, which ensures you'll be flying "clear on top" throughout your life. ($17.95 cloth)

HOW TO GET WHAT YOU WANT FROM ALMOST ANYBODY, by T. Scott Gross, shows how to get great service, negotiate better prices, and always get what you pay for. ($9.95 paper)

TEAMBUILT: Making Teamwork Work, by Mark Sanborn, teaches business how to improve productivity, without increasing resources or expenses, by building teamwork among employers. ($19.95 cloth)

THE BIG APPLE BUSINESS AND PLEASURE GUIDE: 501 Ways to Work Smarter, Play Harder, and Live Better in New York City, by Muriel Siebert and Susan Kleinman, offers visitors and New Yorkers alike advice on how to do business in the city as well as how to enjoy its attractions. ($9.95 paper)